RUSSIA
IS NO
RIDDLE

by

STEVENS

RUSSIA IS NO RIDDLE

RUSSIA IS NO RIDDLE

by
EDMUND STEVENS

NEW YORK
GREENBERG : PUBLISHER

*This book has been manufactured in
accordance with the regulations of the
War Production Board*

PRINTED IN THE UNITED STATES OF AMERICA
BY J. J. LITTLE & IVES COMPANY, NEW YORK

☆ CONTENTS ☆

v

INTRODUCTION

I first went to the Soviet Union early in 1934 to study first-hand what was commonly referred to in liberal-progressive circles in those days as "the Russian Experiment." I had planned to remain for a year at the most, but force of circumstance in the form of marriage intervened and I stayed on for more than five years— until June, 1939, when the Soviet Government granted exit visas to my wife and our son, who had arrived while we were waiting.

In a planned society our marriage had not been according to any plan—either the Soviet Five-Year Plan, my personal plans, my wife's plans, or the plans of the trade union committee at the foreign language publishing house where both of us were working. The trade union committee had simply given my wife as her "social assignment" the task of cheering up a somewhat lost and aloof young American. For the purpose they had staked her to almost unlimited movie tickets and to occasional seats at the theater. Too late did the trade union committee call my wife in and tell her she was rather overdoing it.

As the years passed, my preconceptions about the Soviet Union— born in the slough of the great depression back home—were revised in the light of experience. But together with a knowledge of the Russian language and Russian culture, I acquired through daily contact and observation, a lasting admiration and sympathy for the Russian people. This experience is not peculiar to myself. It has been that of practically every American who has lived for any length of time in Russia, regardless of his politics. Russians who come to the United States acquire much the same feeling toward Americans.

It is indeed remarkable how readily average Americans and Russians find a common ground. The most striking evidence I saw of this was at the American airbases in the Ukraine, where G. I.

Joes and Russian Vanyas and Vasyas worked together servicing the heavy bombers. Even the combat crews who flew in from Italy and took over the neighboring town declared that they felt more at home here on Soviet soil—that the people seemed more like home folks—than anywhere else they had been.

Again, if I may be permitted once more to cite my own family, I never cease to marvel at the swiftness of my own wife's Americanization. It is a far cry from the Cossack collective farm in the Urals, where she taught school, to the campus of Wellesley College where she is studying today. Yet she has taken the transition in stride, rearing two children and running a household at the same time. Had our "military experts" known my wife, or any of the millions of men and women like her, they would never have gone off the deep end by predicting the Nazis would capture Moscow in a few weeks.

It is the human equation—the ruggedness, honesty, and warmheartedness of the common man in both countries—that will, I am confident, enable America to live with Russia and Russia with America, despite all obstacles.

Russia, like America, has had its periods of isolationism. And though the premises of American and Soviet isolationism were poles apart, the practical results were remarkably similar. Russian isolationism stemmed from the time just after the Revolution, when the new Soviet Power was treated as an outcast by the other nations—all of whom hated and feared Communism. Lenin, and with him the other Russian Communist leaders, assumed that the October Revolution was but the opening gambit of a world revolution. At that time it was held inconceivable that the world could long exist part-Soviet and part-capitalist. The two systems were inherently and basically irreconcilable. Besides, the Hegelian dialectic, which Marx had borrowed to supply his materialist philosophy and economics with a revolutionary dynamic, made the process of social change as certain and inevitable as the sequence of day and night. Capitalism was all washed up and must give way to socialism, the next higher stage in the Marxist scale of social evolution.

While it was impossible to apply this formula rigidly and predict with any measure of precision the time and place of the next revolution, still in the years immediately following the last war there were strong reasons for hoping that the revolution, instead of becoming localized in Russia, would spread over a good part of Europe.

Despite the collapse of the Bela Kun Communist regime in Hungary and of the short-lived Bavarian Soviet Republic in 1919, despite the triumph of Fascism in Italy and of similar reactionary movements elsewhere, expectations that the world revolution would not long delay persisted in the minds of Russia's ruling party until the failure of the Hamburg uprising in 1923. By a strange trick of fate the extinction of this hope was closely followed by the loss of Lenin, the great guiding brain of the Communist Party and the world Communist movement.

The year 1923 was the crucial year when the Bolsheviks shifted their sights from the distant and lofty goal of world revolution to the more immediate practical task of preservation of the Soviet power inside Russia. Under the newly established leadership of Stalin, the Communist Party grimly girded itself for defense against the tide of counter-revolution that was rising everywhere beyond the Soviet borders.

Contrary to the claims of the Trotskyites, this was no betrayal of the Revolution and of Lenin's trust. One of the secrets of Lenin's greatness had been the ability to reconcile his Marxism with the logic of events. And even before failing health had forced the Master to relinquish the reins of leadership, he himself had made some important modifications in his policy at home and abroad. Internally he adopted the New Economy Policy, renouncing the earlier efforts to impose socialism by force, and permitting a limited revival of private enterprises. Externally he had encouraged the restoration of diplomatic relations with other countries and had even sanctioned such close agreements as the Rapallo treaty with Germany. At the time, these modifications were loudly denounced by the "leftists," as betrayals, just as six years later Stalin's policy of building socialism in one country was denounced by the Trotskyists.

The shift in the "Party line" did not take effect overnight. For several years the Comintern continued to work at cross purposes with Soviet diplomacy, and Foreign Commissar Chicherin's best-laid plans were often spoiled as a result. Only gradually, as the

Soviet state grew stronger internally, were the Comintern and *Narkomindel* policies synchronized, and the interests of the world revolution brought into line with the international prestige and security of the Soviet Union.

But despite tactical concessions to the times, the basic postulate of fundamental antagonism between two systems remained, as did its corollary, the fear of capitalist encirclement—an awareness of the ever-present danger that the capitalist powers might sink their squabbles and combine for an attack on the Soviet Union.

It was the task of Soviet diplomacy to play upon the differences within the capitalist camp for the purpose of averting such an anti-Soviet alliance; to side temporarily with one group of capitalist powers and then with another; to oppose whatever power or combination of powers was momentarily the chief threat to the Soviet Union.

In the decade after the Revolution and right up to the rise of Hitlerism to power, the biggest threat to Soviet security seemed likely to come from the Western Powers. Britain and France had planned the intervention against the new regime. America steadfastly refused to recognize the Soviet Government. In all these countries the tone of the press was strongly anti-Soviet. Hence Russia had been drawn toward Germany—like herself an outcast. And despite political antagonisms and the German repudiation of Communism, economic and military collaboration between Soviet Russia and the Weimar Republic had proved advantageous to both. But the advent of Nazism changed all this completely. Fanatical opposition to Communism had been largely instrumental in putting Hitler in power. Hostility to Russia became a cornerstone of Nazi foreign policy.

Realizing that Nazi Germany had become the greatest threat, the Russians hastened to cement better relations with the Entente Powers on the basis of common opposition to the Germans.

It was at this point that diplomatic relations were re-established with the United States and Russia joined the League of Nations. The Soviet policy toward capitalist countries underwent a radical change. Whereas previously all types of government in capitalist countries had been regarded strictly as the "dictatorship of the bourgeoisie," and therefore equally abhorrent to Communists, the Russians now began dividing the sheep from the goats. Fascism, which was synonymous with Nazism, was recognized as the most reactionary, militarist type of capitalism, as opposed to bourgeois democracy, which was the more progressive, "peace-loving" variety.

The re-establishment of diplomatic relations with Russia by the then brand-New Deal heralded by Litvinov's trip to Washington seemed about to usher in a new era of Soviet-American good feeling. Few newly appointed ambassadors have ever assumed their posts under better augury than William C. Bullitt, first United States Ambassador to the Union of Soviet Socialist Republics. The President's choice of Bullitt was welcomed in both countries as a happy one. Had not Bullitt, sent by Wilson to Russia in 1919, reported back that, like it or not, the Bolshevik regime was there to stay and had the overwhelming support of the Russian people? Had not Bullitt at one period in his matrimonial career been married to the widow of Lenin's American friend John Reed?

A veritable new broom, Bullitt swept into Moscow prepared to carry all before him. His scheme to build a magnificent country-club embassy residence, complete with dairy farm, somewhere beyond the Lenin Hills was early abandoned; but he added a ball-room wing to the Spasso Mansion which was turned over to him by the Foreign Office, and his parties were extravaganzas for which bears and other denizens of the Moscow zoo were procured.

Alas, this honeymoon period of Soviet-American relations soured all too soon. The ins and outs of this obscure chapter in diplomacy have never been adequately aired. Evidently the political and commercial results of recognition had failed to come up to American expectations. There was no follow-up in Moscow to the conversations opened with Litvinov in Washington over the settlement of the old Tsarist debts. Also, there was disappointment at Russia's failure to take a strong line with Japan. Instead, in the face of Japanese expansion the Russians successively yielded up their positions in Northern Manchuria, the culmination coming in 1935 with the sale to Japan of the Chinese Eastern Railway—the direct link with Vladivostok. Many people in Washington had expected that with American encouragement the Russians would even risk war

xiv   *Introduction*

with Japan to halt such encroachments on their vital interests. What they failed to understand was that with the star of Nazi Germany fast rising in Europe and threatening an anti-Soviet coalition, Russia could not challenge the Japanese alone, especially as the industrialization and agrarian collectivization programs were still in their critical stages.

In 1935, after a lapse of seven years, a Comintern Congress convened in Moscow. Among those present were representatives of the American Communist Party, and Earl Browder made a report before the Congress on the activities of the American Party. This seemed to be a flagrant violation of that clause in the Soviet-American Agreement, signed by Litvinov in Washington, whereby both countries pledged themselves to harbor no organizations that were seeking to overthrow the lawful government of the other. Actually this clause was a dead letter from the start, since scores of anti-Soviet White Guard Russian organizations continued to function and print publications in the United States before and after the agreement.

The Browder report to the Comintern proved the last drop in Bullitt's cup of disillusionment. Filing a protest with the Soviet Foreign Office, which was in due course rejected on the stock pretext of no connection between the Soviet Government and the Comintern, Bullitt shook the dust of Moscow from his heels for good. At one time called a "fellow-traveler," he became one of America's most bitter Soviet-haters. But before his change of heart he had taught the Red Army the game of polo, and it has survived his apostasy.

Fortunately the Administration and the State Department proved to have more balance and ballast than their individual emissaries. In 1937, after a two-year interregnum, President Roosevelt appointed another Ambassador to Moscow, this time hard-headed lawyer-businessman Joseph P. Davies. There was never any phony-pinkish aura to this consort of the Post millions; but his forthright profession of the capitalist faith, combined with fair-minded admiration of the achievements of Russian socialism, won him respect among the Soviet leaders. For the first time, Soviet-American relations had their feet on the ground and not in the clouds.

The Davies era in Moscow, besides being the most successful period of prewar American-Soviet relations, is also the best publicized, thanks to the Ambassador's own book, *Mission to Moscow,* and its somewhat overdone film version.

Throughout the middle and late 1930's, relations with America were to the Russians of secondary importance compared with the diplomatic game then being played on the chessboard of Europe.

For America was outside the League of Nations, which the Soviet Union now hoped to convert into a united front against aggression. Prior to Hitler's coming to power, the Russians had kept out of the League, which they suspected as an instrument of Anglo-French policy and the potential nucleus of an anti-Soviet world front. But the exodus first of Japan and then Germany from the League now brightened the prospect of using its framework as a means of consolidating the forces opposed to international lawlessness. And now the Soviet Union, through its able spokesman Maxim Litvinov, strove to infuse new life and ardor into those cold, vaulted, marble halls in Geneva. For the first time Russia emerged from her isolation, and formulated and preached the doctrine of the indivisibility of world peace.

But though Litvinov's speeches and formulations were warmly applauded, they were seldom acted on. Each succeeding year brought mounting acts of aggression while the League remained passive and impotent. Thus in 1935, one year after Russia joined the League, Italy invaded Abyssinia. The following summer brought the civil war in Spain with its tragicomedy of "Non-Intervention" that enabled the Fascists and Nazis to help their puppet Franco to the hilt while the lawful republican Government was denied the means of defending itself.

The fact was that Britain and France still preferred appeasing Hitler to unity with Russia whom they yet regarded with deep suspicion. The Russians continued their efforts to rouse the Western European powers to the common peril. They attempted to supplement the weakness of the League as a buttress against aggression by a series of bi-lateral non-aggression and mutual-assistance pacts. In the fall of 1938, when Hitler had turned the heat on Czechoslovakia, the Russians stood ready to fulfill their treaty obligations to the Czechs provided the French did the same, and for a moment it looked as though at last the Western Powers and Russia would combine to meet the Nazi challenge. But only for a moment. At the Munich Conference, to which the Russians were not invited, Neville Chamberlain sold the Czechs in exchange for one more year.

It is the irony of history that the League of Nations, which had failed to expel other members for deeds of aggression and which the Russians had fruitlessly sought to galvanize as an effective means of averting war, expelled the Soviet Union over the Finnish issue. That was the League's parting gesture, after which it gave up the ghost. But the Russians have not forgotten that act. The recollection of it has made them chary lest any new international organization develop a similar anti-Soviet bias, especially in view of the fact that about twenty of the countries eligible the membership have not yet extended recognition to the Soviet U. These misgivings, expressed in the attitude of the Soviet delegates at the Dumbarton Oaks Conference, must be allayed if any new world peace organization is to have a chance of success.

It is beyond the scope of the present book to rehash the controversial issues of the German-Soviet Pact and the Finnish war. In the light of subsequent events many hasty judgments have since been revised. Present Red Army successes argue forcefully in favor of Soviet policy, whose object then as now was the preservation of Russia. Suppose the German invasion had come a year earlier? Suppose the starting line had been the prewar Finnish frontier, twenty miles from Leningrad? As it was, Finland's entry into the war made possible the two-and-one-half years' blockade of Russia's second largest city—a siege that cost the lives of about 1,500,000 civilians, which is equal to approximately half Finland's total population.

Soviet policy of 1939-40, while it did not avert the war from Russia's shores, gave her both the precious margin of added time for preparation and the additional territory along her western frontier for cushioning the Nazi onslaught. It was a margin that spelt the difference between victory and defeat in the heartbreak months and years that followed. It meant, finally, that Russia was not called on to face Hitler's armed might alone, but as part of a powerful world coalition.

The blood and sweat it took to weld that coalition defy historic comparison. It was achieved the long, hard, and costly way. The burning villages of Abyssinia, the blood-soaked battlefields of Spain, the siege of Warsaw, the fall of Paris, the beaches of Dunkirk, the blitz on London, the assault on Belgrade—all these and more besides must needs have come to pass before the Western Powers and Russia took the obvious step of combining against their common enemy. And then it was Hitler who cast the deciding vote. By his invasion of the Soviet Union on June 21, 1941, the Fuehrer succeeded, where all diplomats and negotiators had failed, in uniting his enemies.

TO MOSCOW WITH CHURCHILL

☆ ☆ ☆ ☆ ☆ ☆ ☆ ☆ ☆ ☆ ☆ ☆ ☆ ☆

I WONDER if every diplomatic or military mission that journeys to a foreign capital to conduct important negotiations takes along someone to look for secret microphones? If only the walls of the Guest House of the Soviet Foreign Office had tongues as well as ears, what a story they could tell! What a procession of statesmen-politicians has passed through the portals of the compact little mansion on Moscow's "Dead Alley" in recent years!

The list would begin with "honest broker" Pierre Laval, who came to Moscow in the summer of 1934 with a honeyed smile on his heavy lips and black treachery in his evil heart to sign the French-Soviet Mutual-Assistance Pact. The following year President Eduard Benes came to sign a similar pact between Czechoslovakia and the Soviet Union, the implementing of which was contingent on the fulfillment of the Franco-Soviet treaty. Then through the years sundry American, British, Chinese, German, Finnish, Polish, and Turkish representatives.

In the summer of 1939 it had accommodated the leaders of the British Military Mission that fumbled the world's last chance for peace.

The negotiators were still deadlocked over the refusal to agree to Russian troops entering Poland in the event of a German invasion. The Russian press was still trying to transliterate the impressive monicker of the head of the British delegation, Admiral Reginald Plunket-Ernle-Erle-Drax, when Ribbentrop suddenly blew in with his suite and was put next door to the Guest House in the former Austrian Legation. The Nazi Foreign Minister promptly agreed that Russia should march into Poland when the Germans attacked from the west, thus meeting Russia's security requirements. Over the low garden wall the British delegates could hear the noise of their new neighbors celebrating the signing of the Soviet-German agreement. The British left the next day in a state of nervous collapse.

The following March, Finnish Prime Minister Rysto Ryti, Juho Paasikivi, and the other members of the Finnish peace delegation stayed at the Guest House while negotiating the termination of the Soviet-Finnish winter war. Recent Finnish peace delegations as well as Romanian and Bulgarian have also stayed at the Guest House. In the war period it has accommodated numerous British and American representatives and visitors, including Lord Beaverbrook, Averell Harriman, Wendell Willkie, and Patrick Hurley. During the Hull-Eden-Molotov conference of October, 1943, the American Secretary of State stayed there.

Friend, foe, and neutral have enjoyed the same unstinted measure of Russian hospitality while at the Guest House. In August, 1942, I stayed there with Averell Harriman and the other American members of the party who accompanied Prime Minister Winston Churchill on his first trip to Moscow.

The Prime Minister was put up out of town in a sumptuous *dacha* or summer house and, like a high Soviet official, was whisked back and forth between there and the Kremlin in a heavily curtained, bullet-proof American limousine of the type Chicago gangsters made famous, so that the ordinary Muscovite never caught a glimpse of him.

Harriman, Brigadier General Spaulding, Major General Russell Maxwell, then Commanding U.S. Forces Middle East, his aide, Naval Lieutenant Sumner Gerard, and I in the role of "Technical Advisor" were accommodated at the Guest House. The day of our arrival Gerard and I were presented with a four-page, typewritten list by the chef and asked to check the party's gastronomic preferences. Without distracting our superiors from affairs of state with such trivialities, Gerard and I checked off the items we liked. The lavishness of the resulting menus would have been shocking anywhere, let alone in war-grim Moscow.

Every meal consisted of at least four courses, and the table was always embellished with a huge basket of tempting fruit. Only with the greatest difficulty could we persuade our hosts that our party did not want champagne for breakfast.

Once we invited the American press representatives to supper, and when they saw the food, especially the fruit, they asked us if we had brought our provisions with us. Many months later, when I had sampled Hotel Metropole fare, I understood why.

Even the American Embassy staff (and they are better off for food than the correspondents), not excepting the Ambassador, Admiral Standley, found meals at the Guest House a real treat during the period of our four-day stay.

Thanks to Harriman's zipped lips, virtually no news leaked out during the actual Churchill-Stalin talks in Moscow. Churchill avoided the press completely. Only after we had flown back to Cairo was the curtain of censorship lifted to let out the bare fact of his visit. Churchill's press conference back in Cairo was singularly uninformative—consisting mostly of generalities about how well he and Stalin had got along with each other. Not till later did the gossip gradually leak out about the unfavorable impression caused at the Kremlin banquets by the Prime Minister's appearance in a siren suit—the Russians are sticklers for form—by his grumpiness during the toast-making, and by the unceremonious way he sat on his own Ambassador, Sir Archibald Clark-Kerr, when the latter proposed a toast to Stalin's health. Churchill told Sir Archie that as Ambassador he could address himself only to Molotov, the Foreign Commissar.

That first Churchill visit to Moscow coincided with the low ebb of Allied diplomatic and military fortunes. On the Russian front, Sevastopol had fallen after an eight-month siege. The Germans were pushing ahead in the Caucasus and beyond the Don elbow toward Stalingrad. Rommel was on the threshold of Alexandria. In the Far East the battle of the Solomons was raging indecisively; while the Japs had gained a foothold in the Aleutian Islands. Feeling in Russia was bitter over the failure of the Second Front to materialize despite the promises presumably made to Molotov on his trip to London and Washington. So bitter was it, that members of Allied military missions who appeared on the streets in uniform were jeered by the population. Jokes were passed about the Anglo-Americans having established their Second Front in the front row at the ballet. While official circles withheld their comment, the papers were full of reports of mass meetings by labor groups and leftist organizations in Britain and America, petitioning for the immediate opening of a second front. There was little effort at sober evaluation of Second Front possibilities in terms of forces and, more particularly, shipping. The Russian people did not know that out of a convoy of forty-eight ships bound for Murmansk in June, 1942, forty-five had been sunk, and that when as much as one-third of a convoy managed to get through, it was considered a good showing. They also tended to overlook or minimize the heavy Allied naval commitments in the war against Japan. However, such oversights are understandable in view of the fact that the Nazis were still gnawing their way deeper and deeper into Russia's living flesh. The turning in the road was not yet in sight. The long bitter agony and slaughter of Stalingrad was still ahead.

Before the two men and the countries they stood for could trust each other either militarily or politically, there were many suspicions and misunderstandings that needed clearing up.

Stalin had not yet forgiven the British for Munich, when the Chamberlain Government, so the Russians thought, had virtually invited an anti-Soviet coalition of Britain, France, Germany, and Italy; while Churchill's stand in favor of the fascist puppet Franco in the Spanish war ill accorded with his present role as leader of a democratic coalition to fight Fascism and Nazism. They also remembered Churchill's role as a prime instigator of intervention in the Russian civil war. Too, the Russians were still deeply suspicious of the Hess episode. They were convinced that Hess had flown to Britain, not on his own, but as Hitler's emissary in a bid to enlist Britain's support for his forthcoming anti-Soviet crusade. The Russians resented British reticence on the subject and the fact that Hess was getting what they considered lenient treatment ill suited to his guilt as one of the top war criminals. In the Kremlin mind there still lurked the suspicion that the Hess request for a *de facto* armistice in the West had been granted and that Britain might even now, as on previous occasions, be playing a double game— encouraging both Russia and Germany to exhaust each other while she stood on the sidelines preparing to reap the spoils. Was not that what the London Poles, who had the support of the British Government, were openly hoping for? General Anders, commander of the Polish forces in the Soviet Union had, with British approval, declined to fight on the Eastern Front alongside the Red Army. The lack of a Second Front confirmed these gnawing doubts and, added to the growing seriousness of the Russian position on the Eastern Front, came as near as anything ever came to shaking the Man of Steel's confidence in ultimate victory.

Churchill for his part deeply resented the Russian failure to comprehend and appreciate the British war effort, their constant sniping on the Second Front issue, their failure to give the British people due credit for weathering the grim months of the blitz when they alone defied the conqueror with unbroken spirit in the face of seemingly hopeless odds. He had not forgiven the Stalin-Ribbentrop pacts, nor the period when Russian policy seemed oriented toward Germany, when Russian wheat and raw materials helped the *Wehrmacht,* when the Communists in Britain and elsewhere sabotaged the war, so he thought, at Moscow's bidding.

On the basis of the reports of his own military experts, Churchill had fully expected the Russians to collapse in the first few months of the German invasion. Even now, despite the admittedly heroic show they were putting up, he was by no means sure they could or would continue to hold out. He, like Stalin, was haunted by the specter of a separate peace.

A few months before he left London, Churchill had talked to General Anders, just come from Russia. Anders, as Commander in Chief of the Polish Army in the East, had enjoyed unusual opportunities for travel and observation inside the Soviet Union. What he had to say confirmed the Prime Minister's worst suspicions. The Russians were at the end of their resources. Transportation and internal economy were in complete chaos. Morale on the home front was cracking. By the end of the summer the Germans would be beyond the Volga. At the same time they would complete the conquest of the Caucasus. Baku with its oil would be theirs.

It was on this basis that Anders sold Churchill the plan for pulling his Polish troops out of Russia, where they had been trained and equipped with the help of the Red Army for eventual service on the Russian front. If they stayed on in Russia, Anders argued, they could not affect the issue—the country was already foredoomed to defeat. They would simply be needlessly sacrificed for a lost cause.

But if they were pulled out of Russia in time, they could strengthen the garrison of the Middle East against the inevitable day when the Germans would bear down from the Caucasus.

Churchill not only agreed to the Polish exodus from Russia; he was so impressed with what Anders had to say about the imminent peril of a German attack through the Caucasus that he switched large Indian forces to Iraq and Persia out of Burma.

On his way through Cairo Anders had told the same story to the thirty-odd generals and eighty-odd brigadiers who garrisoned British GHQ Middle East, and had thoroughly convinced them, too. At that time he and most of the other Government Poles were full of the expectation—unconscious product of their wishful thinking—that Germany and Russia would destroy each other completely like the Kilkenny cats, leaving a vacuum into which the Poles might march and re-establish "Greater Poland" to the Dnieper.

Later, when it became all too evident that Russia would not be destroyed, many of these same Poles conceived the necessity for a war between Russia and the Western Powers and shifted their tactics accordingly.

That was in the winter of 1942-43. But in the spring and summer of 1942 the Poles were still confident that Russia would be defeated, and they were doing their level best to convince the British and Americans. That was the real purpose of General Anders trip direct from Russia to Cairo and London.

Presumably he had come to negotiate with the Allies for uniforms and equipment for his army. The Russians had even provided him with a special plane for his trip to Cairo. It waited two weeks to take him back and then flew off without him. Anders never did return to Russia and in due course the Russians learned what he was really up to.

Against this background, small wonder both Stalin and Churchill resorted to strong language. Neither man is used to mincing words and it was almost twenty years since Stalin had spoken to any statesman of equal rank. Churchill, though his tenure of office had been shorter and his power more circumscribed, is in his way as domineering and intolerant of opposition as Stalin. And now he was up against a man whom he could neither bully with his strength nor mesmerize with his eloquence—strained as it was through a flannel-mouthed interpreter.

At those meetings in the zero hours—during his four-day stay Churchill, in conformity with Stalin's custom of doing all his heavy work at night, arrived at the Kremlin around eleven and stayed on till five o'clock in the morning—the P.M. stormed a bit; Stalin kept coldly calm, though his steely surface sometimes gave off sparks.

The British aristocrat and the Georgian cobbler's son were like positive and negative currents of the same high voltage. But though their background, training, outlook, and temperament bred antagonism at almost every point, historic necessity and their common hatred for the Berchtesgaden paperhanger held them together.

In the end, Stalin was made to understand just why the Allies could not invade France for some time to come. He was told about the forthcoming North African expedition which would have to serve as a second-best Second Front. The Soviet Marshal was far from satisfied, but thereafter the Russian press noticeably abated the Second Front needling campaign—all but Ilya Ehrenburg, that is, whom no one seemed able to silence.

Churchill, for his part, received assurances that the end of the German advance in Russia was in sight and that the Kremlin had no intention of negotiating a separate peace. The little that he saw of the Red Army and of the spirit of the Russian people during his visit seemed to confirm these assurances, and almost grudgingly he revised his estimate upwards. The two men, though they could scarcely be called bosom friends, at least understood and respected each other now. The anti-Hitler coalition had weathered its first severe political crisis.

RETURN TRIP

☆ ☆ ☆ ☆ ☆ ☆ ☆ ☆ ☆ ☆ ☆ ☆ ☆ ☆

I N THE fourteen months that intervened between Churchill's trip to Moscow and the Hull-Eden-Molotov conference in the Soviet capital, the back of Nazi striking power had been broken on all fronts. The victory at El Alamein and the landings in North Africa had been followed in mid-winter by the Russian triumph at Stalingrad. And in the spring came the Allied victory in Tunisia and the ousting of the Axis from Africa. The Stalingrad and North African operations had each cost the Germans over 300,000 men in killed and captured alone. The *Afrika Korps* and the Sixth Army —flower of the *Wehrmacht*—were wiped out. And then in July, 1943, while the Americans and British were scrambling ashore in Sicily, the Nazis launched their last major offensive of the war, the Kursk offensive on the central sector of the Russian front. For nearly six weeks the lull had been so complete that one could hear the birds twittering peacefully in no man's land under the sultry summer sky. And then all hell broke loose. The artillery opened up. The clouds of Stukas descended on the Russian lines and finally the *Panzers* crawled out, spitting fire and steel. For fifteen miles they crashed ahead, chiseling a narrow corridor, so they thought, through the Russian defenses. Then suddenly, seemingly out of nowhere, the Russian artillery replied with a fire power unequaled before in the Eastern campaign. With deadly accuracy the shells rained down on the narrow Nazi salient. The Nazis stepped up their own artillery and a terrific duel ensued for a matter of over a week.

And then, almost as suddenly as it had begun, the firing ceased. "I think the most terrible moment of my life," a captured Nazi artillery officer told me some months later, "was that morning when our heavy guns slackened off and fell silent. Stalingrad had been awful, yet even then there was still hope of a comeback. But when the order came through to use up our ammunition and pull out our guns, then I knew our last big offensive, for which we had prepared so long and on which we had pinned such hopes, had failed. From that moment the war was as good as lost."

Allied political relations had continued to improve with their military fortunes. Even though the invasion of France, for which the Russians had bargained, had failed to come off, in September the British and the Americans were ashore in Italy, Mussolini had been deposed by his own Fascist Grand Council, and shortly after Italy capitulated. From the Soviet rate of advance on the Eastern Front, it was apparent that before the end of the year the Germans might be pushed back into Poland.

I heard the opening of the Moscow Conference over the ship's radio one night in mid-Atlantic. I was on my way to Moscow, and fate in the guise of the War Department had placed me on a ship bound for the Persian Gulf with a cargo of nothing more explosive than frozen turkeys for the Thanksgiving dinners of the men of our Persian Gulf Command, who ran the overland supply route to Russia.

One of my roommates was a young Polish naval lieutenant on his way to Cairo with a shipment of typewriters, radio sets, and refrigerators for the Polish Legation there. He had been in England when Germany invaded his country and had neither seen nor heard from his wife and child since the war started. In most respects he was a sane, intelligent, humorous, and thoroughly likeable chap; but when the talk shifted to international politics, he became irrational. He declared there was no possibility of a Polish-Russian accord; and he frankly hoped that, after the defeat of Germany, Britain and America would fight Russia—views which I had heard from other Poles. When the news came through that the Moscow Conference had been a complete success, I assured him that doubtless some accord had been reached on the Polish issue—a bit of unfounded optimism on my part.

The news of the Moscow Conference made me impatient to reach

my destination. Our ship was a fast new vessel which up to our
present voyage had always traveled alone, trusting to its superior
speed and armor. But now we were tied to a slow convoy. Our
skipper—a red-headed, beetle-browed Dane who had run away to
sea at the age of fourteen—champed like a hobbled racehorse, and
the crew laid bets that the "Old Man" would find a way of cutting
loose. But the orders had apparently been strict, and there were
sinister rumors of a new Nazi secret weapon, the "acoustic torpedo."

And then one night as we were nearing the African coast, the
routine of our voyage was suddenly interrupted. I was about to
wriggle into my bunk, when the lights flickered and went out.
The darkness was pierced by the jarring clang of the alarm gong
and I was aware that the rhythmic throbbing of the engines had
stopped. My trousers—the only article of clothing I took off at night
—were hanging on the same hook as my life jacket, to which my
passport and other personal papers wrapped in oilskin were securely
tied for just such an emergency. During boat drills I had carefully
timed how long it took to get from my bunk to my lifeboat station
on the boat deck three flights up—a minute and a half. (There is
an expectancy of three minutes from the time a torpedo hits until
the ship goes down.) This time I must have cut my traveling
speed by a good thirty seconds. As I sped down the companionway,
I brushed past others in the darkness who were coming up from
the engine room. As I reached the level of the dining saloon, there
was a violent jar; and the ship, quivering from stem to stern,
lurched over on her port side at a forty-five-degree angle. There
was a crash of smashed crockery and a tinkle of broken glass from
the pantry. Then the ship righted itself and there came another
gentler shock.

On deck a thick fog had swallowed the blue running lights of
our neighbors. But on our top deck the lurid red lights of
the "Christmas tree" were flashing a distress signal. The crew members were standing by their boat stations. One of the officers gave
me a fill-in on what had happened. It seemed that the ship's electric generator had suddenly gone dead. When the power failed,
the elaborate steering mechanism had ceased to function. The

engines stopped and the ship went completely out of control. Wallowing helplessly in the trough of the waves, she had yawed out of line; and before we could signal in the dark, a tanker in the next line was bearing down upon us. Only by the most cunning seamanship had the skipper of the tanker averted cutting squarely into us amidships. He had managed to veer and instead had sideswiped us. One of the tanker's lifeboats had been scraped off and was nesting crazily in a tangle of ropes, davits, and twisted railing on our cargo deck. But we only saw that the next morning. Meanwhile one of the fast little destroyers came alongside in answer to our distress signal and asked if we were in serious trouble. By now the generator was again functioning and the ship responded.

Besides the captured lifeboat, the morning light revealed a gaping hole in our prow, where the tanker had cut into us. It was well above the waterline and was soon patched up with boards and caulking, but our skipper hesitated to take a damaged ship through the Mediterranean where convoys were often attacked by air and sea. Accordingly he requested and received permission to put into Gibraltar for repairs. Two days later when our convoy strung out to thread the narrow straits, we were placed at the tail end of the line, and instead of following the others we broke off and headed for the towering rock still visible in the gray November dusk, even though a myriad lights had already begun to twinkle at its base.

In the first year of the war the Rock was blacked out, with the result that it was clearly silhouetted against the lighted Spanish coast. Accordingly lighting was restored. We presently heaved to while the pilot and representative of the port authority climbed aboard. The latter, a dour Scot, cautioned our captain that the anchorage here was not a cozy place.

"We'd a spot of trouble last month," he said. "Several ships at anchor here were blown up. 'Twas time bombs that did it. Fastened to the hull they were, below the water line. One of the ships spotted the man that did it swimmin' around in the water. Thinking he was drowning, they fished him out. Spoke nothin' but Spanish— or if he did, he didn't let on. And bloody awful scared he was. But they figured it was just from fright after the narrow squeak he'd had from drowning. So they lowers a boat and puts him ashore, very obligingly. Two hours later the ruddy alarm clock goes off. You'll see her layin' on her side off shore in the morning."

He handed the captain a sheaf of mimeographed instructions labeled "Most Secret." They cautioned: "While in Gibraltar, behave as though you were in hostile territory. Remember, right across the border is Spain, which has friendly relations with our enemies. Thousands of people pass back and forth across the border daily. It is impossible to keep check on every one of them. Some are doubtlessly enemy agents. From LaLinea they can pick up a telephone receiver and in a few minutes they are through to Berlin and can transmit any information they have gleaned." It went on to caution the captains of ships in the anchorage to double their lookout against possible saboteurs. The Scot warned us particularly to beware of the little rowboats that put out from the Spanish shore ostensibly with something to sell. As most of the anchorage was Spanish territorial waters, there was nothing one could do to interfere with them, except, he said, keep them away from the sides of the ship.

"Keep a fire hose handy," he advised, "and if they come in too close, just give them a squirt. Many of them may be just honest smugglers, but some are sure to be in the pay of the German admiral stationed across the bay in Algeciras."

He then proceeded to tell us a story which eloquently illustrates where the sympathies of the "neutral" Franco Government lay. Ever since Mussolini declared war, an Italian tanker had been riding at anchor off the shore of Algeciras. The British soon learned that this ship served as headquarters of the sabotage activities against British and other Allied shipping in the roadstead. Repeated protests to the Franco authorities, both locally and through the Embassy in Madrid, were unavailing; and regularly each month a number of ships were either scuttled or severely damaged by these enemy agents operating from neutral territory with the connivance of the authorities. Then, when Italy surrendered, the crew of the tanker voluntarily moved her from the Spanish to the British side of the anchorage and turned her over to the British, who found in the hold a complete workshop for the production of time bombs equipped with suction pads which made it possible to fasten them to the hull of a ship below the water line.

All night long as we lay at anchor in the roadstead, our sleep was shaken by the unpleasant metallic plonk of depth charges, sometimes far away, out in the straits, but at other times close enough to jar our teeth loose. This we later learned was done partly to prevent possible sneak attacks on the anchorage by submarines, but principally as a precaution against enemy saboteurs. No man in the water, intent on fastening a bomb, could survive the crushing pressure from the near-by blast of an "ashcan."

In the morning we found ourselves anchored less than two hundred yards from the Spanish shore, which fairly bristled with barbed wire, coastal batteries, and machine guns—all pointing, most impolitely, in our general direction. The surrounding water was swarming with gaily painted rowboats, two men in each. One of them rowed with a curious standing-up, pushing motion; the other reclined in the stern, holding up bits of merchandise for our inspection—everything from shawls to bottles. But our Captain was not a man to be trifled with. The fire hoses were already out, neatly coiled and connected, ready for instantaneous action should one of the rowboats brashly venture too close; and every two hours we scraped a line under the keel of the ship, from stem to stern, to feel for any time bombs that might possibly have been attached. It was feared that because our ship was a new and superior design, it would be singled out for sabotage. A fast Diesel-powered patrol boat, flying the Royal Navy ensign, pulled alongside and a cheery Northcountry voice hollered through a megaphone, "Hope we didn't keep you awake last night with our charges. Keep an eye on those bastards in the rowboats. Don't let 'em come alongside. See you later. Cheerio!" And with that it streaked off into the bay. The rowboats, which at the approach of the patrol boat had scurried for shore like frightened water beetles, swarmed out at us again.

That morning I went ashore with the skipper, who had to make arrangements for repairing the ship. Most of the casualties from the Mediterranean theater came limping into Gibraltar—some on their own power, others on a tow line. The motor boat taxi that took us in stopped at one American Liberty Ship with her prow so badly stove in that it was a wonder she kept afloat. The Captain, who came ashore with us, told of being torpedoed just off Bone as he was setting out for home with a hold full of Italian prisoners. Many of the poor devils had been killed by the explosion; their bodies were still swishing around in the flooded compartment, although it had all happened early in June. They had been on the way to Gibraltar ever since and had only just made it that same morning. I thought the faces of the crew I saw along the railing, dirty and unshaven, had developed a sort of prison pallor, despite exposure to the sun and weather.

Gibraltar is one of the few fortified strongholds of the world that looks just as a fortified stronghold should—thick, gray, crenelated walls encompassing a huddled little town whose main dimension is vertical rather than horizontal. And over and beyond it the brooding mass of the Rock, literally honeycombed with passages, living quarters, and storerooms, so that in the event of siege the entire defending garrison might go underground and hold out indefinitely.

In the recent past the Rock was overrun with monkeys—Barbary apes—but of late their number has dwindled to the point of extinction. Investigation revealed that some of the nasty old grandpa apes were tossing the young progeny out into the void. Now the apes are carefully protected, especially the young, and their numbers are gradually increasing. The officer entrusted with supervising their welfare is a brigadier. An old tradition says that so long as the apes endure, the British will rule Gibraltar. . . .

Even a cursory visit to the rock fortress discloses some of the difficulties the authorities are up against in coping with espionage and sabotage. Some six thousand Spanish workers employed in the shipyards and dock area daily commute back and forth from the neighboring Spanish town of LaLinea. Hundreds of peddlers, hucksters, and peasants with their carts also pass in and out between the Rock and the Spanish mainland. There is so little room on the Rock that when Gibraltar became a link in the wartime air route from the United Kingdom to the Middle East, an airport could be built only by encroaching on the "Neutral Zone," the flat narrow isthmus connecting the Rock with the mainland. The highway to Spain runs through the middle of the runway; so when planes are either landing or taking off, traffic is temporarily halted.

The far side of the airfield is flush with the Spanish border, and through a high wire fence Spanish sentries are visible pacing back and forth. From such a vantage point it is as easy for German agents to keep tab on the air traffic through Gibraltar as it was for the German admiral with the spyglass in Algeciras to count the convoy ships as they steamed through the Straits. The German agents in La Linea must have fairly scorched the telephone wires to Berlin when General Eisenhower's headquarters for the invasion of North Africa was stationed on—or rather in—the Rock.

The situation in and around Gibraltar ill-accorded with some of the nice things said about Franco by some of the important people in London and Washington. It tended to confirm the Russian thesis that the Spanish fascist dictator had not changed his spots.

Despite the desire in certain quarters to make the Caudillo look respectable, the Russians continue to regard him in the same light as they do his Nazi and Fascist masters who placed him in power.

The Russians have not forgotten that the Nazi-Fascist aggressors used Spain as a proving ground for the present war. They recall that General Franco, while turning his mask of neutrality toward the Western Powers, along with the other Quislings gave his full support to Hitler's anti-Soviet crusade.

They have not forgiven Franco for the crimes committed on Soviet soil by his Blue Division, which he raised to serve with the Nazis on the Eastern Front. Franco is on the Russian list of war criminals; and when the time comes, it is likely they will insist that the arm of retribution shall not be stopped by the Pyrenees.

The Russians regard fascism as a world evil that must be stamped out root and branch everywhere if the peace is to be secure. If Spanish fascism survives, the Russians are convinced Spain will be the incubator for future fascist revivals.

We soon learned that the ship might be tied up in Gibraltar indefinitely. For once the repairs were finished, she must wait for another convoy. The boys of the Persian Gulf Command would not have their turkeys in time for Thanksgiving. They would be lucky if they got them for Christmas. But that didn't worry our crew members. For them, lying over in Gibraltar was just so much gravy. Though not a bomb had dropped on the Rock since it was raided by disgruntled Vichy Frenchmen after the naval battle at Mers-el-Kebir, Gibraltar was still regarded by the War Shipping Board as a combat area. Merchant seamen drew an extra five dollars a day just for being there—which made the Navy boys of the gun crews feel pretty burned up. Rather than wait, I arranged to fly on to Algiers the next morning.

A RUSSIAN IN ALGIERS

☆ ☆ ☆ ☆ ☆ ☆ ☆ ☆ ☆ ☆ ☆ ☆ ☆ ☆

THE SHELVES in the local shops of Algiers were covered with dust. The Germans, it seemed, had cleaned up everything.—*Pas de militaires, vous comprenez,* a merchant explained apologetically, *des commerçants en civile. On envoyait toute chose en Libie, chez Rommel. Après, quand les Allies sont venus, les Américains, on espérait que cela changerait les affaires, on espére toujours, mais*—and then the conclusion, accompanied by the appropriate shoulder shrug, —*que voulez-vous? C'est la guerre.* Ronnie Stead, the *Monitor* correspondent in Algiers since the invasion, told me how once, immediately after a bombing, he saw an old French couple literally walk out of the ruins of their house after a bomb had crashed into it and dismiss their terrifying experience with a shrug and the inevitable remark. It ran so utterly true to form that Ronnie felt amused despite the tragedy.

As in so many wartime cities, the one touch of color relieving the drabness and shoddiness of unpainted houses, dirty streets, and ungarnished show windows, was the infinite variety of uniforms. There were spahis with scarlet cloaks and jangling spurs; there were admirals festooned with gold braid. While I was having a haircut one morning, into the coiffeur's walked a young captain of the Foreign Legion. He was as ornate as a Christmas tree, with his ribbons, his medals, and sundry little silver baubles (a miniature cutlass, some sort of bird, some tiny crossed pistols) dangling from the pocket of his beautifully tailored tunic. There was a glance-neither-to-the-right-nor-to-the-left aloofness in his manner that let you know he was distinctly someone above the run. He easily and effortlessly established his priority over the cringing civilians awaiting their tonsorial turn, and with perfect timing advanced on a chair that happened to be vacated at that moment.

17

"A veteran of Bir Hacheim, one of Koenig's men," my barber explained in an awed whisper. I mentally compared this gorgeous creature with the disheveled, battle-stained members of the Bir Hacheim garrison whom I had seen in Libya just after their heroic stand. Yes, the French had come a long way since then.

By comparison the Americans were much less dressy. But there were far more of them, and they were everywhere. In the broad thoroughfares of the European city and in the narrow alleys of the Arab quarter, their light khaki drill was sprinkled through the swirl of burnooses and nondescript European garb.

And the amount of saluting you had to do, wherever you went, definitely took the joy out of being a war correspondent in uniform. In this respect it was quite unlike the good old days in Cairo where, despite the perpetual military parade, there was almost no saluting. That was because there were Australians around who said they'd be damned if they'd salute a blankety blank Englishman, even if he happened to be a b——dy brigadier.

But though the American Gee Eyes might salute their French Allies, they never spoke to or fraternized with them. It wasn't only the language barrier. They just weren't interested. Though they were physically in Algiers, most of these American boys were mentally thousands of miles away. When they thought of the French at all, it was with vague irritation—or at best, condescension. Even an officer said to me, "These frogs are all right in their own way, I suppose. Only it isn't our way. They're different. More like children, spoiled children, and that's how you've got to treat 'em. Humor 'em sometimes, scold 'em at others." Few of the official Americans had a kind word for General de Gaulle.

The press room, several floors up in a large modern building, was like a college classroom during a charwoman's strike. There were row upon row of little desks, a portable typewriter on each; maps, bulletin boards, and posted announcements cluttered the walls haphazard. Here every evening at a set time some two hundred accredited correspondents foregathered to hear the communiqué on the day's operations in Italy. They listened breathlessly to the words of the military spokesman, scribbling notes the while. Then and there they pounced simultaneously on their waiting typewriters; and for the next hour or so a staccato pandemonium broke loose, in the course of which the skeleton communiqué was clothed in reams of copy and in two hundred unique styles. For most of the correspondents this was the whole story. They were utterly wrapped up in the military news and, with a few outstanding exceptions, totally ignorant of, or indifferent to, the French political scene.

Yet a great nation was being reborn under their very noses. Here, in the sole section of metropolitan France free from the Nazi yoke —for Algeria, though in Africa, is legally an integral part of France—the mold of France's political future was being cast. At the time of my visit, delegates from the French Underground were meeting in Algiers. These men who had smuggled themselves past the Gestapo to voice the will of the French people provided a graphic preview of liberated France—the utter repudiation of Giraud and other rightist elements, and the overwhelming endorsement of de Gaulle and a swing to the left.

The members of the French Committee of National Liberation were bubbling with indignation at having been left out of the Moscow Conference. The local French press was brimming with passionate prose on the subject, reminiscent in its temperature of the hotter sessions of the Chamber of Deputies back in Paris. This, regardless of the issues involved, was a healthy sign that Frenchmen were indeed pulling out of the slough of apathy and defeatism, and regaining their old Gallic spunk and temperament. They also resented the indifference and condescension of the Americans. It stung their pride more sharply than outright hostility could possibly have done.

The British, by comparison, were far more considerate of French feelings and tried not to give offense. The daily American newspaper, *Stars and Stripes,* was strictly a house organ for the AEF. And though it came out with an Algiers dateline, it never so much as mentioned the momentous meeting of the delegates of the French Underground. But its British counterpart, the *Union Jack,* reported on the meeting at some length.

Consequently in Algiers there was a gradual rise in British stock, inversely commensurate to the steady decline in American popularity. A year before, when the Americans headed the North African landings, they had stood ace-high with the French. Hence they encountered a minimum of resistance; whereas the British, had they been in the forefront, would doubtless have met determined opposition. The anti-British poison skillfully injected into France's fevered brain after Dunkirk was still working. Furthermore, the French had not yet forgiven the British attack on the French fleet at Mers-el-Kebir.

Ever since the Allies set foot on North African soil, the British had been watching their step. They kept their skirts carefully clear throughout the maladroit attempt to foist General Henri Giraud on the French Liberation Movement in place of General de Gaulle. They also took pains not to irritate the French unnecessarily in small matters. In Franco-American disputes they assumed the role of mediators seeking to reconcile the Americans to the French viewpoint. And despite the fact that lingering French rancor was fanned from time to time by mistrust of British motives in Syria—a portion of the French suspected the British of secretly encouraging the Syrian and Lebanese demands for complete independence—Franco-British relations had begun to improve. By making amends for past mistakes and washing away the bad blood between the French and English, Churchill sought to pave the way for a renewal of that close alliance that had long been a keystone of British policy.

The British and Americans no longer had the diplomatic field in Algiers to themselves. A third power had appeared on the scene and was throwing its mighty weight around, quite gently for a start. In Algiers I hastened to call on Alexander Bogomolov, the newly arrived Soviet representative. For three hours we sat in his room in Algiers' swank Hotel Miletti, now an army billet for colonels or better, but looking about as seedy and run-down as the rest of the town. Part of its façade, damaged in an early German air raid, still boarded over.

In the low candlepower light we munched tropical fruit that had been presented to Bogomolov that afternoon and discussed the international situation. Also present was a young fellow with the build of a football tackle, whom Bogomolov once or twice addressed as Misha. Throughout our conversation Misha lounged on the couch and said nothing, though he listened intently to every word.

Bogomolov was convinced that the Western Powers would find it economically profitable to maintain good relations with the Soviet Union and to forge a strong postwar collective security system.

It was the economic base, he said, that determined policy and outlook. Take the Orthodox Church in Russia, continued Bogomolov (his name in literal translation means "Praygod," suggesting that he had had highly devout ancestors somewhere along the line), in the old days, as the established State Church, its economic base had been the Tsarist system. The Revolution cut its economic roots out from under it, so for years it was against the Soviet system. But now the Soviet Government has made terms with the Church and provided it with another economic base, albeit a more modest one; so now the Orthodox Church had a stake in the Soviet system and would work for it. That was the whole secret, he added confidently.

"But how about the Marxist assertion that religion is the opium of the people?" I objected.

"Oh, that," answered Mr. Praygod deprecatingly, "is a matter for individual opinion. Our Soviet Constitution stands for freedom of conscience, you know."

Bogomolov, perfect diplomat, was careful to say nothing to me that might be construed as criticism of the Allies. After all, North Africa was their theater. But he hinted that the Fighting French, all too weary of their weakness and dependency on the big powers, did not enjoy being constantly reminded of the fact. And the patronizing attitude of many of the Americans was constantly rubbing salt into their wounded pride.

"You know what French pride is," Bogomolov remarked. "At present it's about all they've got left. No wonder they're a bit hypersensitive."

The Russian was frankly disturbed by the presence in Algiers scot-free of a number of ex-Cagoulards and other gentlemen who in peacetime France had taken no pains to conceal their fascist sympathies. Bogomolov hoped that the Allies would come to realize that halfway measures were not enough to rid the world of the Fascist and Nazi menace. If any sort of stable peace was to follow this war, a clean sweep must be made. That was why Bogomolov and his Government were also perturbed by the political setup in the portions of Southern Italy then under AMG control—which none of them had been allowed to visit as yet.

There was something mildly professorial about Bogomolov's spectacled oval countenance and his soft-spoken concise delivery. It suggested the scholar rather than the man of action. His fund of background knowledge was encyclopedic and his logic, in his own Marxian terms of reference, unassailable.

Alexander Bogomolov was a comparatively young man. Unlike Maxim Litvinov, Ivan Maisky and other Soviet diplomats of the older generation, Bogomolov had not known Lenin or Trotsky. He had no pre-Revolutionary political past to make or mar him. He had matured under the regime.

His career in the Soviet foreign service had been brilliant. In 1932 he was appointed Soviet Ambassador to China, holding that post through the critical years of Japanese expansion into Manchuria and Inner Mongolia. Bogomolov had successfully weathered the purge of 1937-38 that had wrought such havoc among his colleagues, and in 1939 he succeeded Potemkin as Soviet Ambassador to France. After the French capitulation of June, 1940, he followed the rump regime to Vichy.

That was during the period of Soviet neutrality, but on June 26, 1941, the fourth day of the German attack on the Eastern Front, the Petain Government without much argument yielded to Hitler's pressure and severed diplomatic relations with the Soviet Union. Bogomolov was next appointed Soviet Ambassador to the European Governments in Exile, with headquarters in London. There he formed many valuable personal contacts. He was especially cordial with Dr. Eduard Benes, head of the Czech Government; under his tutelage, Czech-Soviet relations soon recovered from the setback of the now defunct Soviet-German Pact, and the old cordiality was restored. In Vichy, Bogomolov had never cultivated the personal intimacy and confidence of aged, rabidly anti-Soviet Marshal Petain, but in London he was soon on the friendliest footing with another French officer of monarchist and Catholic antecedents, General Charles de Gaulle. The Fighting French leader, smarting from the snubs he received with such regularity from his British patrons and their American Allies, responded swiftly to the overtures of Bogomolov, who alone of the representatives of the three major Allied powers treated him with full equality as the representative of a first-class sovereign power. In cementing these good relations with de Gaulle and the Fighting French, Bogomolov was by no means acting solely on his own initiative.

With characteristic judgment and foresight, the Russian Government early recognized that de Gaulle, whatever his political antecedents, had become the voice and leader of conquered but undefeated France. Regardless of what London or Washington might think of this irascible and not always tactful soldier, the Russians recognized that he was all things to all Frenchmen whose spirit had not been blighted by the Nazi caterpillars. They perceived that his courage and pride were those of France, his voice that of France. The very foibles which his critics sought to magnify and exploit— his touchiness and addiction to histrionics—were French foibles.

In the early days of the North African campaign, when de Gaulle was getting kicked around a bit by the American and British Governments, the Russians kept carefully out of it. The Darlan-Peyrouton-Giraud tragicomedy had no repercussions on relations between the Russians and the Fighting French. The Russians were not even present.

But as soon as de Gaulle's ascendancy had been vindicated and the former Vichyites ousted, the Soviet Government promptly recognized the French National Liberation Committee in Algiers as the "representative of the state interests of the French Republic and as the leader of all French patriots fighting against the Hitlerite tyranny," a far more sweeping recognition than was ever bestowed by either Britain or America.

The Russians complained that Bogomolov's arrival in Algiers to take up his duties had been deliberately held up for a considerable period by Allied red tape. The French believed this story. In any event, with his coming, a direct link was established between the

Soviet Government and the French Committee of National Liberation. Relations between the Russians and the Fighting French,
already good, became even better.

The strengthening of the Soviet influence in Algiers had tangible
repercussions. Already, at the time of my visit, stringent measures
were being taken to smoke out former Vichyites and other suspect
elements, and to bring traitors to justice. A few weeks later the
Russian delegation to the Inter-Allied Mediterranean Commission
arrived, fifty-strong, headed by rapier-minded Deputy Foreign
Commissar Andrei Vyshinsky. Perhaps Vyshinsky, who was state
prosecutor during the famous Soviet treason trials, gave the French
a few helpful suggestions on how to run their purge. At any rate,
thereafter it gathered momentum, to the grim satisfaction of
French patriots everywhere; and General de Gaulle's popularity—
though showing no increase in Washington and London—soared
to new heights among his fellow-countrymen.

The Russian policy of closer ties with the French has been aided
by the military situation. For a long time the Red Army was the
sole army fighting the main bulk of the *Wehrmacht* on the European Continent. And during the months when there was no Second
Front, Soviet propaganda—as well as the French Communist Underground—exploited that fact to the utmost. In the night of
oppression the only light of hope seemed to come from the East.
Even the Allied air war redounded to Russia's favor. For it was
inevitable that in raids directed against Nazi military objectives
in France (such as the Renault Automobile Works outside Paris),
French civilians should also suffer.

The same applied to the bitterness that sometimes addled French
joy at being liberated by the Allied armies after the invasion of
France. For war is a nasty business regardless of the purpose, and
a lot of French towns were knocked to pieces and a lot of Frenchmen killed in the process of being liberated.

By contrast, no French civilians were killed, no French houses
hit, by the Russians. To the French, the Red Army offensive was
a war against *le Boche* pure and simple.

The Russians, for their part, always gave full credit to the activities of the French Resistance Movement. And after the Allied land-

ings in France, they approved and supported the Fighting French demands for more of a part in the military operations.

From the outset relations between the Soviets and the Free French were helped by the fact that the Free French saw a distinct advantage for themselves in closer contacts with Moscow. To this end they sent a picked group of French fighter pilots to the Soviet Union in the autumn of 1942. These were the members of the Normandie Squadron which has made a name for itself in Russia, flying with the Red Air Force through every major campaign of the last two years.

Improved contact with Moscow aided the Fighting French in many directions. It enabled General de Gaulle to some extent to follow a stronger line in his dealings with Britain and America. An occasional hint was enough to frighten the Western Powers with the prospect that the Free French, if not handled gently, would gravitate into Russia's orbit, which would be especially upsetting to Churchill's dream for a postwar renewal and strengthening of the Anglo-French alliance as the cornerstone of British Continental policy.

The object which recently took General Charles de Gaulle to Moscow was much the same as the motive behind President Raymond Poincaré's visit to St. Petersburg in 1914. Then as now France and Russia were drawn together by the common threat of Prussian militarism. Today the French look to the Soviet Union as the one great continental power with the means and the will to keep Germany in check and prevent a new German comeback. The Russians realize that they can rely on France to back them on their policy of a stern peace for Germany.

The seeds of the Franco-Soviet Pact, which de Gaulle signed in Moscow, were being sedulously tended by Bogomolov at the time of my Algiers visit.

AMERICANS AND POLES IN PERSIA—
WILLKIE AND AFTER

☆ ☆ ☆ ☆ ☆ ☆ ☆ ☆ ☆ ☆ ☆ ☆ ☆ ☆

FOR ANYONE like myself who had been in Egypt in Eighth Army days, to return to Cairo late in 1943 was an anticlimax. The flight from Algiers took me over territory I had traced and retraced during the see-saw desert war against Rommel. Now even the areas of heaviest fighting were as empty as a theater locked up for the night after the audience has gone home and the stage has been cleared. The shifting sands had filled in the old trenches and bunkers, and were slowly engulfing the rusted hulks of vehicles, tanks, and planes that alone recalled the fighting.

But, Cairo—it had taken Rommel and the *Afrika Korps* camped on the doorstep almost to rouse that noisy, sleepy, fabulously wealthy, poverty-plagued, Oriental, Western metropolis from its habitual routine.

Its ears were too full of its own noises, its nostrils too full of its own smells, its eyes too full of its own colorful sights for anything short of a major catastrophe to disrupt the animated aimlessness of Cairo's daily life. Through sluggish millenniums this Nile Valley, like the fabled Lotus Island, had ever imposed its own habits and outlook on successive alien conquerors. And now in the shade of the banyans at the Gezira Club, among the palms of Garden City, or on the terrace of Shepheard's Hotel overlooking the bustle of peddlers and dragomans in Suleiman Pasha, the old poison seemed to be at work on the incumbent foreign masters, the British.

In the days of the desert battles, the war effort had provided a powerful antidote, though even then the poison of Egypt slowed down efficiency. But now the war had moved away from Africa and the old incentive was gone. GHQ Middle East, though it continued to employ a huge staff, had slipped back into the easygoing ways that had been so rudely interrupted by Italy's declaration of war in 1940. In those days there had been a certain feeling of expectancy in the face of a future ominous with threats; now even that exhilaration was lacking. For Cairo the future held nothing.

The correspondents on the scene had little to do but follow local games of Balkan politics, played endlessly in a vacuum by Governments in Exile that shuffled and reshuffled the same old packs of cabinet ministers. And both correspondents and exiled politicians waited forlornly for a British expedition that would set them ashore in the Balkans.

Diplomatic relations had been established between Egypt and the Soviet Union and the Soviet minister and his staff were expected shortly. This was a far cry from the autumn of 1941, when the Egyptian Government, haunted by the specter of any threat to its rotten-to-the-core social order, had not only refused to establish relations with Russia, but when Litvinov was scheduled to pass through en route to the United States, had at first withheld permission for him to land in Egyptian territory. Finally, under Allied pressure, the authorities had agreed that he might land but would have to spend the night in the plane. Any embarrassment this might have caused was avoided, however, as British Airways in Teheran contrived to fumble the Soviet envoy's priority and left him grounded. Furious, Litvinov had flown via the Pacific instead—only a few days ahead of Mr. Kurusu.

More recently, there had been in Cairo an amusing bit of contretemps with another Soviet through-passenger, a Soviet press correspondent homeward bound from the United States. Some of the British Airways officials with a none too pro-Soviet cast of mind had decided the fellow could jolly well cool his heels on a low priority. Each morning the Russian dutifully called the Airways office to be told laconically they were sorry they couldn't take him that day. After which he went forth into the city determined to make the best of his enforced stay. In the course of two weeks, he contacted the editors of all the Arabic papers, wrote several articles for them, and arranged for them to take the Soviet news service; interviewed most of the leading Egyptian political figures; and was engaged in collecting vital statistics—when the British suddenly caught up with his activities. There must have been some fast exchanges between the higherups and the Airways office! For one day at noon—in the morning he had been given the usual runaround—the Airways office called him and announced that they could take him first thing in the morning.

After calling on a few old friends, I was ready to leave Cairo with no regrets. Contrasted with the aimlessness of Cairo, John Payne Field was a beehive of purposeful efficiency. The fumes that drugged the British at GHQ in Garden City did not reach this American built and operated airport which, though geographically in Egypt, was a transplanted corner of the U. S., in no way different from the scores of similar airports with which our Air Transport Command has circled the globe. Within six months concrete runways, a big modern terminal building, and neat rows of brick barracks had mushroomed on a bare expanse of desert.

The seven-hour, non-stop flight from Cairo to Teheran gives a bird's-eye picture of some of the most storied lands in the world.

Sinai, Palestine, the garden terraces and white walls of Jerusalem, the deep sink of the Dead Sea with the green margined Jordan wriggling into it. Then Mesopotamia, land of two rivers, the Modern Iraq, once the granary of the ancients, most fertile part of the Fertile Crescent, now languishing neglected, its irrigation ditches and rich soil choked with drifting sand. Then rows of sharp jagged mountain ranges and the central Persian Plateau— another barren, water-starved country.

At the northern end of this tableland, rimmed by the lofty Elborz Mountain range, stands Teheran. On clear days the snow-crowned cone of Demavend dominates the far horizon, but through the arid summer months it is curtained by the dust haze. At four thousand feet elevation, Teheran is blessed with a climate far healthier than the sunbaked lowlands of the south along the Persian Gulf. But the rarefied atmosphere causes newcomers to complain of dizziness for the first few weeks before they get acclimatized. Save for irrigated patches, the country around Teheran is as bald as the Sahara; though in the fall rainy season it is often pelted by cloudbursts. There is no vegetation to hold the moisture in the soil, and so it runs off with no beneficial effect. Not so very long ago as history is measured in this ancient land, this area was clothed in forests and grass. But the people cut down the trees for firewood and the goats sheared the grass faster than the new shoots could grow. Some agricultural experts whom the "Old Shah," Rheza Khan Palehvi (father of the present Shah, whom the Russians and British forced to abdicate in 1941), brought in for consultation, devised a reforestation scheme, but the old Shah lost interest when he found that the transformation would not be effected in his lifetime.

Teheran—the new part of the city—was built as the old Shah's conception of what a modern European city must be like. The old Shah, a self-made despot who rose to his high station from shepherd boy, had never been out of Persia, but that did not cramp his style. It all began one day when his expensive new Renault limousine became wedged between the walls of a Teheran thoroughfare, scratching the fenders and blocking his further progress. In a rage the Shah ordered that by sundown next day the street should be widened. And the Shah's word was absolute law. Therefore his architects got busy. Foreigners were called in and in the course of a decade the main part of Teheran was transformed from an Oriental maze into the present city of broad straight avenues and spacious squares flanked by imposing public buildings. The plan required that every house must have at least two stories. In many cases the owners got around this by simply building up a false front with windows painted on it—which seemed to meet the specifications. In fact, much of Teheran's modern exterior is a false front.

The city is totally lacking in that most elementary prerequisite of a modern city, a sanitary water supply and sewage disposal system. At various times of day, water is flushed through gutters along the sides of the streets. The people dip their drinking jugs, wash their feet, scrub their clothes, and pour their slops in this same ditch. This combined water and sewage system is vindicated by a passage in the Koran to the effect that running water purifies itself every seven feet. When some Swedish engineers once tried to sell the old Shah on installing a clean drinking-water system, he dismissed the proposal with the remark that he never drank water anyway, but only tea.

The Old Shah had other vagaries. At Ab Ali, some sixty miles from Teheran, where mineral springs bubbled out of a fissure in the Elborz Mountains, he decreed a luxurious hotel similar to those he had heard existed at Europeans spas. The hotel in due course was completed, with long lobbies sumptuously hung with Persian rugs, but with room accommodations for only a score of guests.

Despite his eccentricities, Shah Reza did much to modernize the country. He built roads, and perhaps his main achievement was the construction of the Transiranian Railway. This line was the Shah's own brainchild. He had spurned suggestions of linking it up with the Iraqi Railway and hence with Turkish and European systems, or with the Russian line to Tabriz in the North, or with the Indian Railways in Baluchistan. To underscore his independence and show the world that he had no intention of providing his powerful neighbors with a highway of penetration, he built his new railway at right angles to the course of commerce—from an arbitrary point on the Persian Gulf to another arbitrary point on the Caspian. The road was not built primarily for commercial purposes; it was the Shah's personal plaything. He had his own private train which was kept in constant readiness, with the steam up, ready to take him for a ride whenever his royal fancy so desired.

Little did the Shah realize that this toy of his would prove ideally suited for the Lend-Lease supply route to Russia.

It was in Teheran that inter-Allied military collaboration was first successfully undertaken—more than two years before the Stalin-Roosevelt-Churchill meeting there. In August, 1941, Britain and the Soviet Union by joint agreement sent their troops in to the country from the north and south in order to clean up the nests of Axis espionage and intrigue, and secure the country as a corridor for supplies to Russia.

Soon after America entered the war, Britain and Russia decided to take her into partnership in their occupation of Iran. The reason was that the Allies were anxious to secure the maximum co-operation of the Persians, and they decided the Americans were best suited to this purpose. The Persians, in the past oft divided by their powerful neighbors into spheres of influence, were antagonistic to both Russia and Britain. But Americans shared none of this heritage of suspicion. Most Persians literally thought of Uncle Sam as a benevolent if somewhat eccentric elderly gentleman with whiskers—an opinion based on the fact that the occasional Americans who visited their country in peacetime had been for the most part missionary-educators, archaeologists, astronomers, and globe-trotting philanthropists. And twice in the past, American college economists—Dr. Schuster in 1907 and Dr. Millspaugh in the early twenties—had made well-intentioned, if not too successful, efforts to unsnarl the country's finances and balance the national budget.

And now again the Persian Government asked for, and got, American experts to help reorganize everything from its currency to its traffic system. By accident rather than design, they also got American officers to train and modernize their army. In February, 1942, an American military mission of twenty-odd members, headed by Major General Greeley, arrived in Teheran en route to Moscow. They were to pick up their Soviet visas in Teheran; but apparently there was some misunderstanding, for the visas never materialized. After six months of fruitless waiting, they were redesignated "U. S. Army Mission to the Iranian Army."

On my previous visit to Teheran in September-October, 1942, the first of the American experts had just arrived. But already they were running into difficulties.

An American Army doctor, Lieutenant Colonel Neuwirth from New York, had been installed as advisor to the Persian Ministry of Health. Because of the polluted water supply, typhoid, dysentery, and other enteric diseases took a regular monthly toll; while Asiatic cholera was a periodical visitor. Neuwirth's untiring work on behalf of the community soon won him a high decoration from the Shah. Nevertheless, the task confronting him would have discouraged a less determined crusader in the cause of progress and enlightenment. Besides material handicaps, at every turn he encountered entrenched prejudice and corruption, sometimes in strange quarters.

The British Legation had its own spring water piped in from the mountains. For years this British Legation water was reputed of surpassing purity and was peddled all over town by a fleet of donkey watercarts. Then one day Dr. Neuwirth analyzed it and pronounced it contaminated. The charge was, of course, denied by those who had anything to do with the sale of water. But the charges and counter-charges evoked sharp discussion, and illustrated the tremendous difficulties that face the attempt to improve primitive sanitation.

One of the early American experts to arrive in Persia was Colonel Schwartzkopf, the former New Jersey police chief at the time of the Lindbergh kidnaping case. His job was to reorganize the Persian Gendarmerie, or national police, which had been a center of Nazi influence. Its main function was presumably to keep order in the country among the wild tribesmen. Since the removal of the stern hand of the Old Shah, they had been getting obstreperous, often taking potshots at the supply convoys which were beginning to wind through the mountains in ever-increasing volume. On one of his earlier inspection tours, Schwartzkopf discovered that his Gendarmes were sometimes more of a menace than the tribesmen, that they were in the habit of extorting tribute from travelers and staging their own holdups.

An equally tough job was that of reorganizing the Teheran City Police. This fell to the lot of L. S. Timmerman, a man with many years' experience overhauling the police departments of American Midwestern cities. His first difficulty, and one he never quite solved, was to get a competent interpreter. His second was the fact that his Persian Chief, who had to sign all the papers and issue the orders, was doped with opium most of the time.

Tim's first efforts were directed toward eliminating bribery by securing a living wage for his cops. He discovered that the ordinary Persian flatfoot got the equivalent of eight dollars per month if he was illiterate (and 90 per cent of the force was) and twelve if he could read. The first reaction from the Persian higher-ups to Tim's proposal for a wage increase was blank amazement. Of course the men took bribes! So did everyone. They always had, they always would. What was wrong with it? It saved the Government a lot of expense.

One day Tim staged a surprise inspection trip to the Teheran prison. He knew that if the prison authorities got wind that he was coming, they would arrange a conducted tour for him and he would see nothing of true conditions. As it was, the warden almost had apoplexy when Tim and Neuwirth, whom Tim took with him, arrived. His hands shook so that he could hardly manipulate the keys. Conditions defied description. The prisoners, having been robbed of their clothes, walked around wrapped in filthy blankets that crawled with vermin. Though this was nominally a jail for people detained while awaiting trial, some of the inmates had been there for five and six years—so long that neither they nor the jailers could remember what the charges against them were.

On the other hand there were a few favored prisoners, mostly officials and favorites of Reza Shah, arrested after his abdication. These had comfortable quarters to themselves, were allowed out on parole, and could bring women in. Among these privileged inmates was Mukhtari, former police chief under Reza, who had been sentenced to eight years' imprisonment.

His crime was that for years he had murdered the Shah's political enemies by the ingenious method of injecting air bubbles into their bloodstream with a hypodermic syringe. At the time of the inspection, Mukhtari was in town shopping.

Two years later Tim keeled over in the traces, still battling for law and order.

In September, 1942, I flew to Teheran with Wendell Willkie, who had invited me to join his party aboard the plane *Gulliver* at Jerusalem. During his four-day stay in the Iranian capital, Willkie discovered that professional Iranian politicians are even more slippery and evasive than their American counterparts. In those days the Germans were still camped at El Alamein on the threshold of Alexandria and the Suez Canal, and they were driving through the Caucasus towards the Caspian and Baku, not so very far from the Iranian border. And though Iran was under Allied occupation, many Iranians were still banking on a German victory. Willkie, after his interview with the Premier Saltani el Gawam, reported that the latter had agreed to make a pro-Allied declaration before the Mejlis—the Iranian parliament—in his speech the following day. Imagine Willkie's and our disappointment when the Prime

Minister confined himself to an attack on "grafters." Of the Allies,
not a word. An old-timer in Teheran explained to Willkie that an
Iranian will promise a visitor anything for the sake of politeness
and hospitality, but that the promise is in no way considered bind-
ing. To these Asiatics, frankness and veracity were not virtues;
they were signs of a feeble intellect.

"Never try to do business with an Iranian that way," an Armenian businessman and friend of mine once explained. "The Iranian
always expects and prefers the indirect approach. Suppose, for example, I have some sugar that I want to sell to an Iranian merchant.
Before offering him my sugar, I begin my conversation with him
on some entirely unrelated subject such as his brother-in-law's
health, or the latest parliamentary debate. Then, by degrees, without giving him the least inkling as to my purpose, I try to find
out whether he wants sugar. Having ascertained this to my satisfaction, but still without enlightening him, I remark in passing
what a pity it is that sugar is so scarce and expensive. Gauging his
reaction, I pass on to some totally irrelevant subject and wait for
him to revert to the subject of sugar. If he shows the proper interest, I then remark that unfortunately I have no sugar, but, being
pressed, I tell him that while I have no sugar myself, I do have a
friend who may perhaps have a little which he doesn't want to
sell. I then add that as a personal favor I might undertake to try
to persuade my friend to part with a little of his precious sugar.
And thus by slow degrees our verbal sparring proceeds until a
transaction is agreed upon. It is complicated by the fact that my
merchant is himself no novice at the game. He, too, is constantly
trying to trip me into revealing my intentions by a careless word,
thus giving him the psychological advantage. In such ceremonious
haggling, time is no object; it can drag on for days before the deal
is consummated."

This exposé seems to confirm a common saying in the Middle
East that it takes an Armenian to understand and outsmart an
Iranian. It also explains why Americans found Iranians difficult
to understand and deal with. Teheran and Rushville were both in
"one world," but they still were worlds apart.

With one Iranian, however, Willkie got along famously. That

was young Shah Mohammed Reza. The Monarch seemed deeply impressed with the Hoosier's sincerity and his assurances that America was pledged to safeguard the rights of small nations, both during the war and at the peace conference table. The sequel to a pleasant open-air luncheon at the Shah's summer palace (at which the servitors backed away with the empty plates so as always to face the Presence) was a spin aloft in *Gulliver*—the first time the King of Kings had ever been airborne. So perhaps there was still something to be said for the American direct line of approach, even in Iran.

At that time Americans were still but a handful in Teheran— far outnumbered by the British and Russians. During the day one saw Red Army uniforms walking in twos and threes through the center of town, but for the most part they kept strictly to themselves. For the bulk of the Russian troops, who were quartered near the airport, the city was off limits. One never saw an intoxicated Russian soldier, and the only Russians who were free to visit the restaurants and cabarets were airforce pilots assigned to ferry back American Lend-Lease planes as a respite from combat duty. By contrast, the British and the few Americans about were often mixed up in bar brawls and street fights.

But the most conspicuous foreigners in Persia at that time were the Poles whom General Anders was evacuating from the Soviet Union through Persia. The underlying reasons for the evacuation have been discussed in a previous chapter. Anders was far more concerned with getting troops out of Russia than civilians. It was strictly not a case of women and children first. By September the evacuation was virtually finished. Some eighty thousand soldiers had been brought out of Russia, and most of them had already been shipped on to Palestine and Iraq. Of the thirty-five thousand noncombatants who came out, about ten thousand had been sent off to Kenya by ship from the Persian Gulf.

The remaining Poles showed little desire to go to Kenya. They were quite content, it seemed, to sit the war out in Persia—so long as the liberal flow of British and American funds and American Red Cross supplies continued. Over the protests of the Persians, some of them had taken jobs or gone into business in town. But the local shops and restaurants vied for their custom, and notices in Polish began to appear in every window on the Lalazar, Teheran's long, narrow, main shopping street. Local wits renamed it the "Polish Corridor."

American Red Cross foodstuffs, clothing, blankets, and surgical supplies were arriving in Teheran at the rate of one thousand tons monthly. They were to be forwarded to the Polish refugees in Russia through the Soviet Red Cross. The Poles, however, objected to dealing through the Soviet Red Cross, declaring that if the supplies got into Russian hands the Poles would never see them. It was therefore decided that the Polish Red Cross would take over the shipments in Teheran and forward them to its own delegates in Russia. But the Poles themselves, with what assistance the British could give them, could not handle more than 450 tons monthly. The result was that through the spring and summer of 1942 huge quantities of American Red Cross supplies piled up in Teheran warehouses.

Inevitably some members of the Polish Red Cross succumbed to the temptation of inflated prices in Teheran. In the middle of July some 5709 sacks of high-grade American flour were turned over to the Polish Red Cross by Bill MacDonald, the tall lanky American Red Cross representative. The Poles moved the sacks from the railway yards to a large warehouse at Polish Civilian Camp No. 2, outside Teheran. There was no way of locking up the warehouse. But a guard was on duty so that presumably the flour could not be removed without authority. In the first week of August, MacDonald on a routine checkup visited the warehouse to find that the flour had disappeared. Kolat and Stiburski, the Polish Red Cross representatives who had signed the receipts for the flour, denied all knowledge of its whereabouts. Their manner toward MacDonald was distinctly unfriendly.

MacDonald next did some sleuthing on his own and soon traced the flour to a Persian warehouse where it was being mixed with local flour and sold commercially.

At the same time, though the baking of white bread was illegal for Persians, large quantities of white bread were being sold openly in the more expensive bakery shops. This MacDonald traced to the Polish camps that had stocks of American Red Cross flour. For his pains, MacDonald incurred the bitter animosity of the Poles. They began pulling strings in Washington, demanding his recall because of his "anti-Polish sentiments" and seeking his replacement by someone more pliant to their purposes. A few months later MacDonald was recalled.

Meanwhile, word was received that all the Polish Red Cross delegates in the Soviet Union had been arrested and would shortly be expelled from the country. The Russians charged that they had caught two of the delegates red-handed using their official duties— which enabled them to travel about quite a bit—as a cloak for gathering military information.

The Teheran Poles were violently indignant over this latest "affront" to their national pride and publicly protested that this would leave hundreds of thousands of Polish women and children to perish by starvation and exposure. I discussed the pros and cons of the case with a senior British liaison officer attached to the Polish Army, whose bias if anything was pro-Polish.

"The trouble is," he said, "that our Polish friends are so confoundedly inept—it's a deuce of a mess about those delegates. But there's nothing we can do about it. The Russians have definite proof of the charges, you see."

In Teheran there was a sizable group of old-school Polish officers and former Government officials who openly declared that war with the Soviet Union was not only inevitable, but desirable.

With the Willkie party I visited one of the Polish camps for civilians. In the vast bare rooms of a drafty building that once must have served as a school of some sort, hundreds of families squatted on the floor, barricaded from their neighbors by their bundles of belongings. All had recently come out of Russia, and while we were there we saw a bus from the Caspian port of Pahlevi deliver a new batch. They were marched off with their bundles to the fumigating station.

Neither the incumbents nor the new arrivals seemed in bad shape. Most of the young girls had a peasant, apple-cheeked look that made Willkie want to be photographed with them. To the commandant who had been showing us around, expatiating the

while on the ill-treatment of the Poles in Russia, I remarked on
how healthy most of the people seemed.

At my comment he frowned slightly, rubbing his jowl, and
answered, "If you come around and bring your camera another
day, I'll· guarantee you some vivid photos of how terrible our
people look when they come out of Russia. I'll fix up anything
you like. You're a reporter, you publish your pictures. It'll be sensational, yes?" he ended insinuatingly. It was some moments
before I caught the full impact of his meaning.

I observed the commandant with new curiosity. His stocky
form was encased in a British-issue, officer's summer uniform, but
with the insignia of a *pulkownik*—a colonel in the Polish Army—
fastened to the shoulder tabs. A black patch curtained the empty
socket of one eye, but not the deep gash in the cheek below. "The
Bolsheviks gave me that," he said, answering my unuttered question.

"In 1939?" I asked blandly.

"You're twenty years off," he replied. "I got that in 1919 serving
with Denikin below Oryol."

Only then did I note that his Russian, save for an alcoholic
wheeze, bore no traces of a Polish or any other foreign accent.

When he learned that I had lived for several years in the Soviet
Union, he asked, "And were you never in a prison camp?"

He seemed surprised when I told him I had not been, and added,
reflectively, "You must consider yourself fortunate that you got
out and are not now rotting in a prison camp. That's Bolshevism
for you—a concentration camp run by Jews."

Later I found that this *pulkownik* was on terms of intimacy with
an American major of Polish extraction who was in town gathering data on the Poles for G 2 in Washington. Before he was commissioned, he had been a physical training instructor in a small-
town high school and was enormously proud of his chest expansion. When he was on the point of returning to Washington, he
showed me some lurid photos he was taking back with him.

"I guess that'll burn 'em up!" was his comment.

I mentally recalled our mutual friend, the *pulkownik,* and the
photos he offered me.

From the standpoint of these anti-Soviet Poles, publicity in America for the alleged piteous plight of the refugees and their inhuman treatment by the Russians served a twofold purpose. First, it ensured that the generous, and to them profitable, flow of American Red Cross supplies would be maintained. Second, it tended to align American public opinion against Russia.

Through the American major of Polish extraction I met a Polish officer who told me the story of a Polish prisoner of war conspiracy in a Soviet camp, boasting of his leading part in the plot.

Before the war, the officer had lived in Detroit for a time, so his English was colloquial. Like many other officers, he had been captured by the Russians in September, 1939, and sent to a camp on the banks of the Pechora River in the vast subarctic forests of the Komi Autonomous Republic. Having obtained an assignment as a semi-trusty, which allowed him considerable freedom of movement between adjacent camps, this man functioned as the link in a large plot, hatched immediately after the German attack on Russia. The plan was to overpower the guards, seize their arms, and then appeal by radio for German aid in the form of planes and paratroops.

This plan is less fantastic than it appears at first sight, when one recalls that in that vast and sparsely populated region planes are the sole means of rapid communication. The prison guards were comparatively few in number, and the conspirators were counting on a general revolt of the criminal and political prisoners as well as the prisoners of war. At that time the Germans were advancing rapidly, and the air-distance from their bases in northern Finland was only a few hours. Only the release of the Polish prisoners under the terms of the Polish-Soviet treaty forestalled the conspiracy.

THROUGH RUSSIA'S SIDE DOOR

☆ ☆ ☆ ☆ ☆ ☆ ☆ ☆ ☆ ☆ ☆ ☆ ☆ ☆

FOR ALLIED diplomacy and war materials the road to Moscow in the present war has led through Teheran—a roundabout route no matter how you hold the map. In wartime a straight line is seldom the shortest way.

In prewar times, as part of my job as Moscow representative of a big steamship company, I used to meet large contingents of American tourists who "did" the Soviet Union in the summer. Their booked tour usually included the Scandinavian countries, with stopovers in Copenhagen and Stockholm en route to Leningrad. Despite its directness and the added attraction of the white nights, I always thought this approach placed Russia and the Russians in about the worst of all possible lights.

For after the bandbox tidiness of Stockholm or Copenhagen even the best Russian cities looked a bit shabby, as few of the tourists failed to remark. The worst feature was probably the plumbing. Strange as it seems now, in those piping days of peace the American tourist abroad tended to measure human progress and civilization mainly by the plumbing, which was definitely not a factor in Russia's favor. Many a time I had to listen to caustic comparisons with Stockholm, where things were different, and in my official capacity had to transmit to the management indignant complaints about the bathroom facilities or, rather, the lack thereof. This unfavorable first impression of the Soviet Union tended to stick to the tourist, the more so as it usually confirmed his preconceptions and his conviction—often the product of wishful thinking —that socialism wouldn't work. It also encouraged the assumption of a sneering attitude toward the Russians and their efforts—which in turn confirmed the Russian's own dislike and distrust of foreigners.

The war in Europe not only stopped the tourist trade, of course, but it also sealed the Scandinavian route and all other lines of approach via Europe. Since then Moscowarding foreigners, from Winston Churchill to Eric Johnston, have traveled through Asiatic Teheran, which was reached via the Middle East. This approach sets the Soviet Union off to far better advantage. And it is with the East, rather than the most advanced parts of Europe, that Russia deserves comparison. For the ignorance, poverty, and oppression of the masses in old Russia was far nearer the Asiatic than the North-European standard.

After the starvation, the filth, the human degradation that meets the eye everywhere on the journey through North Africa, Egypt, Iraq, and Iran, the Soviet Union, with its youthful confidence and spirit, is indeed a contrast.

In my days with the Eighth Army in Egypt, I was indelibly impressed with the utter indifference of most of the native population to the issues and the outcome of the war. Even in the days when a victorious Rommel was moving on Alexandria, the Egyptian *fellaheen* remained completely impassive. Since before the Pyramids were built, countless invasions had rolled over their backs without satisfying their gnawing hunger or slaking their parching thirst. One set of masters had simply replaced another.

Millenniums of hopelessness seem to have drained the vitality from both the people and the soil itself. Through most of the Middle East the flyspecked apathy of the inhabitants is matched by the dust-choked, sunbaked barrenness of nature. Even from ten thousand feet up in the air, the land presents an appalling sight. The hazy cubic miles of yellow emptiness extend almost uninterrupted from the West Coast of Africa to Teheran.

By contrast, the Russian countryside, viewed from the air in spring or summer, is a lush green carpet patterned with forests, rich meadows, and fields of waving grain—all interwoven with broad winding rivers. The snow-mantled winter landscape is as clean and fresh as an unwritten page.

When I reached Teheran en route to Moscow a year after my first visit to Iran, I found great changes. The Poles were practically gone and forgotten. The Russians were still around as big as life; the British were huddled in the wings; the Americans held the center of the stage and ran the show. For by now the Transiranian supply route from the Gulf of Persia to Teheran was completely in the hands of the U.S. Army's Persian Gulf Command. Under the able direction of Major General Donald Connally, American railroadmen from the New Haven, the Pennsylvania, the New York Central, and the Union Pacific operated the railway with American locomotives and rolling stock brought over for the purpose. They were hauling Lend-Lease supplies for Russia at the rate of 200,000 tons a month or better, while additional thousands of tons came up by road in giant Studebaker six-wheeler trucks that were themselves assembled by Americans from Detroit in American equipped assembly plants at Khorramshar and Andimeshk in southern Persia for consignment to Russia.

To house its thousands of troops in the Teheran area, the Persian Gulf Command had constructed two large camps: Camp Atterbury for the railwaymen, below the town down by the railway yards; and Camp Amirabad, three miles above the town near the foot of the mountains, for the other categories. There were row upon row of brick billets with hot and cold running water, a luxurious officers' mess hall with clubrooms, and an even bigger and more elaborate recreation center for the enlisted men, with a theater, a library, a cafeteria, a gym, and many social rooms. Dances were held once a week both at the officers' mess and at the recreation center—but on different nights, because the supply of girls was limited and the same girls attended both. Most of them were Polish girls—about the only Poles left in Teheran—who lived and worked at the camps, serving in the mess, cleaning up the billets, and doing the washing. Besides dances, there were movies several times a week, and an occasional USO show got this far. The reason for all this entertainment was to discourage the men as much as possible from going to town and possibly picking up VD or getting into some other trouble. In general the medical staff was about the hardest-worked outfit on the place. They had to keep a constant eye on the water (which was heavy with chlorine) and be ready to repel an invasion of any of the dozens of complicated diseases in the town. The problem was not a simple one, even for those who were conscious of what more enlightened methods could do to raise the sanitation and physical standards of this area. One can have nothing but admiration for the long hours and the selfless labor which went into the effort to hold in check this weird assortment of ills. So determined were the medical men to avoid contamination that the Commissary purchased nothing locally; everything from the canned butter to the eggpowder omelettes came from America. Even the delicious melons for which Persia is famous were declared taboo.

From Teheran to the Caspian port of Pahlevi I traveled overland, having joined forces with the two State Department couriers on the Moscow run, Charles Walson and Ashton Clark. Their baggage consisted of ten pouches of diplomatic mail and about two tons of freight, mostly motion picture reels for the Embassy in Moscow. They were extremely conscientious couriers and spent their time checking and rechecking the load piece by piece against long typewritten lists, until soon there was no more room left in the margin for additional pencil marks.

For the trip to the Caspian the Army lent us a Studebaker six-wheeler. It was not one of their best, and when we got to Kazvin— our first overnight stop—thoroughly saturated with white Persian dust, we put the truck in shop for a complete overhauling. This included replacing several gears and a wheel, and putting on a complete set of new tires all round. As Kazvin was the final servicing and repair point where the Americans handed over their trucks to the Russians, there were plenty of parts to be had.

Beyond Kazvin we would be in the Russian occupied zone, where Americans had seldom ventured. Clem, our Negro driver from Virginia who had never spoken to a Russian in his life, did not relish the prospect of having to drive back alone.

The lieutenant colonel in command at Kazvin agreed to lend us his Russian-speaking interpreter, a sergeant who was only too glad for a chance to see the forbidden country of the Russian occupation zone.

And so, with three of us riding atop the pouches and freight and one in the cabin with the driver, we started off on the final lap of the trans-Iranian trail to Russia.

A few miles north of Kazvin, rounding a bend, we suddenly bore down on the first Red Army check post. Standing in the dead center of the road in front of us was a big buxom girl in an olive drab Red Army blouse and a blue denim skirt. Great bunches of unruly flaxen hair cascaded from under her cap, while grasped firmly in her capable hands was a tommy-gun whose muzzle at that moment was pointed in our direction. The glint in the eye that was drawing a bead on us was anything but friendly.

Clem jammed the brakes to a lurching halt.

"Put dat pistol down, babe," he implored the Amazon, who in fact lowered her weapon the moment we stopped. Giving us the cool once-over, she stepped up to the driver and asked him in Russian for our documents. I produced the courier letter from the American Legation in Teheran, directing her gaze to the affixed written authorization of the Soviet Embassy. She read the inscription to herself in a half-whisper, and then, with the inevitable Russian "seechahss" (which literally translated means "this hour" and in practice implies almost anything from two minutes to infinity), disappeared into a small house with a hammer and sickle over the lintel.

After five minutes a lieutenant appeared in the doorway.

"Which of you speaks Russian?"

"I do," I answered.

"Please step inside a moment."

I followed him inside. The small room, not much more than an alcove, contained, beside a kerosene stove, portraits of Lenin, Stalin, and Berya; a battered purple-ink-stained table; and two officers of the Border Patrol Service—one of them, a major, seated; the other, a captain, standing.

"Is that the only document you have?" the captain asked me.

"No, we also have our personal passports all visaed for the Soviet Union," I answered.

"Yes, but what about the truck, have you no visa for it?"

"The truck is not going into Soviet territory," I answered, deliberately misconstruing his meaning. "It's only taking us to Pahlevi and then returning."

The captain pondered this an instant.

"The truck," he said, "should have a special permit to enter the zone of Soviet occupation."

"We inquired about that before starting," I answered. "We were told by the Soviet Embassy that would not be necessary."

"You should have consulted the Soviet Military; they, not the Embassy, make the rules," he fired back.

But at this point, just as things seemed nearing an impasse and I had grim visions of our being turned back to Teheran, dust-choked and dejected to face the scoffers, the major, who had thus far kept silent, intervened.

"After all, Anton Palich, we should not be too sticky and formal. They're Allies."

With this the captain's objections collapsed completely and he beamed accord. He had not been overruled. He had simply been relieved of the responsibility for making a decision, by a superior officer.

Now that business matters had been settled and the tension eased, both officers were friendly and talkative. What did I think of the liberation of Kiev a few days before? Wasn't the Red Army wonderful? When would the war end? How were things going in Italy? "You Americans don't seem to be making much headway there. What's wrong?" All leading up to the inevitable "When will the Second Front be opened in France?"

On most of these questions all I could tell them was wait and see. Besides, I knew my companions must be getting restless. We had over 130 miles of narrow, dusty, winding mountain road, clogged with truck convoys, to negotiate before nightfall.

As we started off, our lady roadblock, now shifted to one side, gave us a winning smile and waved farewell in a most unmilitary manner. During our journey we met many more of these Red Army girls on duty at the many check posts. Later, in the Soviet Union, I was to find them doing the same job on the frontline areas, directing traffic at intersections and river crossings, making the vehicles stay in line and keep their distance, trying to prevent traffic snarls that would delay supplies vitally needed up forward or make targets for roving enemy planes. They stood for hours in icy winter snows and under broiling summer suns. Thousands had been killed at their posts by bombs and machine guns.

Flanking the spurs of the Elborz Mountains, the road dropped dizzily toward the Caspian in an endless succession of hairpin turns, and usually at every turn there was another Studebaker six-wheeler coming at us from around the corner. More than once when we were crowded to the edge of the narrow road, I saw the wreck of some truck that had toppled off into space lying far below in a dry watercourse. But we had to make time. Clem manfully wove our juggernaut in and out of the long, slow-moving supply convoys, earning the curses of the Russian, Persian, and Central-Asiatic drivers. (I presently observed that many of the Soviet troops assigned to driving on this run had the flat Mongoloid features of the Uzbek and Kazakh.)

As we neared the shores of the Caspian, we emerged into a different world. The desert bareness of the Persian plateau country suddenly gave way to lush vegetation. Thick, dark green forests climbed the slopes to meet us, but down lower the vegetation had a steamy tropical character. There were palms and acacias and swamp pine festooned with lichen moss. The fields, divided into squares by little earthen causeways, were ankle-deep in water that nourished the slender rice shoots. But though nature was more generous here than in southern and central Persia, the people looked just as ragged and undernourished—if anything, a little worse off. Almost everyone had the emaciated, fever-racked look of the malaria victim.

Pahlevi was a dreary hole. It had once enjoyed a boom as the gateway of trade between Europe and Iran; but when the railway, by the Old Shah's royal whim, had been built to the eastern corner of the Caspian, the town's future was seriously compromised. For the moment, however, it was one of the main trans-shipping points for Lend-Lease goods; there they were transferred from trucks to ships that took them to the Soviet ports of Baku and Makhach Kala. It was a trans-shipping point for us, too, and our first call was at the office of the Soviet Steamship Agency. The director, a swarthy gentleman with Oriental features and the picturesque Russified name of Mahmoud Hassanovich Ibrahimov, proved most obliging. The passenger steamer to Baku had left only two days previously. We could either wait for the next trip, which would be a week later, or else take pot luck and rough it on the first available vessel. But, he warned us, it wouldn't be luxury traveling.

We immediately chose the second alternative. Within the hour we had unloaded all our baggage except the diplomatic mail in a warehouse well surrounded by Soviet sentries. The pouches had to be carried up several flights of stairs to our hotel room, because the couriers could never leave them for an instant—those were the rules. We took turns mounting guard. The Hotel Imperial, Pahlevi's sole hostelry, a big, rambling agglomeration of planless buildings round a courtyard, had no conveniences but was tolerably clean for Iran. It was owned and operated by a Greek family from Salonika. They had been there for several generations, yet until the war, they had kept close contact with their homeland. The head of the clan and of the establishment was a monumental matriarch in ruffled black chiffon that matched her eyes and hair. A huge ring of massive keys dangled on a chain from the folds of her dress. The key ring somehow harmonized with her heavy plain-gold earrings. Obviously such a woman would be a force in any community, and Pahlevi was a very small puddle. There was a bevy of daughters— lesser, paler editions of their mama—who did most of the work around the place. Two sons, I learned, had volunteered and were now with the Greek Army in the Middle East.

This family of Greek hoteliers reminded me of other Greeks I had met in the jungle outposts of the Sudan, living in thatch huts and trading calico and trinkets with naked savages who came out of the bush with rings in their noses. No one but Greeks, I reflected, would have the persistence to stick it out in a dump like Pahlevi.

The matriarch proved a gold mine of local information. Before the Russians were in the war, the town had been full of the agents of German business firms. They handled the Reich's extensive trade with Iran. Besides providing a market for German goods, the Shah's kingdom had been an important loophole in the economic blockade of the Reich, thanks to a treaty with Russia which provided for duty-free trans-shipment.

When the Russians marched into Persia in August, 1941, one of their planes had dropped a small stick of bombs on Pahlevi. They had all fallen in the dock area among warehouses crammed with German goods. A year later a German plane had flown over the town, causing considerable panic. But instead of bombs, it had dropped leaflets that nobody could read because they were printed in Turkish instead of Persian.

Pahlevi wasn't exactly a gay spot for young girls. Were it not for the war, the lady implied, her daughters, instead of hanging around the hotel, would be with relatives in Salonika on the lookout for husbands. Marrying a Persian was, of course, unthinkable for Christian Greek girls. Why, Persian wives were worse than chattel slaves—even spinsterhood was preferable. Now, she added, with the Russians here, things had livened up. There were Soviet movies, or shows and concerts by traveling Soviet troupes almost every week—never before had there been so much cultural life in Pahlevi. And the Russians were quite nice, many of them. Several of their officers lived and boarded at the hotel. They paid their bills regularly, were clean and well behaved—this last said almost wistfully, as though they rather overdid the good behavior. They never consorted with anyone other than their own nationality, women not excepted, even though they presumably belonged to the Greek Orthodox Church.

The Russians' conduct was a distinct surprise. The news of their coming had started a frantic exodus of the wealthier Persians. To unpleasant memories of the first World War, when the Tsar's troops had occupied this same region, were added fears of sovietization. Instead there had been complete order. The Russians had not meddled in the local administration or confiscated property. Gradually the refugees had come drifting back. At present the richest man in town was getting very handsome rent from the Soviet Shipping Agency which had leased his docks and warehouses for the duration.

The main landmark of Pahlevi was the Shah's Palace, a rather derelict and hideous Oriental adaptation of the late nineteenth century, standing on the bay shore in a weedy garden enclosed by an iron grating sadly in need of repair. In the bay beyond the palace a large luxury yacht rode at anchor, gleaming white in its shipshape trimness. You could guess without being told that this was the Shah's royal yacht. It was built in France at the Old Shah's commission. Neither the old man nor his son, the present Shah, had ever set foot on board. But during the old man's reign it was sometimes used by his favorites for orgiastic pleasure cruises. The town of Pahlevi proper lay beyond the Palace on the far side of the bay from the docks, and thus outside the main stream of commerce. Our hotel faced a small square opposite the main entrance to the dock area which the Russians had fenced off. No one got past the gates without the proper *propusk*—pass. The traffic jam which pivoted about the base of an equestrian statue of the Old Shah in the center of the square defied description. The nearest comparison that comes to mind is Forty-Second Street and Broadway during the theater rush hour. But the vehicles in the Pahlevi crush were monster six-wheeler Studebaker trucks instead of New York taxicabs, and none of the drivers ever let up on their horns. The bedlam lasted from dawn till midnight.

Yet the confusion was more apparent than real. Freight was trans-shipped at Pahlevi with an efficiency that seldom permitted supplies urgently needed by the Red Army to pile up. The man who kept things moving was our friend Mahmoud Hassanovich, and in due course he moved us out of there, too.

The morning after our arrival he advised that he could put us on a ship the following morning. Again he warned us that the accommodations "would not be those of a cabin liner." Again we assured him that this mattered not at all, that our one interest was to get moving.

And so early on the morrow we carried our ten mail pouches— average weight well over one hundred pounds—down from our third-floor room, loaded them on a truck provided by Mahmoud Hassanovich (our truck had turned back with Clem and the sergeant the previous morning), collected our other two tons of freight at the warehouse, and headed for our embarkation.

Our first sight of the S.S. *Spartak*, which was to take us to Baku, proved that Comrade Mahmoud Hassanovich had meant every word when he apologized for the accommodations. Not even on her maiden voyage could the *Spartak* have contended for the title of flagship of the Caspian merchant fleet—and that had been back in 1871. She had been steadily going to the dogs ever since. The captain explained that she had been consigned to scrap before the war. But now every available bottom was desperately needed, and so even this superannuated hulk was pressed into service.

She creaked indignation at this outrage in every seam. As an added protest on the trip down to Pahlevi the main engine bearing had burned out. But there was no time for repairs, and so we would be returning to Baku on a tow line and with a cargo of steel ingots in the leaky hold.

"Unless we get in a storm and the tow hauser snaps, we should make it all right," the captain opined reassuringly.

But in any case by that time our ten pouches of diplomatic mail and two tons of freight—all duly rechecked—were in the hold on top of the ingots, and so it was too late to turn back.

The *Spartak*'s decks and quarters were in keeping with her character. Every inch of exposed surface was caked with oily soot that left an indelible smudge on everything that touched it. Again the captain explained: "No time to stop and paint—we've got to keep moving." The only sitting space indoors was in two ward-rooms below decks that served as the officers' and crew's messes, respectively. The walls in both were decorated with pictures of the Political Bureau of the Communist Party.

We were assigned a little stateroom off the officer mess aft, with three bunks in it and room for nothing more. For once Watson and Clark could not sleep with their mail pouches. But the stateroom had been made tolerably clean, and everyone from the captain down seemed eager to make us as comfortable as possible.

The most remarkable feature of the *Spartak* was its crew. The captain, Vassili Ivanich, a stocky young man of twenty-seven, had been invalided out of the Navy for wounds received on the Sevastopol run the year before.

He was just beginning to recover the use of his right hand and arm, the ligaments of which had been severed by machine-gun bullets when the destroyer on which he served as gunnery officer was strafed from the air. Every day he eagerly tested the articulation slowly returning to his stricken limb. He dreamed only of when he could return to combat duty and quit this "paddling about in a mud puddle on a stinking wreck with a bunch of women, kids who ought to be in school, and grandpappies who should be warming their bones on top of a stove."

"But," I objected, "the job you're doing now is tremendously important for the war, you know."

"Perhaps," came the rejoinder, "but it isn't my job. My job is killing Germans. There's thousands of people could plow this old tub through this irrigation ditch, but good gunnery officers are needed in our Navy."

"I see your point," I replied, "and hope you get your wish. But you can't go on killing Germans all your life."

"Of course," he said, "we won't go on killing Germans indefinitely. We've killed a lot already. But they're a lot more that need killing before we can stop."

"But when the shooting does end," I persisted, "and it will, sooner or later, then what would you like to do?"

At this point he squared his chin and shoulders and a note of pride came into his voice:

"I serve the Soviet Union. I shall go wherever my Party and my Government send me and do as they order me."

"But," I insisted, "your Party and your Government assigned you to be captain of the *Spartak*, and though you do it, you don't enjoy it. What I meant was, not where would you be sent, but what would you like to do if you had the choice?"

Vassili Ivanich's face, which had been scowling through the first part of my remark, suddenly lit up. "If I had my choice," he almost shouted, "after the war I should like to be captain of one of those new, luxurious Diesel ships that will ply between Vladivostok and San Francisco. Have you ever been to San Francisco?"

But before I could answer, the rosy vision faded from his eyes. With a deprecatory smile and indicative nod toward the shabbiness around us, he said, "I've got to get to work; the tug'll be here any moment to take us off."

The mate of the good ship *Spartak* was easily twice the captain's age—a likable old ruffian with a salty tang.

"I was born in Baku," he told me. "If you've never been there, you haven't missed much. Terrible place, oil in everything—in the air you breathe, in your food, in your hair, on your clothing. You can't get away from it. I first tasted oil with my mother's milk and I haven't been able to get rid of the taste since." He spat disgustedly into the tar-streaked scum that lapped our side. "I doubt if all the vodka in the world would rinse it from my mouth and I've used my share in the attempt."

Uncle Fedya, as the other members of the crew called him, had been at sea ever since he was twelve years old.

"Started out to see the world, I did," he commented sardonically, "and what did I see? Astrakhan, Kislovodsk, Makhach-Kala, Pahlevi. Forty years I've swum circles around this landlocked pond, like one of those sturgeon that spawn their caviar in the mouths of the Volga once a year. Only now I'm past my spawning season and I don't suppose I'll ever see the ocean. Tell me, is it true the water there is a deep, clear blue—not dirty-gray like this Caspian of ours?"

The peak of Uncle Fedya's career had been back in 1918, when as a young man he had worked for the British, who were then occupying Baku. They had given him a slick motorboat all to himself. And his job had been to take parties of officers out fishing.

"Save for one or two of the senior officers," he reminisced, "they were all young fellows, about my own age. High-spirited, they were, always laughing and joking in English among themselves. Sometimes their jokes were on me, but since I couldn't understand, it didn't matter. In any case it was all good natured. Our luck with the fish wasn't always good. But that didn't seem to spoil their fun or dampen their spirits. They'd ask me to sing—I had a pretty good voice in those days and I sure let them have it. They'd whoop and stomp and try to lend their vocal support. Several times we almost tipped the boat over."

Uncle Fedya had also learned a few English expressions, few of them printable, though he used them in all innocence.

With ear-rending whistle blasts, two steam tugs nosed into us. The *Spartak*, inert and powerless, was slowly prodded into the channel where the ship that was to tow us to Baku was waiting.

It took over an hour to fasten the tow line, which, when it was finally unsnarled and taughtened, looked woefully slender. The *Spartak* was so heavy with steel ingots that the main deck was not more than a foot above the waterline. Slowly, painfully, we gathered momentum until we were scudding through the muddy gray water at our ceiling speed of four knots per hour. We cleared the harbor breakwater at noon, but at sunset the rococo turrets of the Shah's palace were still visible.

The work of getting the ship under way had been performed entirely under the direction of the young captain and the old mate by boys in their middle teens. They were a noisy, quick-tongued, high-spirited crew clothed in ragged, patched-up hand-me-downs—almost to the last detail like any bunch of tough kids on a waterfront anywhere in the world. Several turned out to be refugees from the invaded Ukraine, whose families had perished or had been caught behind the German lines. One snub-nosed, freckle-faced redhead was from Stalingrad, where his house and parents had been blown to bits by a Nazi bomb before his eyes. But close contact with slaughter and the soul-searing horrors of war had not destroyed their essential childlike simplicity and innocence, for which their outward air of toughness was a not too convincing camouflage. The boy from Stalingrad took a fancy to Ash Clark, to whom he bore an amusing facial resemblance, and applied himself to teaching Clark simple words in Russian, laughing uproariously at his mispronunciation.

There were four women aboard. Two of them, the navigator and the radio operator, were officers. The other two ran the galley. Though we had brought along our own provisions for the trip, the captain insisted that we share the cabbage soup and potatoes of the officers' mess. We agreed, provided they permitted us to contribute something; and so we produced canned peaches and pineapple and graham crackers for dessert—delicacies which none of them had ever tasted before.

That was at dinner the first night out. Thereafter there wasn't much eating done on the voyage. For long before morning a storm blew up that shook our ship like a terrier shakes a rat. For the first time in many thousands of miles of ocean travel I was sick that morning, but my mortification was mollified when I found that practically the entire crew was in similar straits. Angry mountains of gray water seemed to converge upon us simultaneously from all directions. It was a sea without rhyme or rhythm in its motion. That, I was told, was because the Caspian's landlocked shallowness left no elbowroom for a deep broad groundswell, and even during a raging storm the water simply slopped from side to side as in an agitated bathtub, which made it the more treacherous.

The tow line didn't snap; the *Spartak* didn't founder; and we woke up the morning after our second night aboard to find ourselves lying in Baku Harbor. The clustered houses of the ochre-colored town climbed the surrounding hills. The skyline was broken by the tall silhouettes of public buildings that were under construction at the time of the German invasion, when work on them had been suspended for the duration.

In the course of the morning we hove alongside a dock to unload our mail pouches and freight. Again the list was carefully rechecked as each item came out of the hold. An Intourist man appeared with a truck which would take everything to the hotel. In the customs shed my luggage received a perfunctory examination from a charming lady customs inspector who had majored in American literature at the University of Leningrad. She asked me if I had anything in the way of American magazines that I could leave with her for reading practice. She had had a big library of English books at her home in Leningrad where she had spent the first two years of the war as a fire fighter, living through the famine and blockade of the frightful winter of 1941-42. Her husband, she mentioned in passing, had been killed at the front, fighting to defend the city. Her house had been demolished by a shell from the long-range German siege guns that bombarded the beleaguered city day in and day out for more than two years; and finally, her health undermined, she had been ordered to evacuate and had been given this quiet job, far from the fighting, in order to recuperate.

"I don't enjoy it," she apologized. "It makes me feel as though I were making others pull my weight when there's still so much to be done."

At the big, modern Intourist Hotel we spent the next two hours rechecking the pouches and the freight. The pouches had to be carried up to our rooms; the freight we had to turn over to Intourist, who would forward it to Moscow by train. We would leave for Moscow in the morning by plane.

Back in our rooms we ordered dinner. In the midst of the cabbage soup there was a knock on the door and an individual strode in wearing a dark blue uniform strongly reminiscent of a New Jersey motorcycle cop, with boots and riding breeches. Embroidered on his sleeve was an American spread eagle, almost lifesize, clutching a shield with the stars and stripes, and underneath—as though that weren't enough—a big "U.S." in gold thread. A similar crest adorned his hat.

"Not bad, eh?" the visitor inquired proudly as he followed my glance to the insignia. "Designed it myself."

He turned out to be a technician, sent in by his employer firm to help the Russians install American-made Diesel engines in submarines. When he first arrived in Russia, he'd had himself a hell of a time hanging around Moscow for two weeks with nothing much to do. But then they'd sent him down here to the shipyards in Baku. The town was an awful dump, without one decent cabaret or anything else in the way of entertainment except movies. The people were real friendly-like though—most of them—especially the dames. And there were some nifties. If only they had the clothes. If any of us wanted dates, he knew girls who had plenty of friends. He could fix it up in no time. There weren't many joints you could take 'em to, though. The best place in town was the Naval Officers' Club, where they had a bar and an orchestra of sorts. He and his pal had gone there the other night with a couple of girls, but they hadn't felt any too welcome; and the next time they tried going, they wouldn't let 'em in. But probably if we all went, they wouldn't keep us out. It would be worth a try anyway.

We thanked him for the invitation but excused ourselves on the grounds that we had to be up at five in the morning for the long drive out to the airport.

Early next morning, after rechecking the pouches to make sure none had walked off in the night, we drove in the dark for two hours through shadowy forests of oil derricks to the Baku airport.

Our fellow-passengers in the bucket-seated C-47 were Red Army officers. We skimmed along the Caspian and the barren, saline Kalmyk steppe to the port of Astrakhan on the mouths of the Volga, landing on a bleak airfield where the mud snowballed round the balloon tires of our landing gear and caked on the ailerons. Only with the greatest difficulty did the plane get off the ground again with this weight of mud added to its load of diplomatic pouches. Following the broad silvery band of the Volga, we reached the ruins of Stalingrad. For miles in all directions, zigzag trenches and circular gun emplacements scarred the ground. We hedge-hopped along a railway line where the ravages of battle seemed still fresh—charred hulks of freight cars toppled against signal towers, a locomotive sprawled on its back in a ditch. . . . Gaining a little altitude, we passed the tumbled ruins of factories and apart-ment houses. But everywhere among the destruction were signs of returning life. The remains of tanks, planes, field guns, trucks, cars, and other scrap had been gathered from the battlefields into enor-mous junkpiles. Forests of wooden scaffolding had grown up around the empty shells of gutted buildings, many of which already had bright new roofs.

All this we saw in a few seconds. Then, just as we were prepar-ing to land, low-hanging clouds which had kept us close to the deck all the way from Baku, swallowed us completely, blotting out Stalingrad and its airport. After a few minutes of futile floundering, our pilot gave up the search and nosed the plane in the direction of Moscow. Our one Stalingrad passenger took the news with Russian stoicism. He curled up in his bucket seat, tucked his sheep-skin around him, and went to sleep.

I have had some harrowing plane rides in my time, including flights to the front line with loads of ammunition and high octane gasoline, and a forced landing in the trackless desert in an old Blenheim Bomber. But all was tame compared with that flight to Moscow in a C-47. The Russian pilots do not fly on a beam, but rely on landmarks for guidance. On the Stalingrad-Moscow run their usual course was to follow the railway. They flew so low that once one of their planes actually scraped a train. By a miracle no serious damage was done. But the pilot insisted that the accident was the train's fault. It was off its timetable and had no business to be where it was!

Visibility, which had closed down on us at Stalingrad, grew worse as we flew westward, until we were literally plowing our way through a heavy blizzard. But our pilot, still flying by landmarks, instead of climbing over the storm, continued to hug the ground. Now and then a jagged hole in the white blanket would reveal treetops rushing by outside the cabin windows, swaying in our slip stream. But most of the time we saw nothing and just hoped. Once there was a sickening lurch as our pilot yanked the stick barely in time to avoid clipping a church tower. But Fate was kind, and over Moscow the sky cleared in time for us to land in the fading winter twilight. Another hour and the balloon barrage would have been up, sealing the airport for the night.

MOSCOW LIFE

☆ ☆ ☆ ☆ ☆ ☆ ☆ ☆ ☆ ☆ ☆ ☆ ☆ ☆ ☆

FOR THE newly arrived foreigner, getting grooved into Moscow life takes plenty of footwork and paperwork. The inmates of the Metropole were spared most of this. They simply handed over their passports to the Intourist Service Bureau, who took care of all formalities. But those such as I, who lived off that reservation, had to fend for themselves. Getting a residence permit was simple enough. I went to the proper office armed with a slip from the Press Department of the Foreign Office, presented myself at the Registration Bureau, filled out a questionnaire, and within the half-hour was handed my permit signed and sealed. But the district where our house was located was rather out of the way. The local police precinct had had scant practice dealing with foreigners, so getting registered involved several trips and a number of phone calls. All this was remarkably like prewar days. But now the paper work was greatly complicated by rationing.

Once I had been accredited to the Press Department, I was eligible for a ration book to the special diplomatic store. The monthly food allowance for us privileged foreigners was generous by any standards—30 kilos of bread, 5 kilos of meat, 4 kilos of butter, 5 kilos of fish, 5 kilos of sugar, 30 eggs, a variety of other items depending on the season and the supply available, and enough soap for a reasonable standard of personal cleanliness.

Compared to the allowance of the average Russian, this was real abundance. The Russian civilian also got a food card. The main item it entitled him to was bread, and the size of the ration varied with his category—worker, white-collar employee, or dependent. There were also coupons for meat, sugar, butter, and other items, but in smaller quantities and not always honored. Articles not available on the food-card at Government prices could be purchased on the open market at prices that defied the imagination. Eggs were comparatively cheap at twenty rubles each—four dollars by the official exchange rate. But a pound of butter on the open market cost forty dollars. The price of meat varied with the supply—between seven and thirteen dollars a pound. Milk cost eleven dollars a quart. Yet even at these prices there were eager buyers, and the peasants who trudged into market each morning with their produce slung over their shoulders did a thriving business.

These peasants who sold their surplus produce on the open market were the nearest Soviet equivalent to war profiteers. Taxes took a heavy toll of their assets, but still left them with vast hoards of paper rubles which they could either sew up in their mattresses or invest in Government lottery bonds. There was little else they could do with their new-found paper wealth, for consumer goods were virtually non-available at any price. Not until the following spring did the Government open up commercial stores where suits, shoes, overcoats, and other clothing could be purchased at astronomical prices.

When that happened, even though a suit cost six or seven hundred dollars and other prices were scaled accordingly, the peasants queued up for them. Having lived through the inflation that followed the last war when the ruble, like the mark, lost all value and prices were calculated in millions, the peasants thought that durable goods at any price were a safer investment than paper money. The Soviet Government judged peasant psychology shrewdly. During the war it had financed its internal expenditures largely by printing unlimited quantities of paper rubles. The commercial stores were established for the deliberate purpose of raking in these vast piles of banknotes that were in the hands of the peasants—the only people with anything to sell—so that most of this paper could then be retired and the ruble gradually restored to something like its prewar purchasing power.

My immediate problem, more urgent than food or anything else, was firewood. The winter firewood shortage in Moscow was far more acute than any coal or fuel oil shortage in any American city. To the local population it was literally doled out by the stick. During the two previous war winters, my mother-in-law had sealed off

all but one small room of our home. There she installed a tiny
stove—an ingenious contrivance made from an empty kerosene can.
In it she literally burned one sliver of wood or wisp of paper at a
time—paper was also at a premium. By this method she managed
to get the full benefit of every fraction of a calorie, together with
most of the smoke. All winter she huddled against the stove,
wrapped from head to foot in a heavy, fine-spun woolen shawl that
had been in her trousseau, tending her tiny flame like a vestal
virgin. The preceding winters had been severe, and inevitably part
of my library and all of my files had been sacrificed to the little tin
Moloch.

As a privileged foreigner, I got enough firewood to operate on,
but going through the regular channels involved first applying for
coupons and then for a truck to fetch it from some farthest suburb
—all of which left time enough to freeze in the meanwhile.

At this point the Embassy came to my rescue. They provided me
with coupons which I could return later, with a truck in which to
go for the firewood, and with Morris, the Embassy's number-one
wangler and factotum, to go along and superintend the job. Every
American Embassy or Legation the world over has its Morris. He
is invariably a native who at one period of a somewhat checkered
career lived in America long enough to learn a broken but highly
fluent variety of Brooklynese and assimilate the mores of poolroom
and lunch counter society. Then having saved up a dollar nest egg,
he returned to the old country to impress the local yokels. Presently,
however, this began to pall, or his savings gave out, or were claimed
by a grasping government; so he decided he would like to go back
to America. He accordingly went around to the American Embassy
or Consulate only to find that his claim to American citizenship or
a re-entry permit had meanwhile expired, and that his allegiance
had been reclaimed by his country of origin. Hoping to find some
way out he then applied for a job at the Embassy or Consulate as a
local employee.

Morris' story conformed to this general outline, with the added
particular that his repatriation had been purely accidental. He had
left Russia in the early twenties as member of the crew of a Soviet
ship which he had jumped because he liked the looks of San Fran-

cisco. After working his way across the continent at odd jobs, he had again taken ship, this time to Rio, had knocked about South America for a couple of years, and had then taken ship back to the States. This pleasantly varied life of alternate spells on land and sea continued until 1934. That year he shipped as steward—a cushy job if you are a good businessman—on a tramp freighter. One of the ports of call was Odessa. Morris went ashore for a look around and to arrange for the purchase of some provisions, but his fluent Russian aroused the interest of the authorities. He was held for questioning. His papers were examined, and the manner of his previous departure from the country was ascertained. He was informed that he was still a Soviet citizen and must therefore stay in the country. Then it was that Morris wept bitter regret that he had neglected to acquire American citizenship when he had the chance.

By now his tears had long since dried. He had married, fathered a daughter, and done tolerably well for himself financially and otherwise as Embassy factotum, making all the food purchases for the Ambassador's table. There was nothing, he boasted, he could not obtain by some means or other, and though Morris was a notorious braggart, people had to admit that he delivered the goods.

This time Morris knew of a woodyard which had just received a trainload of good dry birch—not the green or soggy pine and spruce logs one usually got. The checkmaster, who could tell by a glance of his professional eye whether you had loaded your full quota, was a friend of his and was also very fond of coffee—"Now if I had a little extra. . . ." Also, Morris warned me, we would have to get the wood loaded onto the truck. The girls who did this job for Soviet organizations that drew their wood supply from this yard were not obligated to serve us. He doubted if they would take money for the job, but if I could take along some sugar, chocolate, or cigarettes. . . .

Thus was I initiated into the system of barter which had sprung up in wartime Moscow because money had so largely lost its purchasing power. I soon discovered that one couldn't get anybody to do anything, from laundry to shoe repairing or inserting a watch crystal, without some payment in kind. Later, with the opening of the commercial stores, all this changed overnight and money became a readily accepted alternative medium, though usually at a rate so prohibitive that it was still preferable to deal in kind. Thus getting a pair of shoes half-soled would cost you either four hundred rubles or four cans of condensed milk. Correspondents were allowed to get their rubles at the Embassy rate of twelve to the dollar instead of the official bank rate of five to the dollar. But even so, four cans of condensed milk—provided you had them—were a lot cheaper than seventy-five dollars.

Everything went according to plan with the firewood. Morris directed the driver of our truck to the particular pile. He argued and cajoled the girls—a formidable collection of hard-boiled, apple-cheeked mamas whose natural huskiness was exaggerated by their felt-padded, grimy peasant coats—into loading the logs in return for an odd assortment of lumps of sugar, chocolate bars, and cigarettes. He slipped some coffee to the checkmaster, and with a towering load we headed back into town, followed everywhere by thousands of envious eyes.

We took along with us two of the girls who, in return for some extra emolument, had agreed to help with the unloading. We backed the truck up against the fence and the girls started tossing the logs pellmell into the yard with callous disregard of our lilac bushes and anything else they might hit. The noise of this bombardment brought my mother-in-law out onto the back porch double-quick.

"Hold your fire!" she shouted to the girls. "Now, one of you climb down and catch the logs the other tosses to you and stack them neatly over here."

"*Ahnoo, Mamasha,*" said one of the girls, "do you think we've got all day to waste just so you can order us about? We know our job without your telling us what to do. We only came along to help out."

"How much did you give 'em?" *Mamasha* asked, turning to Morris.

Morris enumerated the outlay of sugar, chocolate, and cigarettes. Before he had finished, *Mamasha's* Cossack blood was boiling. A glint came into her eye that made even Morris wince.

"*Mahsháyneetsee*—scoundrels!" she shouted, turning on the girls. "You think anyone who's a foreigner is made for you to cheat and swindle, that we're running a charity bazaar. Come on, you big overstuffed cows, get busy. You're going to do just as I tell you, or else—"

She didn't have to specify her threat. The girls, assisted by the driver, were already unloading and stacking the wood conveyor fashion.

Ever since I had taken my wife and small son to America in June, 1939, *Mamasha* had faithfully guarded our house. She had, alas, been powerless to save our garden when the city decided to build a large block of flats directly in back. So that now, instead of the country-like silence and seclusion, fresh air and light, we had once enjoyed, we had a broadside close-up of this enormous rabbit warren where women and children, hanging out of windows or over the rails of little balconies, chattered and shouted at each other endlessly from early morn till dusk. Under Soviet law there is no private ownership of land. All of it belongs to the state, which is therefore free to dispose of it anytime as it sees fit. In the cities most of the housing also belongs to the city Soviet or municipal government. Private dwellings such as ours were the exception. Back in the days of Lenin's New Economic Policy, when private enterprise had been given some rein, enterprising individuals who wished to build themselves a house could obtain a plot of land for the purpose from the Government on a long-term lease. The Government was free to break the lease any time it chose, but the actual structure of the house was the property of the individual. And if the Government decided it needed the land on which the house stood, for some other purpose, it paid the owner two thousand rubles for breaking the lease. He was then at liberty either to move his house somewhere else, or dispose as he saw fit of the lumber and other building material in it.

We had bought our house, or rather half of a house, from its builder in 1938. Previously the premises had been rented to various foreigners—to a councilor of the French Embassy and eventually to a line of Herald-Tribune correspondents.

The building was a long, rambling, one-story affair with heavy log walls. The two halves were quite separate. In the other half the builder, Matvei Nikolayevich Timofeyev and his wife, occupied two small rooms and rented the remaining space. In his day Matvei Nikolyevich had been quite a lad. One of the last of the N.E.P. businessmen, when the private sector of trade had been squeezed to the wall completely, he got a job as purchasing representative for some retail merchandizing organization—state-operated, of course. His position gave him an opportunity to travel about a bit—to the textile centers of Ivanovo and Kalinin and to the shoe factories in Leningrad. There was nothing to stop him taking along small stocks of personal purchases on his trips, and if they happened to be articles that were much in demand and commanded a high price in Kalinin, or Yaroslavl, or some other town where his position took him, why so much the better. Thus Matvei Nikolayevich eked out his very modest salary until such time as his superiors got annoyed and fired him. Then he would take it easy until he got another similar job.

The war had brought to a sudden end all of Matvei Nikolayevich's lucrative little sidelines. Unwilling to become an office drudge at four or five hundred rubles a month, he had gone into a rapid mental and physical decline. The injunction "He who does not work shall not eat," which is written into the Soviet Constitution, found literal application in the case of Matvei Nikolayevich. For in wartime Moscow only those who worked were eligible to foodcards. Yet not even hunger nor the taunts of his razor-tongued wife could rouse him from his despondency and drive him to work. At the time of my arrival he was no longer able to lift himself from his sagging, grimy bed. His wife would go off for whole days at a time, simply locking the door to the room where he lay and taking the key with her. The neighbors would hear his piteous cries for food, but could not reach him. After my arrival, I told *Mamasha* that, after all, we shouldn't let him go hungry. *Mamasha* was a contradictory combination of peasant frugality and the almost overpowering generosity of a tender heart that bled for all suffering, with the latter quality invariably getting the upper hand. But that, of course, didn't keep her from grumbling about wasting precious food on "the old scoundrel." Still, it was thanks to *Mamasha* that he lingered on.

Then one wet, chill morning in mid-March there was a knock on the door. Matvei Nikolayevich's wife stepped in, her sallow horse-like face unusually lugubrious in a black lace shawl. Matvei Nikolayevich had passed away quietly in his sleep that night and could I lend her one thousand rubles for funeral expenses?

Our garden was gone, but everything inside the house, with the exception of the files and some of the books which had gone to feed the stove, was in its place. Even a few old toys we had forgotten in the rush of packing were gathering dust where they had been left. The furniture was just as it had been, save that the upholstery was a bit faded and soiled.

The roof leaked in one or two places where ack-ack shrapnel had pierced the tin, and the plaster was badly cracked from high explosive bombs that had demolished several blocks of buildings a quarter of a mile away. Our house was near a railway station and therefore in a target area during the German raids on Moscow in the summer, fall, and winter of 1941-42. The big sheltered market opposite the station had been burned to the ground by incendiaries, and our house had only survived thanks to my eldest brother-in-law, who night after night stood watch on the roof dousing firebombs.

In the panicky days of mid-October, when the Germans were bearing down on the gates of Moscow and everyone with any means for going was evacuating the city, *Mamasha* refused to be stampeded from her post—even when my brother-in-law brought her railway tickets.

"If Stalin can stick it, so can I," she retorted to those who tried to persuade her to leave.

Thousands of people abandoned their possessions in headlong flight, and anything in the way of furniture could be had for the asking. My mother-in-law had her eye on a grand piano and was all set to buy it for next to nothing. But Evgeni, the eldest and only son of the family left at home, talked her out of it.

"At a time like this, with the Germans in the suburbs and bombs dropping everywhere, you decide to buy a piano. When any morning you may wake up and find yourself playing a harp!"

In days to come, *Mamasha* never forgave Evgeni for having made her miss the opportunity of a lifetime.

A skilled worker, Evgeni had been exempted from the Army. But like everyone else in Soviet industry in wartime, he worked under militarized conditions. He was on day and night shifts on alternate weeks, and was lucky if he got a day off more than once in two months. During the weeks when he was on day shift, he was up and out of the house by six-thirty in the morning and never home before eight-thirty. His night shifts also ran fourteen hours. In addition to this, he was often called to the factory outside of working hours on an emergency assignment. When the end of the month rolled around and his factory sought to fulfill its monthly quota in a last minute rush, Evgeni never came home at all for days on end.

As a skilled worker, Evgeni's earnings averaged around one thousand rubles a month. From this was deducted his subscription to the war loan, his trade union dues, and other contributions totaling about 250 rubles. A few months after my arrival, Evgeni was promoted for his good work to shop foreman. This meant a couple of hundred extra rubles in pay and no more night shifts. But because of the added responsibility his working days were now longer than ever, and more often than before he was called to the shop outside hours on emergency assignments.

Yet neither Evgeni nor his working comrades ever complained. No matter how hard they worked, they were, they realized, better off than the men in the trenches. It was equally their duty to give their last ounce of strength to the war effort. Falling down on the job would be akin to desertion at the front. And as for striking for shorter hours or better pay, the thought, had it ever occurred to them, would have seemed monstrous—a form of treason that would have been dealt with accordingly. If you didn't like it, you could join the Army.

Both of the other two brothers had gone into the Army. The youngest, Leonid, had not been heard from since August, 1941, when he wrote his last letter home from somewhere near Staraya Russa. At twenty-one he was a lieutenant in a tank brigade and was presumed killed, though no official notification had ever been received and *Mamasha* still lived in hopes that maybe, when the war ended, he would turn up somehow from somewhere. But even official notifications of loss in action were no final proof, as was proved in the case of the middle brother, Pyotr, Petya for short, a sergeant in the infantry. At the time of the German invasion his unit was stationed near the Romanian border in Bukovina. They held up the German advance on their sector for a time, but were outflanked and cut off. For two years *Mamasha* had no word of Petya. Then one morning in May, 1943, a postcard arrived, the usual form: "We regret to announce that Senior Sergeant Bondarenko, Pyotr Andreyevich, reported missing since July 10, 1941, was killed in action." That appeared final. But that same afternoon, when *Mamasha* was still as near prostration from grief as she could ever allow herself to be, the doorbell rang. It was a nurse. She informed *Mamasha* that she had come from the military hospital to which Senior Sergeant Bondarenko, Pyotr Andreyevich, had been brought as a patient the previous evening; that he was wounded but on his way to recovery; and that if she would call between certain hours the next day, she could see him.

The next day she went and there in a white hospital bed was Petya, large as life—rather larger than in prewar times. He told quite a remarkable story. After his unit had been encircled, it had split up into small groups that tried to filter past the enemy lines to reach the Russians. Once he was captured but managed to escape. By that time, however, the front had moved far to the east. So he no longer tried to get back to the main forces, but instead joined up with a group of partisans, composed mainly of soldiers who like himself had been cut off. Working their way northward, they reached the fastnesses of the Pinsk swamps and for the next two years harried German garrisons and lines of communications by sudden forays. After their raids, laden with spoils, they retired to the safety of the swamps, where no German punitive expedition ever pursued them. It was a free and easy life. Captured German supplies plus what they received from the sympathetic peasantry more than filled their wants. They had all the meat, milk, cream, bread, and other foodstuffs they could eat—which accounted for Petya's chubbiness. In fact, Petya had been having the time of his life until once during a night raid a German mortar shell fell too near him and blew a hole in the small of his back. The vertebrae had been injured and he was unable to walk or even stand. But the Partisans never left their living wounded behind, knowing full well that the Germans would torture them—partly out of sheer sadism and partly in order to wrest information from them. So Petya had been gathered up and for the next three months had been dragged flat on his back in a sleigh as his unit moved from place to place. For extra blankets he had traded a gold wrist watch and other valuables he had taken from a captured German officer.

In the spring his detachment had cleared deep in the swamps a secret airfield on which transport planes could land with ammunition. The empty planes were used for taking back the severely wounded. When Petya's turn came, he was put inside a plane and flown five hundred miles back to Russian-held territory.

A month later Petya was discharged from the hospital, unfit for military service, but able to walk. The prospects of return to civilian life bored him beyond tears. He had a perpetual faraway look in his eyes, and talked and thought of nothing but his two years with the Partisans.

Compared with many Russian families of my acquaintance, my wife's family had been fortunate in the loss of only one brother out of three. Households in which all the males of two generations had been wiped out were not exceptional. I remember one neighbor of ours, an old woman, who had lost five sons. One day she came to see my mother-in-law. She was sobbing so profusely it was some time before we learned the cause of her grief. Notice had just come of the loss of her daughter's husband. This left her a total of fifteen fatherless grandchildren to care for without any visible means of support beyond an allowance from the Government.

Never had I seen so many cripples anywhere as in the Moscow streets, trolley cars, and subways. Everywhere there were crutches, wooden legs, empty, dangling sleeves, and—most horrible of all— the tap, tap, tap of seemingly endless numbers of blind men. Such things, more than any amount of written information, brought home to one the tremendous suffering and sacrifice of the Russian population.

Yet, despite the untold suffering of the past two and one-half years, Moscow put on a brave appearance. Considering the difficulties of obtaining clothing, the people looked surprisingly presentable. The clothes of most were shabby, but it was a proud and clean shabbiness. The old shiny suits were carefully mended and patched, the cracked shoe leather polished. And the drab monotony of civilian dress was everywhere relieved by the sparkle of new officers' uniforms with the brilliantly colored or gilded epaulettes that had just been introduced. Even the officials of the Foreign Office, the *Narkomindel,* were now in pearl-gray uniforms, also with dressy epaulettes and brass buttons. These Foreign Office, or "Diplomatic Service," uniforms were so unfamiliar to the average Russian that whenever we went off somewhere on a trip, the escorting official of the Foreign Office Press Department was invariably taken for a visiting foreign general.

The appearance of Moscow's buildings matched that of the inhabitants. There was an over-all dinginess reflecting lack of paint and materials. But bomb damage had been repaired, cleared away, or skillfully camouflaged. Already public buildings were being spruced up. It was a cheering sight to Muscovites to see the camouflage paint being sandblasted from the Kremlin's venerable, crenelated, red-brick walls and from the white face of the Building of the Council of Labor and Defense, Moscow's nearest approach to a modern skyscraper. Only the huge old shapeless pile of the Metropole Hotel continued slowly to disintegrate. The lobby got grimier and grimier and the roof leaked, which didn't really matter unless you happened, like Eddy Gilmore of the Associated Press, to have a room on the top floor. And then you were liable to wake up in the night with most of the ceiling plaster on top of you.

At our house, whenever there was a thaw and the snow on the roof began to melt, we set out tin basins all over the living room floor, and often nights were rendered hideous by a steady drip, drip, drip—like an old Chinese torture. But most of Moscow, including the American Embassy and Spasso House, was similarly afflicted. So who were we to complain?

The war had put a complete stop to all housing construction. Everywhere buildings in various stages of completion stood lifeless and boarded up. All the other improvements of Moscow's ambitious city planning program had been suspended with one important exception: the building of additional lines of the Moscow Subway, on which work proceeded without interruption. Shortly before my arrival a new line had been opened with a station only two blocks from our house. That put us within five minutes traveling time of the center of town—a veritable godsend in view of the complete disappearance of taxis and the overcrowded street-cars which you boarded at dire peril to life and limb. The new line, which passed beneath the Moscow River, was a very deep one. Up-and-down escalators carried passengers into and out of what seemed like the bowels of the earth. The stations were as shiny and elaborately decorated as those built in peacetime, with a martial motive in the frescoes and statuary depicting scenes from battles ancient and recent.

Never, not even in the piping days of peace, had Moscow seemed so teeming with people. Even the subway, which in former days had always been fairly roomy except at rush hour peaks, was perpetually packed. This wartime crowd differed radically in composition from the Moscow peacetime crowd. It was far less citified, with a preponderance of peasant women with hayseed in their hair, and on their shoulders huge bundles that were perpetually getting jammed in the subway doors and escalators. They shoved, pushed, and pommelled with such violent vigor that getting on and off the subway was like bucking a football scrimmage line or being pulled through a clothes mangler.

The causes of this influx of people to Moscow were economic. If there was almost nothing to buy in the city, there were no consumer goods whatsoever available in the villages. So day after day these peasants with money in their packs flocked to town and made the endless rounds of the markets, looking for someone with a pair of old boots or an ancient coat to sell. The chief source of such clothing was the relatives of those killed in action. So great was the need that a mere sentimental attachment seldom deterred a woman recently widowed from disposing of her husband's wardrobe. Even my mother-in-law, who loved her children dearly, had sold all the clothes of her two missing sons. So that when Petya returned, there was nothing left for him to wear. The Russians, for all their depth of feeling and emotion, are a practical people and consider that the best way of honoring the dead is to help the living.

Such individual commerce was on the ragged edge of legality. The police did not actually prevent it, but they kept a close eye on the open markets. Anyone who was seen there too often, or whose appearance otherwise excited suspicion, was liable to be stopped and closely questioned. The one practice which was severely prosecuted was the sale on the market of foodstuffs or consumers' goods obtained on ration coupons at Government prices.

Yet even this could not be prevented altogether. And near the railway station in our neighborhood a curbstone market in such contraband had developed. At certain hours of the day the street was so thronged with vendors and customers that the trolley cars could hardly barge through. People with something to sell kept their wares in their pockets or carefully wrapped up in market bags, and furtively whispered their wares in the ears of prospective customers. It was business on a very small scale indeed—a quarter of a loaf of bread, a roll, a sliver of butter, five or six lumps of sugar, a pinch of tea, half a box of matches, broken packages of cigarettes at so much a smoke. If a policeman wandered into the throng, all commerce in his vicinity ceased. The people just pretended they were waiting for a streetcar. But as soon as he had moved on out of earshot, trade was resumed. It was impossible for the police to make an arrest unless they actually caught the people red-handed at the moment of transaction. Otherwise they were just people on their way to and from shopping.

The Government sought to limit the wartime influx into Moscow by prohibiting all travel in or out of an area within a radius of one hundred kilometers (roughly sixty miles) of the capital without special authorization. But the capital was such a powerful magnet that people by the thousands managed to slip through anyway, in spite of careful police check ups on the papers of all train and vehicle passengers entering the area.

Important in determining the character of the city's wartime population was the circumstance that a very fair proportion of Moscow's peacetime population had been evacuated to remote parts of

Siberia and Central Asia, together with the factories or institutions in which they were employed. As the Government intended that much of this translocation of plant equipment and personnel should be a permanent part of the eastward shift of the country's economic and cultural center of gravity, many of these former Muscovites found their bridges burned behind them. Yet such was the attraction of their native city and so little did they relish the prospect of settling permanently in the hinterland that a fair portion managed to filter back despite all the legal impediments and the higher salaries or wages in the new location. More often than not they found new tenants in possession of their apartments and what furnishings they had left behind, and the dockets of the civil courts were full of eviction cases.

Among those Moscow residents who smuggled their way back to Moscow was Katya Duranty, Russian wife of the former New York *Times* correspondent, and her twelve-year-old son, Mike. She and the boy had been evacuated to Gorki back in October, 1941, and had lived on a collective farm outside the city. They managed to get back to Moscow thanks to a friendly railwayman who hid them in a compartment intended for the transport of household pets. Once in Moscow, Katya soon got her residence legalized by obtaining from the British Embassy a letter to the effect that she was the wife of a British subject. She regained tenure of her old apartment.

Despite endless working hours, meager food, threadbare clothing that could not be replaced, heatless rooms, leaky roofs; despite an endless list of hardships that would have exhausted the will and stamina of a not so hardy or determined people; despite the fact that the end of their ordeal was not yet in sight, average Russians managed for the most part to keep their courage and good humor.

Sometimes they spoke wistfully of all that had been built at such sacrifice and then destroyed, of the millions who would never see the victory for the sake of which they had given their lives. They were saddened by the thought that the war had come just when things were getting easier, just when some of the blessings of life they had dreamed and worked for ever since the Revolution were coming within their grasp for the first time. And then, even as they were about to clutch it, happiness was snatched from them. It would take another lifetime to rebuild. But their faith in the final outcome was unshaken. The generation of the living had been denied. The coming generations would carry on and achieve the goal. Meanwhile one tried to make the best of things. And the best way of doing that was to consider how much worse things might have been than they actually were. Suppose the Germans had captured Moscow, for example? Suppose Stalingrad had fallen, or Leningrad?

Not all Russians showed the same degree of stoicism or spiritual fortitude. I had one friend, a writer of considerable distinction, who had lost his only son as a result of the evacuation. The child had traveled for many days through the chilling Russian autumn in an unheated boxcar. It was more than his physique could stand. Death of his son had extinguished all the light in the father's eyes. He was haunted by his loss continuously and had paid money to the Orthodox, Catholic, Jewish, and Moslem clergy to pray for his son according to their rites. Gradually his grief became an obsession. In the midst of an ordinary conversation he would suddenly break off the thread and say, apropos of nothing, "I had a son. But now I haven't any. I buried him. Tomorrow I must go and put fresh flowers on his grave." And he took flowers out to the cemetery almost every other day, even in winter time.

THE CROSS AND THE SICKLE AND HAMMER

☆ ☆ ☆ ☆ ☆ ☆ ☆ ☆ ☆ ☆ ☆ ☆ ☆ ☆ ☆

THE HUMAN craving for comfort and consolation had turned many folk back to the faith of their fathers at the exact time when the Soviet Government, for reasons of its own, had decided to give religion a bit more leeway. In this respect the war had merely speeded up a process that had been going on for years. Government-sponsored atheist propaganda was on the wane. To large sections of the population—those most directly under the influence of the reigning Communist ideology—religion had ceased to be an issue in which they were interested one way or the other. The devout, far from being weaned from religion by the activities of the Godless League, were simply outraged and antagonized by the affront to the objects and beliefs they most cherished.

Hence the Government—while in no way renouncing its official atheist philosophy—had gradually come around to the view that in time, as the Soviet way of life developed, interest in the Church would decline of its own accord; and that active atheist propaganda served no useful purpose, but on the contrary adorned the Church with the crown of martyrdom.

To defeat the Germans the Soviet Government had to rally all the forces of the country, not on the basis of a single social philosophy, but on the common denominator of national survival. The response of the religious communities had been prompt and patriotic. In the Orthodox Church prayers were said for the victory of the Red Army and the health and welfare of Stalin and the Soviet Government. Large sums were collected for the national defense fund. Money was raised for the arming of special tank units' which should be named after famous Russian heroes, such as Alexander Nevsky or Dmitri Donskoi, who were also saints of the

Church and therefore acceptable to everyone. The clergy urged their flocks to do their utmost for the war effort.

The Government responded by publicly thanking and commending the Acting Patriarch Sergius. Then in September, 1943, with one of their characteristic sweeping strokes, the Government authorized the Orthodox Church to choose a Synod, the highest church governing body, and elect a Patriarch. At the same time a complete quietus was placed on the activities of the Godless League.

Besides ensuring the widest support of the war by the religious portion of the population, the new policy deprived the Nazis of one of their strongest propaganda lines. It was now the turn of the Soviet to denounce Hitler as the enemy and persecutor of religion. In these denunciations the Church readily joined.

An added incentive to the policy of tolerance was the desire to incur the good will of public opinion in the Western Powers and remove stumbling blocks in the way of full understanding and co-operation.

Two days after I arrived in Moscow a dramatic finis to the era of religious persecution was written by the passing of Yemelyan Yaroslavsky, old Bolshevik and one of the last of Lenin's generation of revolutionaries. Yaroslavsky had been Party Historian and author of many books on Party history. But he was chiefly known for his activities as Chairman of the Godless League and spearhead of the Bolshevik war on religion. For nigh onto two decades, year in and year out, Yaroslavsky had inveighed against the alleged corruption and ill-doings of the clergy and against religion as a form of superstition. He was the author of innumerable pamphlets and booklets on the subject, as well as of quantities of articles printed in the pages of weekly and monthly publications of the Godless League.

But as the Party line toward religion was modified, Yaroslavsky's voice grew noticeably more muffled until its tone changed completely and he started writing articles attacking the Nazis for their persecution of religion. In September, 1941, his Godless League publications folded up. The official reason given for their discontinuance was wartime newsprint shortage. Presumably his quota was later reassigned to the Patriarchate for its new *Journal*.

A considerable amount of religious energy was released overnight, once the pressure was removed. A number of leading operatic singers, for instance, lent their voices to the services on the big religious holidays. (After all, some of the finest music of Tschaikovsky and other great composers had been written for the Church.) Yet there is no sign of the mass religious revival conjured by some writers and speakers.

From the first, the Government recognized the pre-eminence of the Orthodox Church as by far the largest single denomination, and a special State Commission for the Affairs of the Orthodox Church was formed under Georgi Karpov. While there was no restitution of even a fraction of the fabulous wealth confiscated from the Orthodox Church at the time of the Revolution, further conversion of church edifices to secular use ceased. And though such renowned Churches as the Cathedral of St. Isaac in Leningrad, and Basil the Blessed—that garish collection of onion-topped spires built by Ivan the Terrible at the far end of the Red Square in Moscow—are still "Museums of the History of Religion" (in earlier days "Anti-Religious Museums"), some churches, previously taken over, have now been reconsecrated. Legally all church edifices belong to the State, but they are "leased" to the religious communities in perpetuity.

Through the offices of Karpov's organization the material requirements of the Church were looked after: building supplies were obtained for repairs to church buildings; paper and printing facilities were procured for the monthly *Journal* of the Patriarchate as well as for prayer books and Bibles; wax for the candles that are such an important item in Orthodox worship was supplied by the Church itself. The Church now opened its own candle factory, and the proceeds from the sale of the finished product, duly blessed, again became a source of considerable revenue.

There was, of course, no religious instruction in any of the public schools or state institutions of higher learning. Religious instruction of children was allowed in private homes only. But to train its priests, the Orthodox Church was permitted to establish a theological seminary for adults eighteen or over.

To the average Russian this new policy toward the Church was a source of never-ending surprise. Many as have been the changes in policy since the Revolution, none so completely amazed him. When in September, 1943, Stalin received the Acting Patriarch and other Church dignitaries, it was as sensational as would be the news in America that the Chicago *Tribune* was backing Earl Browder for President. One of the most incredible (to the average Russian, that is) features of the new setup was the publication of the monthly *Journal*. The *Journal* was not handled by the *Soyuzpechat* agency which distributes newspapers and periodicals throughout the Soviet Union. Hence not many Muscovites of my acquaintance had ever heard of its existence; and when I showed them a copy, they almost refused to believe their eyes.

The Patriarchate was housed in the palatial former residence of the German Ambassador, where it employed a large staff. Under the strict Soviet wartime rationing system the clergy and employees of the Patriarchate received the same food cards as employees of the Soviet Government. The Patriarch drew the same rations as a member of the Council of People's Commissars, including the gasoline allowance for his Soviet-made ZIS limousine.

Though the Soviet Government stresses the separation of Church and State, it is virtually impossible for anything to exist apart from the State under the Soviet system. And now the Soviet State, which professed Marxist materialism, was to all appearances equipping the Church to fight against its ruling philosophy. In practice, however, the Church took great care not to bite the hand that was now feeding it. It fully realized that in return for the favors bestowed the State expected the Church to give its firm support to the system and to operate within certain limits. The tradition of centuries as the official State religion was deeply rooted in the Orthodox Church, and it therefore slipped very naturally into its new role of close collaboration with the Soviet Government. Its priests exhorted the faithful to support the regime; prayers were offered for the health of the Soviet leaders; and the highest praise was lavished upon them from the pulpit.

Thus it was that in November, 1941, on the anniversary of the Bolshevik Revolution, the late Acting Patriarch Sergius referred to Stalin as "the divinely appointed leader of our armed and cultural forces leading us to victory." Not long after this the present Patri-

arch Nikolai, who at the time was Metropolitan of Kiev and Galicia, was appointed a member of the Government Commission to
Investigate German Atrocities—the first time since the Revolution
that a prelate had been appointed to serve in an official Government
capacity. Meanwhile the Church had taken steps to excommunicate
and anathematize those members of the Orthodox clergy in the invaded regions who had collaborated with the Nazis.

In addition to supporting Soviet home policy and thus strength-
ening the war effort, the Orthodox Church became a valuable
adjunct of Russian foreign policy, as it had been in Tsarist times.
For the Orthodox Church was still dominant among the South
Slavs of the Balkans, as well as in two non-Slavic Balkan countries,
Romania and Greece. Accordingly, members of the Orthodox hierarchy, from 1942 onward, attended the meetings of the All-Slav
Committee in Moscow; and in June, 1943, Nikolai addressed an
All-Slav Congress organized by this Committee. In addition, from
time to time the Patriarch issued messages to the Orthodox Chris-
tians in the various occupied countries.

In another respect the Orthodox Church resembled its old self.
A quarter of century of travail and persecution had not taught the
Orthodox clergy the virtue of tolerance. There was no other way of
construing the fact that the Orthodox *Journal* saved some of its
heaviest ammunition and choicest vocabulary for such dissident
sects as the "Living Church," whose leaders it variously described
as wreckers, provocateurs, and enemies of religion. The phrase-
ology and terms of abuse were grotesquely reminiscent of the
intraparty fight against the Trotskyites. Under such pen-lashings
the separatist factions wilted; and their leaders, after publicly re-
penting, were reinstated in the Orthodox Church with the same
ecclesiastical rank they had held at the time they had strayed
from the fold.

While giving the Orthodox Church religious priority, in due
course the Soviet Government set up a State Council on Religious
Cults, with Ivan Polyansky as chairman, to deal with all other
denominations, including Roman Catholic, Old Believers, Protestant, Jewish, and Moslem. With the annexation of Lithuania and
the former East Polish provinces, Roman Catholicism has now

become the second largest denomination. Though the Kremlin continues to view the political influence of the Vatican in world affairs with strong disfavor, it does not appear to be discriminating against its Roman Catholic citizens on this account.

A Catholic Church, St. Louis des Françaises, has continued to function in Moscow since before the Revolution. Its curate is Father Leopold Braun, Boston-bred Jesuit, who has been in Moscow continuously for the past decade and is generally regarded as the unrecognized Apostolic Delegate. A Catholic Church continued to hold service in Leningrad right up to the famine period, when its curate, Father Marquette, was evacuated. Since the lifting of the siege ring, Father Braun has been permitted to visit Leningrad. The strongest indication that the Soviet Government seeks better relations with the Catholics were the Stalin interviews with the Polish priest from Springfield, Massachusetts, Father Stanislas Orlemanski. But more of that in proper sequence.

The two main Protestant denominations, Baptist and Evangelical, not long ago combined to form a National Council. Similar unification is under way among the various groups of Old Believers—remnants of a seventeenth-century schism in the Orthodox Church—and among the various Moslem sects. The Baptists and the Evangelists maintain a center in Moscow, but are seldom heard of.

While the new liberalism toward religion is a major event in the evolution of the Soviet system and is clearly the expression of an over-all trend, it would be wrong to deduce from this that there has been any change in the official Communist view of religion. There is indeed a far greater tolerance toward religious practices in the ranks of the Party. But this is due, not to altered convictions, but to political expediency plus the fact that religion is no longer regarded as a menace. The very fact that the Communists felt they now could afford to be liberal with religion was an indication of strength on their part, an indication that their position was now secure beyond challenge.

There are no chaplains of any description in the Red Army. There are, however, priests and ministers of various faiths and denominations in the ranks, and they are quite at liberty to minister to the wants of their co-religionists unofficially. A surprising number of the men killed at the front thus receive a religious burial.

Even back in the days when religion was officially frowned on, not all newly arrived little Soviet citizens escaped baptism. In the most "politically conscious" households, where one or both parents were Party members, there was often an old *Babushka*—grandmother—or *Nyanya*—nurse—who would bide her time until the coast was clear and then sneak over to the nearest church with the baby and have it surreptitiously baptized. In many families this happened with the connivance of the mother. In Russia, as in most countries, the women had always been more devout than the men. But even when the husband found out, he seldom felt strongly enough on the subject to make an issue of it. Why not let the women have their way if it made them any happier? There were, of course, exceptions, fanatics, or those who feared that if the fact of baptism in the family became known it might reflect on their Party standing, especially during the purge years.

It was comparatively easy to baptize a child in secret without the neighbors knowing. But a Church marriage was another matter— it was hard to keep that from becoming public property. And so before the Soviet Government signed its Concordat with the Orthodox Church, a civil registration had been the only marriage ceremony for most couples. I recall my own marriage. My wife and I went to the district Bureau of Registry of Acts of Civil Status— colloquially known by its Russian initials ZAGS. The one-room office was bare except for four desks, one in each corner, and a stand in the center supporting some utterly neutral and impersonal potted flowers, equally appropriate for any occasion—christening, marriage, or funeral. At each desk sat a female official, as neutral and colorless as her surroundings, with a big book in front of her. One was engaged in registering births, another marriages, the third divorces; the fourth recorded deaths. Thus all the ages of man from the cradle to the grave converged on this one bare room. My wife and I, having ascertained which corner to go to, told the female our names, dates and places of birth, and other particulars which she listlessly inscribed in ink on slip and a stub. We then paid five rubles, whereupon she detached the slip and handed it to us, and lo, we were man and wife. It was as gay and romantic as the ceremony performed in an American "Marriage Parlor."

But now Church weddings were again decidedly in fashion, partly thanks to the elaborately colorful Orthodox ceremony, with its crowns, incense, candles, and singing. The social stigma had been so completely removed from religious observances that even the daughter of Marshal Ivan Konyev, Red Army idol, could afford to be married in church.

ROMANCE REVIVES

☆ ☆ ☆ ☆ ☆ ☆ ☆ ☆ ☆ ☆ ☆ ☆ ☆ ☆

IN THE Soviet Union, as elsewhere, the war imposed a tremendous strain upon the structure of family life. Everywhere, in town and country, men were torn from their hearths and homes and catapulted into the vortex of war. Even those who survived the perils of the firing line were away from their sweethearts, wives, and children for years at a time. It was only the lucky few that got home leave, even after two or more years of constant service.

But the Soviets soon discovered that in the Red Army, as in any man's army, it was an essential to morale that each soldier be confident that the girl or wife he left behind still loved him and faithfully awaited his return—that his family would be there when he came back.

For a certain portion of the Army it was impossible to provide any such assurance. Their homes had been submerged beneath the Nazi flood, and their only hope of salvaging anything lay in driving the invader out. They could be counted on to put everything they had into the struggle.

The crucial test was when the wife or sweetheart was somewhere in the rear, beyond the reach of the enemy, but not of temptations that tried her love and constancy. As one soldier at the front expressed it in a published letter, "The boys at the front kill Germans with lots more enthusiasm if they know the home front is solid."

And it was on behalf of such men as these that the Soviet Government now swung the concentrated might of its educational, propaganda, and legal apparatus. Contrary to widespread misconceptions abroad, the Revolution in Russia never attacked or undermined the family as an institution or weakened the Russian people's deep-rooted traditional attachment to the family. Though Free Love had been noisily advocated by a small minority in the early days of the New Regime, it had never been encouraged by the authorities. The legal system had from the outset emphasized the responsibility of parenthood. The divorce laws had, indeed, been extremely liberal. But the divorce rate was no greater in Russia than in other countries.

The war brought a new emphasis on continence and monogamy. Once easier to obtain than a railway ticket, divorce now became a tougher and more expensive proposition, involving complex legal procedure. It really had to be necessary to justify the effort and expenditure involved. For repeaters the cost was doubled each time, and the maximum quota was three. Each divorce was entered in the person's passport and after the third time, he or she was barred from re-marrying. Apparently the drafters of the law thought that anyone thrice divorced was hopeless as far as matrimony was concerned and should be kept from further attempts. For Party members, who in morals as in everything else were expected to set a good example, divorce became practically impermissible.

Recently "common law" marriages lost their status. This caused a bit of a shock to those parents who for years had been living together as man and wife on a common law basis, without ever bothering to register. The women were especially alarmed, because the law now absolved fathers of children born out of wedlock from responsibility for their support. Some people complained that this was discrimination against the fair sex, since it released men from what had hitherto been the most effective economic check on promiscuity—namely, responsibility for support of any chance offspring. To this objection the defenders of the law pointed out that the right of consent was always the woman's anyway, and that the law imposed no additional burden on the unmarried mother because she now enjoyed the unrestricted right to turn her child over to a State institution and to get him back whenever she wanted. The law simply protected men from the clutches of designing females who had a child merely in order to get a hold on some man. The fact is that in the Soviet Union, despite the progress made since the Revolution toward equality of the sexes, promiscuity is still more readily condoned in a man than in a woman. Furthermore, both at the front and in war industry with its extended working hours and lack of leisure time, the opportunity and incentive to inconstancy was less for men. It was the women who needed watching.

A nationwide effort was made to inculcate the old-fashioned maidenly and womanly virtues. Banished forever was the mannish, hard-boiled female of the early days of the Revolution. The new Soviet woman, as pictured in the press and in the new literary romanticism, was a paragon of modesty, who blushed when strong language was used in her presence and who didn't speak to strange men. Her hair was no longer close-bobbed, but long and abundant. This did not mean that she was a timid creature. On the contrary she could, when the occasion required, rise to heights of heroism; but never even on the firing line, would she forget the proprieties. The women in the Army were no exception. Writes one officer in a published letter: "There are a good many girls in our unit— telephone operators, nurses, stretcher bearers, doctors, cooks. In time of danger they've all got plenty of guts, but that doesn't detract from their womanliness. Modest in speech and conduct, they manage to maintain a simple dignity. Just try and barge into their dugout unannounced! Politely, but firmly, whatever your rank, they'll tell you off. Once, a sergeant used some strong profanity in the presence of a nurse named Vera. She rose, blushing, and gave the man such a piece of her mind that he went flying out of the dugout like a cork from a bottle. Later he called at the infirmary to apologize." The same officer goes on to tell of a stretcher bearer named Liza. She was a homely, stoop-shouldered little slip of a thing whose sole claim to beauty was her gorgeous golden hair that she kept neatly braided. Whenever anyone tried to tease Liza about her tresses, saying that it was ridiculous to run around the trenches with long braids dangling, and suggesting that she cut them off, Liza answered with a Mona Lisa smile: "My mother cared for my braids ever since I was a tiny girl. She used to come home at night from work, wake me, wash and comb my hair."

It's too bad, complains the author, "that many girls consider braids a sort of bourgeois prejudice."

One day Liza, while attempting to rescue some wounded from exposed ground, was herself injured by shrapnel. Badly hurt, her bloodsoaked braids dangling, she was brought back to the dugout on a stretcher. But even in her extremity Liza remembered the proprieties. As the doctor bent over her to examine her wounds she whispered, "Get the men out of here."

The literary apostles of the new (in reality the old) morality were the young writers of a new romantic school whose leader was the youthful poet, playwright, and novelist, Constantine Simonov. Unknown before the war, Simonov in the darkest hour boldly ventured to return to the old, familiar, but long-neglected love theme —but more of that later.

The rebirth of a new romantic literature was but one more sign of the times. The papers and magazines now devoted much space to True Love and its tonic effect on the fighting forces. Typical is the story of the young naval officer who is impelled to heroic deeds because he feels he must live up to the lofty opinion of him harbored by his lady fair, whose letter to him concluded: "Remember, my dear, that like knights of old you wear on your sleeve a white scarf tied there by the lady of your heart. Treasure it and keep it stainless." Prior to that she assured him that though they hadn't seen each other in three years, she never looked at another man but thought only of him and of his safety.

His envious comrade, to whom the happy lover reads his letter, glumly recalls sundry Valyas and Tamaras whom he'd flirted with or taken to movies, but who never became his soulmates or his sources of inspiration. He makes a mental note that if he doesn't hurry up and find true love, he may miss out on happiness altogether.

In another article a humorist described the misadventure of a traveling salesman who mistook a lady's smile for a come-hither look. After blacking both his eyes, the lady, still beaming, explains she's smiling because she has just received a letter from her husband in the trenches.

A sort of forum for the lovelorn was conducted from time to

time by *Komsomolskaya Pravda,* newspaper of the Young Communist League. Here through the publication of letters and advice in the best Dorothy Dix tradition, the editors seek to find solutions or remedies for misunderstandings, suspicions, heartaches, and estrangements engendered by long periods of separation.

Thus early last spring Lieutenant Grigorienko wrote in from the front telling how, since the outset of the war, the letters he received from his beloved Valya had been a source of warmth and encouragement to him, especially in the trying period of the Leningrad siege. His answering letters from the front had in turn sustained Valya and spurred her to greater production in the Diesel engine factory back home. But then the gossips and scandalmongers had tried to wreck their beautiful friendship, and Valya jilted him. Publication of Grigorienko's letters elicited a flock of letters addressed to him in care of the editor from all over the Soviet Union, mostly from girls, expressing indignation that such things could happen. A collective farm girl writes, "Along with millions of other Soviet girls I read in *Komsomolskaya Pravda* your impassioned exposition of your love. A man who loves as intensely as you do is fully entitled to protection for his feelings. Furthermore, you are at the front and nothing in this world is nobler than safeguarding the peace of mind of a man at the front. We must vent the full force of our anger and contempt on those who don't respect our feelings and the living human truth."

Sure enough, this letter campaign took effect, and recently Grigorienko again wrote to the editor to inform his well-wishing correspondents that everything is rosy once more between him and Valya—that she loves him and believes in him again as before, and will faithfully await his return. The paper also published a photostatic copy of a telegram stating that Valya begged forgiveness for her rashness. The telegram was signed by the secretary of the factory committee of the Young Communist League in the plant where Valya works.

In their effort to strengthen the family, the Soviet authorities tackled the problem of teaching morals, discipline, and manners to children and minors. With the fathers in the Army and the mothers in industry, children get less home attention. Recently there have been warnings that rowdyism and juvenile delinquency were on the increase. Soviet educators are meeting the challenge by discarding newfangled theories and reverting to the timeworn maxim that sparing the rod means spoiling the child. A. Orlov, head of the Moscow School Board, declares that two or three days in the guardhouse is a far more effective method for dealing with serious offenses in the schools than the previous measure of expulsion, which merely encouraged waywardness. If the guardhouse proves inadequate, Orlov recommends commitment of the offender to a labor educational colony. In this connection he deplores what he terms the unfortunate trend to make life in these colonies varied and interesting by the introduction of various games and amusement facilities. All that is lacking, he comments ironically, is to advertise to children and their parents that the only eligibility requirement for entry into one of these pleasant rest camps is to commit some crime.

Orlov also criticizes the fact that special detention rooms for children in police stations have been transformed into cozy recreation rooms with games, story telling, and other pleasant pastimes that make detention a thoroughly enjoyable experience. Such methods, Orlov states, are based on the sentimental fallacy that children are naughty because they don't know what to do with their spare time and that the way to keep them out of trouble is, therefore, to amuse them. This, he says, doesn't develop character, but on the contrary encourages an inclination to avoid doing things that are difficult or uninteresting, thus failing to equip youngsters for the harsh realities of life. Henceforth, all this will be different. Besides introducing penalties in schools, the Executive Committee of the Moscow Soviet has prescribed a complete set of "rules of conduct for children and minors in public places." Among other things, children cannot attend theaters on school days unless they go in organized groups conducted by the teacher. They are completely barred from shows not specifically approved for the young, and an eight-o'clock curfew is imposed on their attendance. They are forbidden to be out on the street after ten o'clock unless accompanied by an adult. They are strictly barred from hawking matches, cigarettes, or other wares on the street and in the market, from hanging on the outside of streetcars or buses, and from skating on the streets or sidewalks. Severe penalties are provided for adults responsible for children's failure to observe these rules, and parents of offenders are liable to heavy fines. These various measures show how far Soviet educational methods have traveled since the early days when student councils ordered the teachers about.

The task of training Soviet girlhood is now the special province of separate elementary schools for girls established last fall at the beginning of the present school year. While these new schools equip their charges for socially useful work in many fields, in the words of M. Butkevich, Director of Girls' Schools in Moscow, "We must also develop womanliness and a strong sense of maidenly virtue and honor. We must always keep in mind that our country's future depends on how we train our girls, the mothers of tomorrow." This, Butkevich remarks, means increasing rather than reducing the curriculum of girls' schools as compared to boys' schools, for in addition to the same subjects taught in boys' schools, girls must also be trained in child psychology and domestic science.

As a rule, Butkevich says, girls aren't as unruly as little boys, and there aren't so many cases of severe breaches of discipline in girls' schools. But since girls are more sensitive and emotional than boys, they do present special problems.

Recently a daily hour devoted to manners was added to the schedule. In that period the girls are taught discipline and the principles of morals and manners—among other things how to behave towards grownups and in public places. As part of their training in domesticity, they take turns sweeping out and dusting classrooms. In addition they are taught darning, knitting, and embroidering. Neatness of attire and cleanliness are stressed, and in every class needle and thread and soap and towel are kept handy for emergencies. The girls are advised to wear their hair combed smooth and braided and to avoid flashy attire. Clearly the product of such training will in many ways resemble her grandmother more than her mother.

Yet this revival of certain old-fashioned tastes and standards in no way implies wholesale reversion to the past. Thus woman's hard-won right to compete with man on an equal footing in practically every walk of life—one of the most important gains of the Revolution—remains unchallenged. Witness the tremendous part being played by woman in Soviet agriculture, industry, and even in the Red Army. The chief underlying change in woman's status is full recognition that in addition to her economic and biological role, woman has a specific morale-building and spiritual function; she is officially restored to her pedestal as one of the chief sources of human inspiration.

With respect to morals, just as in the matter of religious freedom, the war simply accelerated a pre-existing trend. Prostitution had been steadily declining before the war. The V.D. rate was far below the European average. All this was largely due to early marriages.

Closely connected with the new emphasis on the family and morals were the new laws designed to increase the birthrate, the taxes on bachelors (which in view of their smallness were a form of social rather than economic pressure), and the various monetary and honorific inducements for large families, including the title of "Mother-Heroine of the Soviet Union," bestowed on the successful mother of ten. These laws were, of course, war measures. For replacement of its human capital was the major reconstruction problem facing the Soviet Union.

There was one form of marriage which the Soviet Government, without ever forbidding it, has always frowned upon. That was marriage between Soviet citizens and foreigners. The reasons and motives for this are similar to those which have prompted our State Department actively to discourage members of our foreign service from marrying abroad.

Yet time after time both policies have been challenged by the fact that love often refuses to be governed by citizenship, passport, and visa formalities. Again and again the all-powerful agencies of sovereignty have been forced to yield to the human heart, whose ingenuity succeeds in overcoming all the obstacles devised by artful bureaucrats.

There was the classic case of Bryan Grover, the twentieth-century Lochinvar who used a plane instead of a horse. Grover, a British oil engineer, had fallen in love with and married a Russian girl back in the early thirties when he was working for the Soviets in Baku. Having returned to England alone, he was subsequently denied a Soviet re-entry visa. His wife was unable to get an exit visa to join him. Finally, after fruitless years of waiting, Grover devised his plan. He took flying lessons, bought himself a little training plane, and flew with his instructor to Stockholm. Taking off from Stockholm one day on what was his first solo flight, he nosed the plane eastward across the Baltic, climbed into the clouds, and slipped across the Soviet frontier. Somewhere near Kalinin he ran out of gas, landed in a convenient field, and gave himself up to the authorities.

The Russians were very sporting about it. Having made sure Grover was telling a straight story, they gave him a brief civil trial on charges of violating the frontier regulations, found him guilty, and sentenced him to expulsion from the country. His wife was permitted to accompany him. The plane was confiscated.

Actually, despite the difficulties, I do not know of a single bona fide case of a Soviet woman married to a foreigner who has not eventually got her exit visa. There are strong arguments in favor of the Soviet Government's usual policy of applying the time test. For not all the expatriate Soviet wives prove happy in their new homes.

In the course of nature there have also been instances of foreign wives marrying Russian husbands and adopting the husband's nationality. Sergei Prokofiev, the noted composer, is a case in point. We had known him and his French-born wife before the war. They seemed to be an ideally matched couple, cosmopolitan in outlook, frequently visiting America and Europe together. The war changed all this. Prokofiev suddenly went native, shunned the society of foreigners, left his wife and their two sons, and married another woman. Mme. Prokofiev, broken-hearted, still worships his image. She goes to all his concerts and uncomplainingly suffers herself to be snubbed by her spouse and his new wife.

One of the most happily married couples was the well-known modern Soviet playwright Afinogenov and his American wife Jean. Jean had come to Moscow in the early thirties with a group of theater students. She had met and married the handsome young Russian and for nine years they had been ideally happy, sharing together the ups and downs of a Soviet literary career. When in 1937, at the peak of the purge, Afinogenov was attacked editorially in *Pravda* on accusations concocted by his professional enemies, it was Jean who wrote Stalin a letter that bubbled with righteous American indignation. In due course Afinogenov was cleared and vindicated.

In the late summer of 1941, Afinogenov was appointed head of the literary section of the newly established Soviet Information Bureau. In this capacity he undertook to improve relations with the foreign press. When in October, 1941, British and American correspondents were moved to Kuibyshev along with the diplomats, Afinogenov saw to it that leading Soviet writers who were in and out of Kuibyshev got together with them and kept them from losing their wits altogether in that provincial isolation. In December, Afinogenov flew back to Moscow to try to persuade the Central Committee of the Party to permit the foreign correspondents to return to the capital. He was killed a day later when a bomb struck the Central Committee Building.

Arrangements were made for Jean and her two daughters to return to America, but at the last moment Jean decided it would be disloyal to her husband's memory to leave. Accordingly she has stayed on. A special Government decree gave her and the children use in perpetuity of their Moscow apartment and their country house at the artists' colony of Peredyelkino.

Peredyelkino was some twenty miles southwest of Moscow on the Kiev railway line. Though the Germans never got to it, in the critical days it was close to the fighting, and front line Soviet troops had bivouacked in the houses.

The Afinogenov country house was a roomy, rambling structure with gables and turrets copied from pre-Revolutionary Russian suburban style, but with large areas of glassed-in porch and an open fireplace in the living room—both expressions of Jean's American influence. Most of the furniture, as well as the books from Afinogenov's library, had been used for fuel during the critical period of the defense of Moscow. Later the house had served as a sort of rest home for Airforce personnel. They had built a quite workman-like Russian bathhouse in the yard, but to equip it they had torn all the plumbing out of the house itself, as well as the central heating system. The combination radio-record player had also been gutted, but by a happy chance the electric refrigerator had survived in working order—the one link with peacetime.

But at that, the Afinogenov *dacha* had survived in better shape than some of the others. The neighborhood *dacha,* belonging to the writer Vsevolod Ivanov, had caught fire from an overheated stove, when troops were quartered there, and had burned to the ground. However, the owner would get full compensation—the Army would itself undertake to rebuild the *dacha* for him.

Peredyelkino was a veritable literary paradise. The names of the owners and occupants of the various *dachas* provided a complete list of all the leading Soviet authors of the past two decades: Kassil, Katayev, Gladkov, Leyonov, Virta, Vera Inber, Pasternak, Ivanov, Chukovsky. Here amid the pine trees of Peredyelkino many of them lived year-in and year-out, seldom seeing anyone but each other, enjoying a standard of comfort far above the average even for the Soviet intelligentsia.

On one side of the "Writers' Village," as it was called, was a collective farm; on the other a colony of *dachas* belonging to high Government officials and ranking Red Army officers, including the countryseat of hard-riding, mustachioed Marshal Semyon Budyonny. But the writers kept strictly apart from their neighbors, both their inferiors and betters in the social scale. They lacked any community club facilities beyond a boardinghouse run by the Writers' Union. It was supposed to accommodate younger authors not important enough to have their own *dachas,* yet desiring a quiet spot in the country where they might commune with the Muses. Hence it was glorified with the name *Dom Tvorchestva*—in literal translation "House of Creativeness." Most of the writers and their families from the surrounding *dachas* congregated there for their evening meal and a bit of conversation. A week end at Peredyelkino was much like a literary week end anywhere, save that the palisade fences of the Writers' Village seemed to shut out the outside world completely.

Those endless soul-probing discussions for which Russians are famous would extend through the brief hours of darkness into the early dawn. A favorite pastime was to analyze the content of the latest American motion picture, viewed either at Spasso House or at a private showing at the House of the Kino. *Casablanca* was a general favorite—the right admixture of political propaganda, melodrama, and artistry—nothing heavy-handed about the political angle, not overdone, but just natural and logical, in its proper sequence, and hence all the more convincing. These dialecticians were always looking for ideology and political propaganda in every picture, sometimes finding things that were never intentionally put there by the director. Thus it was that grouchy, vitriolic, old David Zaslavsky decided that William Saroyan's *Human Comedy,* with its emphasis on American home life and its lack of class conflict, was a bit of skillful fascist propaganda.

There was considerable excitement over the current vicissitudes of Charlie Chaplin, the Russians' favorite American screen actor. The prevailing opinion—fostered by the noted Jewish actor Solomon Michoels, who had visited Chaplin in the course of a recent tour of the United States—was that pro-fascist elements were seeking to discredit the great comedian on account of his anti-fascist picture—*The Great Dictator*—and his friendly attitude toward the Soviet Union.

All Soviet writers had a great admiration for what they called "American realist literature." They had read everything available of Hemingway's. His last big novel—*For Whom the Bell Tolls*— had been translated into Russian but had never been published.

There was much half-uttered chafing over censorship, and much curiosity over how censorship operated in the United States. Assurances that there was no censorship whatever in peacetime, and that in war it was confined to military matters, always drew polite smiles of incredulity. However, there was general conviction that presently the censorship in the Soviet Union would relax and that some of the manuscripts now gathering dust might see print. As proof of this they cited the fact that even now two Soviet writers, Alexei Tolstoi and Mikhail Sholokhov, who stood head and shoulders above the crowd, were free to write almost anything they pleased and could practically get away with murder in the guise of literature.

"Look at the utterances Sholokhov puts into the mouths of his hero, Pantaleimon Prokofievich," somebody once remarked apropos of the latest instalment of *The Silent Don,* Sholokhov's voluminous and endless novel about his beloved Cossacks. "Why, it's counter-revolutionary! But because it's Sholokhov nobody minds. Is that fair, I ask you?"

"Don't ask me," laughingly answered another. "Send your complaints in to the Central Committee, or drop 'em in the Kremlin mail box, addressed to Yosif Vissarionovich."

Despite such rather good-natured grumbling, these writers, many of them representatives of an older generation of intellectuals which had come of age before the Revolution, were enthusiastically behind the regime and proud of their country. But there was no bumptuous superiority about this pride and enthusiasm. They acknowledged and praised the achievements of Allied arms. And earnestly, hungrily they looked forward to a time when full cultural intercourse with the West should be restored. Therein, they declared, lay the future hope of Russian literature and art. They would bolster these views with endless examples, such as the close affinity between Pushkin and Byron in particular and French and British romanticism in general. They would trace the relation between the great Russian nineteenth-century prose writers and novelists and their Western colleagues. Even in the field of politics and economics, they pointed out, Russia had adapted her structure and ideas from Europe. Free interflow of thought between Russia and the West, they insisted, was the sole guarantee of continued cultural progress. Otherwise sterility would set in.

The voicing of these views augured well for the future of friendly relations between the West and the USSR. Not that these men were in any sense Government spokesmen. But they did represent the most articulate groups in the country—the cultural leaders. Their media—literature, the stage, and now the movies—had traditionally served as the main channels by which the ideas and trends of the outer world had penetrated into Russia. And it was from them and through them that these new influences filtered into the body politic and the Party, eventually penetrating the inner recesses of policy-making. Hence they constituted a very real and a very powerful political force.

CHAPTER NINE ✩ ✩ ✩ ✩ ✩ ✩ ✩ ✩ ✩ ✩ ✩ ✩ ✩ ✩

THE VOLKOVS—A STORY OF FAILURE AND SUCCESS

✩ ✩ ✩ ✩ ✩ ✩ ✩ ✩ ✩ ✩ ✩ ✩ ✩ ✩

THE Volkov brothers, Fyodor and Vlas, were among my oldest friends. Vlas, the younger, was a Party member, typical of thousands of the first generation products of the new regime. His career was a Soviet success story. Fyodor, though more gifted mentally, was of a passive disposition, inclined to avoid the lifestream of events. His natural lack of initiative was fostered by his wife Shura, who hated any kind of change. Even the war, which uprooted so many families, scarcely jarred them in their deep rut.

On my return to Moscow I found the Volkovs living in the same room in which they had lived ten years before when I first met them. They looked about the same and were as well, or as badly, off financially as always. For though Fyodor was a construction engineer and a good one, he had never achieved any degree of success. Luck always seemed to be running out on him; others were always climbing over his head. It was partly, if not wholly, Shura's fault. Even before the war, Fyodor was constantly being offered excellent openings which he could never accept, sometimes because he couldn't get a release from his current employment, but more often because it involved moving somewhere out of Moscow—which Shura wouldn't hear of under any circumstances.

Moscow, Shura contended, was the Mecca toward which everyone in the provinces turned yearning eyes. Why, there were millions of people ready to trade years of their lives for just a corner in some Moscow room. And here she and Fyodor had practically a whole room to themselves. Why, it would be madness to leave Moscow and run the risk of losing the room. It was always easy to leave Moscow, but then just try and get back.

Thus, back in 1938 Fyodor had had a chance to go to Kazakhstan in Central Asia to help build a giant copper smelting plant. The terms were most tempting—three times his present salary and a private apartment upon the completion of the first new modern block of apartments. Fyodor was eager to accept, but Shura was adamant.

Kazakhstan! Who ever heard of anyone going to that hole of their own free will? People would think you were crazy and they wouldn't be far wrong, either. Besides, weren't there poisonous spiders as big as crayfish? She, Shura, would see herself dead before she would ever consent to going out to such a place with Zina. Fyodor argued with her: wonderful opportunity for advancement, the tremendous future of Asia—but as always, Shura got the better of the argument. The same story had been repeated several times in slightly differing versions, and the result was that in all the years I had known them, Fyodor, Shura, and their daughter Zina never had much more to their name than the clothes they had on. When they went to the theater or to a party, Fyodor borrowed his brother-in-law's shoes. The rest of the time he wore old felt house slippers inside his rubbers. Their room, Shura pointed out with pride, was larger than the average—not a bad room as rooms go, in fact, even though it opened on a dark inner court and had not been redecorated since the Revolution. Bedbugs nested in every cranny of the mattresses, walls, chest of drawers, and bookcases, behind the mirror and the framed flyspecked pictures of Pushkin and Gorky. Shura was not the least bit touchy on the subject of the vermin, nor was she bothered by them. There was no point, she argued, trying to get rid of bedbugs. They would only come back; all the neighboring rooms were infested with them; in fact, they lived deep in the walls. The only way to destroy them would be to burn the building. But, she added, they didn't bother her. For that matter, she was quite sure they didn't bite any members of the family.

The first decade of Fyodor's and Shura's married life had been complicated by the presence of Fyodor's father, Boris, who worked at one of the central newspapers, wrapping and tying up bundles of the edition as it came off the presses for shipment out of town.

His working hours were from 1:00 A.M. to 8:00 A.M.; and he habitually slept to within a half-hour of working time, so that evenings at the Volkovs were invariably punctuated by *Papasha's* hearty snoring. But one year before the war, *Papasha,* who had divorced Fyodor's mother long ago, had a sudden spurt of Indian summer, married a young wife, and with this incentive applied for a room of his own. In view of his many years' standing as a worker, it was granted to him in short order.

When I first knew Fyodor and Shura, a small room next to theirs had been occupied by a relic of the old regime—a little, frail old lady who wore a black dress with a whalebone collar fringed with lace. Before the Revolution, she and her husband, a lawyer, had occupied the entire apartment which had now been parceled out— a different family in every room. She had been left this one cubby hole. Fyodor and Shura lived in hopes that when the old lady passed on, they would inherit her room. Once when I dropped in to see them, they were in a state of tremendous excitement. They pointed to a big, red wax seal on the door next to theirs. The old lady, it seemed, had passed away in her sleep two days before. As no one had claimed the body, it had been carted off to the potters' field, and the house committee had sealed the room. Fyodor had been down to the Housing Department of the Moscow Soviet that very morning and had filled out a questionnaire. In the following days he paid several more visits, both to the Moscow Soviet and to the district Soviet, and filled out many additional questionnaires. But before he ever received an answer, the seal was duly removed from the door and a new tenant—an old man with a daughter— moved in. Again they had missed the bus and as usual Shura insisted it was all Fyodor's fault.

As the passing years failed to bring any notable degree of promotion to him or prosperity to his family, Fyodor, by nature one of the kindliest and most even-tempered of human beings, grew a trifle petulant, at times almost sharp, in his domestic arguments with Shura. If she complained of the lack of the wherewithal to buy Zina or herself a new dress, or drew comparisons with their more affluent friends, implying that Fyodor was not a good provider, Fyodor would actually flare up and blame Shura for keeping him back.

"If not for you," he exploded, "and your confounded mistrust of anything new, we'd be out of this rut long ago—why, I might even be a commissar, instead of little more than straw boss on a construction gang."

"Yes," came the tart rejoinder, "and you might be chopping trees in the northern woods, or rotting in some jail. It would be just like you to get shoved into some job with lots of responsibility and then let yourself be made the goat for some gang of imcoppetents or wreckers. At least, I say one's always safer in a crowd. It's better to have an inconspicuous small job with few responsibilities than to get yourself out on a limb where you're exposed and likely to be knocked down."

This same extreme caution and mistrust of responsibility on Shura's part had kept Fyodor from joining the Party. He had been a member of the Komsomol from the age of fourteen and in the Pioneers before that. His record as a Komsomol member had been good, a sufficient recommendation as a candidate for admission to the Party. He had never been mixed up with the Trotskyites or any other deviation. But the years came and went and Fyodor, under Shura's influence, put off his application for Party membership until one day he reached the age limit of the Komsomol and received a notification that he had therefore been automatically dropped from the membership rolls. The easy way into the Party was no longer open, and there he was, suddenly a *bespartiny*—a non-party man. Secretly Shura was jubilant; her cunning Fabian strategy for keeping Fyodor out of the Party had succeeded. Not that Shura was anti-Soviet, but again, she argued, why place yourself needlessly in an exposed position?

Unlike Fyodor, who came from plain working stock, Shura's father had been a high school teacher in St. Petersburg before the Revolution and Shura's mother had bequeathed to her daughter idyllic memories of a time when potatoes had cost three kopeks a kilo.

It was, Shura had told Fyodor, each time he was on the point of putting in an application, never too late to join the Party, but

once you were in, you could never back water. It was much the
same argument as the one she used to dissuade him from accepting
tempting positions outside Moscow: that it was always easy to leave
Moscow but almost impossible to get back. And so, year by year,
life slipped by the Volkovs. The country grew and prospered; the
industrial giants of three five-year plans towered in the wilderness;
Fyodor's classmates at the *technicum* were in the front ranks of the
battle for industrialization; while Fyodor and Shura marked time
in their dingy room with their bedbugs. They had one interest in
life that obscured all else, and that was Zina. Zina was a clever,
fine-featured child with eyes like deep, dark, amber pools. It was a
long standing fiction of the Volkovs that Zina was extremely frail
physically. This gave both parents the excuse to pamper their
daughter, to make those sacrifices whose supreme reward is that
exalted feeling of unselfishness and self-denial which enables parents later to remind their grown children: "I devoted the best years
of my life to you."

Like all intelligent children, Zina soon learned to draw the
fullest advantage from her parents' excessive devotion, and in due
course came to regard their constant attentions as her just due. She
also cultivated the fiction about her delicate health, complaining of
headaches and other indispositions with such frequent regularity
that in time she actually felt the symptoms. Being a precocious
child, she learned to read far too early in life for her own good.
Before she was ten, she had gone through most of the volumes in
the bookcase, including a complete set of Dostoyevsky. And by
the time she was twelve, she and her father would sit for hours in
the dim light of the low-watt bulb, discussing Ivan Karamazov's
philosophical objections to Christianity until the scolding protesta-
tions of Shura, long since in bed, would grow so insistent that they
finally turned in.

When war came, Fyodor was called up, but before he ever
reached the fighting front he was mustered out because his profession of building engineer was on the essential list. For a while he
worked night and day on the construction of a trench mortar and
machine gun factory. Then came the grim days of October, 1941,
when the Germans were driving on the capital with a seemingly

irresistible force. At Fyodor's insistence, Shura and Zina bundled up their personal belongings and joined the exodus. Shura had a married sister somewhere near Irkutsk on a collective farm, and that was where they headed. At least, Fyodor felt, they would be out of danger there and close enough to the soil so they wouldn't starve. To Fyodor, whose grandparents had been peasants, there was something protective and reassuring about the soil. Meanwhile, work on the construction of Fyodor's factory never let up for an instant. Other plants, including airplane factories, automobile factories, electrical equipment factories, were evacuated lock, stock, and barrel to the Urals, with all their workmen. But if Moscow, now a front-line city, was to be defended to the last, trench mortars and machine guns would be required by the defenders. And on the fifteenth of October, the darkest day of the entire war, the new plant went into production. For the first time in his life, Fyodor really felt like part of the scheme of things. He worked with the same will and devotion as nameless millions of obscure Soviet citizens; he took a pride of achievement in his work; he felt a personal stake in the country.

That exaltation had lasted until his first letter from Shura. They had had a long and hard journey. Four times between Moscow and Kazan their crowded train had been sidetracked while endless retching, clanking lines of flatcars loaded with machinery shunted by.

Beyond Sverdlovsk the train had made better time along the trans-Siberian. But by that time the food they had brought with them for the journey had given out, and there was nothing to do but barter their meager belongings at wayside stations. Siberia, almost untouched by the war, was full of food. The Buryat peasants came down to the stations to meet the trains with all sorts of tempting wares. But they turned up their noses at money, saying they already had bales of it. What they wanted was clothes, and not just any clothes, mind you; they were choosy—partial, in fact, to the best silks and woolens. The upshot of it was that by the time they reached Irkutsk, Shura and Zina had, in Shura's words, eaten up everything but the clothes on their backs, including a portable gramophone they had taken along to sell when they arrived.

Irkutsk, despite its remoteness, was already crowded with refugees from all over the Ukraine and western Russia, and they were proving somewhat of a strain on local hospitality. Shura had reached her sister's collective farm only to find there was no real place for her and Zina. Her brother-in-law had been mobilized. Her sister had her own three children to support and look after, and having Shura and Zina there only added to their problems. She, Shura, didn't know the first thing about farm work, and though she knew a bit about bookkeeping and accounting, there was no opening in the collective farm in that field of work. She was further concerned about the state of Zina's health, especially after the long journey. She, Shura, felt terribly alone and friendless.

Under the influence of Shura's letter Fyodor made the crowning mistake of his life. Doubting that he could ever obtain permission to leave his job, he decided not even to raise the issue. And one morning, without notifying anyone, he simply boarded a train, trusting that somehow, in the stress of the times, his desertion might be forgotten. Reaching Irkutsk, he found that, after all, things were not nearly so bad as Shura had painted them in her letter. True, conditions were far from ideal. Living quarters were cramped, but Shura's sister had done her best for them and there was plenty of food. Smitten with pangs of remorse, Fyodor decided to return to Moscow. But at this point Shura objected.

"Either stay here with us," she told him, "or else take us with you. I guess it's safe to go back, all right. If the Germans haven't taken Moscow yet, I don't think they ever will. Besides, whatever happens, it doesn't matter, so long as we're together."

Fyodor feebly objected that when he got back he would at the very least be drafted into the Army for his desertion from his job. At worst, there was no telling what might happen.

Thus in mid-January, in the coldest part of that bitter winter of 1941-42, they set forth on the long return journey. There were no civilians on the trains going west; every car was jammed to overflowing with troops. And so the Volkovs traveled, huddled into the far corner of a "hard" sleeper. (In Russia, train accommodations are divided into "hard" and "soft," class distinctions having been done away with.) But this crowding in with the soldiers had its compensations. Little Zina soon became a general favorite with the men, most of whom had daughters or little sisters that they'd left at home. And these big, raw-boned Sibiryaks—broader and taller than the European Russians——generously shared their army rations and the little bundles of goodies which they had brought along, with Zina and her family.

Somehow they got past the various control points without being removed from the train—they still had their Moscow passports and Fyodor had his factory pass. None of Fyodor's fears materialized. When he reported with trepidation at his old job, it was to find that he had been listed as discharged on account of ill health. He was popular with his fellow-employees and they had covered up for him. Besides, times were too hectic for any careful check up.

But never again could he look his comrades in the eye, much less recapture his old enthusiasm for the job. So instead of going back to the factory, he decided to enlist in the Army. He was goaded to this decision by an inner necessity for self-punishment, plus a feeling that if he was ever to win self-respect, he must get out from under Shura's devitalizing influence. He planned to do it secretly, of course. He would never hurt Shura by telling her he had voluntarily enlisted, for she would guess that he was running away from her. Instead, he would save her peace of mind with a harmless lie to the effect that he had been called up. Even if he were killed in battle, he felt, Shura and Zina would get along. Next spring Zina would graduate from elementary school and enter high school. She was always at the head of her class. Shura would get a job as a bookkeeper. She might even marry again—a more successful husband. And besides, by giving his life at the front, he, Fyodor, would partly atone for the years of passivity, for his past failure to give to his country which had educated him the best that was in him, and for his cardinal breach of desertion.

All these lofty resolves were shattered on the stone threshold of the district military recruiting office. People with his training and qualifications were too valuable, both now and for the postwar period, to be risked at the front.

So with a mingled feeling of relief and disappointment, Fyodor had answered a want ad in the *Vechernyaya Moskva—Evening Moscow*—for a construction engineer. The new position paid less than the job in the defense plant and the rations facilities were decidedly poorer. Fyodor set no store by all these material considerations until Shura jumped on him about it. But by then it was too late. He had already signed up. The project was the construction of a factory for the manufacture of vitamin tablets and food concentrates for Army use. The specifications, formulae, and some of the machinery would be obtained from America. Fyodor was assigned to the construction of a yeast-producing unit.

When I arrived back in Moscow, Fyodor's unit had been completed; but there had been some delay with some of the other units. Meanwhile, Fyodor and his workmen, with plenty of yeast available, had set about making various kinds of home-brew in their spare time. When I had known him, Fyodor was completely abstemious. But now Shura complained that every evening with clocklike regularity he came home from work tipsy from these "experiments." "Not that he drinks heavily," she added hastily. "I don't want you to misunderstand me. But after working all day on an empty stomach, he's in such a weakened condition that the least taste of alcohol sets him up. Also," she added, "since he had to sell his sheepskin coat, he's got to keep warm somehow."

The complete antithesis of Fyodor was Fyodor's younger brother, Vlas. Even when I first met them in 1934, Vlas, though he was Fyodor's junior by two years, looked the more mature. At that time Vlas, who did not have the benefit of a higher education, was working in the same newspaper plant as his father, making photographic cuts. He and his wife Nadya also lived in one room. But it was a cheery room in a modern building and in an apartment equipped with a bathtub and a gas cooking range. Nadya worked in a textile mill and their little boy Miron, aged four, went to a nursery school. Vlas, twenty-four years old at the time, had already been admitted to Party membership. He was deeply interested in photography and was saving up his extra money to buy a camera. One day when I called to see them, with a light in his eyes he opened a small cardboard box and produced therefrom an FED—a Soviet-made, miniature 35 millimeter camera, an almost exact replica of the German Leica. Six months later, the first picture bearing Vlas's byline was published in the paper. Shortly after that, Vlas proudly produced for my inspection a gleaming, genuine, German-made Leica camera with a 1:4 lens.

In the years that followed, my contact with Vlas and his family became extremely tenuous. Those were the purge years, and he feared that association with a foreigner might mar his record. Occasionally I ran into Vlas on the street or at the theater.

As more and more of Vlas's photos appeared in the papers, he became known as one of the leading Soviet press cameramen. In this capacity he was sent to the Far East in 1939 to cover the undeclared war with Japan at Khalkingol on the Outer Mongolian frontier. During the winter war with Finland, he was on the Karelian Isthmus front. In the summer of 1940 he had gone into Latvia and Estonia when the Red Army took over the Baltic States.

At the time of my return to Moscow, Vlas was somewhere on the front. People who had seen him and been with him at the front said that he was fearless to the point of being foolhardy. His exploits had won him a majority and a chestful of decorations.

A year before the war, Vlas and his family had moved out of their one room into their own private three-room apartment in an imposing new block erected for the staff members of his paper. It was substantially, if not attractively, furnished in golden oak. Sundry souvenirs of Vlas's travels were conspicuously displayed. There were squat little bronze Buddhas from Mongolia, embroidered couch and table covers from Bukhara, a complete set of dishes from Riga. A whole arsenal of German trophies hung from hooks on the walls.

From his expedition to the Baltic States, Vlas had brought back two trunks full of clothing, most of it for Nadya, including quantities of silk stockings. But in October, 1941, Nadya and Miron had left Moscow and had spent the next eighteen months at a village near Saratov. She had taken along her Latvian clothing and had traded off most of it for food.

They were in an area only recently vacated by the Volga Germans, whom the Soviet authorities had packed off to Siberia. And not a moment too soon, either. According to Nadya, those Volga German settlements had been honeycombed with Nazi sympathizers. Plans had been completed for landing, with their assistance, a German parachute division in the rear of the then rapidly retreating Russian front. Had the operation come off, the possible consequences might have been serious. The Russians were tipped off in the nick of time by a Russian woman whose German husband had rashly confided in her. That explained the sudden decision to shift the Volga Germans and the swiftness with which it was carried out.

All through the middle thirties the Volga Germans, like the German settlements in the Ukraine, had been the objects of considerable underground Nazi propaganda; not even the purge of 1937-38, which got rid of most of Russia's fifth-column elements, had succeeded in combing these Germans out.

When these people were evacuated, each family was permitted to take along one metric ton of household goods and foodstuffs. Now the Volga Germans were one of the most prosperous farming communities in the whole of Russia—so far above the average standard, that in the days of collectivization an entirely different yardstick had been applied to them to determine those who were subject to expropriation as *kulaks*. This had been partly because as a national minority they received preferential treatment, but also because, had the same standards been applied to them as to their Russian neighbors, virtually the entire community would have been subject to expropriation.

In other words, the one-ton limit on what they could take with them was scarcely a drop in the bucket for many of these German families. Consequently they were forced to leave behind, in addition to their houses, big stores of grain and potatoes, and considerable livestock. Some of this they sold off at sacrifice prices to their Russian neighbors, but they were so pressed for time that much of it was simply abandoned. So the Russian peasants from near-by villages simply moved in and helped themselves to the windfall.

By the time Nadya and other city folk evacuated from Moscow arrived, there wasn't much left lying around; but there were the empty houses, and there was food to be had from the surrounding peasantry at a price. Here, as elsewhere, the peasants preferred consumer goods to paper money; and so Nadya, as she put it, had eaten her way through most of her wardrobe like a moth.

Eventually the Soviet authorities caught up with many of the individual peasants and collective farms that had made a good thing out of the German evacuation. The wiser heads anticipated this by making large voluntary contributions to the defense fund.

Returning to Moscow in the spring of 1943, Nadya was happy to find that her apartment and furniture had not been rifled or taken over by someone else. Vlas, whom she had not seen in all this time, was somewhere on the Southern Front, sending in occasional photographs. His irregular letters were full of the rigors and dangers of front life, and of his latest hairbreadth escapes. A few weeks later he suddenly blew into Moscow. But he stayed home only at odd hours and even then seemed rather absent-minded; when he spoke in answer to a direct question, there was something mechanical and perfunctory in his tone, as though his thoughts were obviously somewhere else. Nadya complained that even when he looked at her, it was as though she weren't there and his gaze was focused on something beyond her. At first she thought it might be another woman. Then from his fragmentary conversation she realized that he was completely and utterly wrapped up in the war and his work. The comparative peace and quiet of home and Moscow made him nervous and fidgety, and he counted the hours until he received his instructions to go back.

Just before I arrived in Moscow, Vlas had again been home for another short, fidgety visit. And though I followed the publication of his pictures in the press and heard of him indirectly from mutual friends, it was not till April that I actually saw him. He had aged greatly; when his face was in repose, his eyes looked incredibly old and tired—though he was only thirty-three. Since the outbreak of war, he had covered the front-line fighting almost continuously. Several times in the early days he had been cut off by the advancing Germans and had avoided capture by a hairbreadth. Once he had crouched hidden under the floor of a peasant hut while the boards creaked and pressed against his head under the weight of jack-booted Germans. At the time of the German capture of Kiev, he

had escaped by driving down an old abandoned dirt road while
German tanks were advancing along the parallel highway less than
a quarter of a mile away. On his latest assignment on the First
Ukrainian Front, somewhere near Zhitomir, a German shell had
landed on the road just behind his speeding car—a German *volk-
wagen* trophy—and a big shrapnel fragment had cut right through
the back seat. "Lucky thing it missed my cameras," Vlas commented when he told the story.

One of his favorite sports was to photograph the German front
lines from a little U-2 observation biplane that had a top cruising
speed of sixty miles an hour. Once he and his pilot had missed the
airdrome and, out of gas, had made a forced landing on a field
where a tank battle happened to be in progress. Under enemy fire,
he and his pilot managed to drag the light little plane behind the
shelter of a convenient hillock—whereupon Vlas sallied forth to
get some good battle scenes. Later, when they examined the plane,
they found that the canvas wings were peppered with bullet holes.

When Vlas and Fyodor got together, which was seldom nowadays, the conversation was awkward and forced, interspaced with
long silences.

Though Fyodor was completely loyal to his younger brother
and invariably praised his courage and ability, there was something
about his mere presence in a room that seemed to make Fyodor
uneasy, upsetting his usual aplomb.

A few days after Vlas's return, we were all invited by Nadya for
one of those traditional Russian evenings of food. The meal began
with sundry *zakuski*—pickled herring, cheese, and smoked salmon.
This was followed by *schi*—sour cabbage soup—and *pirozhki*—home-
baked rolls with cabbage, carrot, and chopped-meat fillings. Besides
Fyodor, Shura, and myself, Vlas's editor and several of his newspaper colleagues were present. When the time for toasts rolled
around, all of us got up and toasted our host and hostess, paying
glowing tributes to Vlas. Suddenly in the midst of it, Fyodor, who
had eaten little and said less through the evening, got up and,
without a word to anybody, left the room. A few seconds later the
front door of the apartment opened and closed.

Nobody made the slightest move to detain Fyodor or call him

back. For once even Shura was too dumbfounded to assert her family leadership. Thereafter the whole mood of the evening was spoiled. Not even a collection of German jazz records that Vlas had picked up somewhere in the Western Ukraine could mend matters, and the party broke up far earlier than is usual in Moscow. Next time I saw Fyodor, he apologized profusely for his exit, explaining that he had suddenly remembered that he had forgotten to leave some instructions for the night watchman concerning the yeast vats. That was the last time Fyodor set foot in Vlas's house, even though Nadya and Shura continued to be friends.

CHAPTER TEN

NAZI CRIME AND PUNISHMENT

A GROUP of Allied pressmen awoke from a chilly sleep in Kiev one morning soon after the city's liberation to blink at several Germans dangling from the hotel balcony outside their room windows. The Soviet newspapers carried no reference to these hangings, and the censors did not allow the correspondents to cable anything about them.

But the inference was obvious. At the recently terminated Moscow Conference the Russians had insisted on a declaration concerning the punishment of the individuals responsible for German atrocities in the occupied countries and areas. The Russians contended that the category of such war criminals embraced everyone from the Nazi higher-ups who issued the general directive for the extermination of Jews and other sections of the population down to the meanest *Wehrmacht* private who mowed down unarmed civilians with a machine gun, or used his bayonet in the gruesome fulfillment of the directives.

The Russians further asserted that any officers or soldiers who committed crimes or atrocities against civilians forfeited their right to be treated as belligerents, and that in the event of capture they could be tried and punished as common criminals. The Kiev hangings indicated that the Russians, with their accustomed zeal for combining theory with practice, were already meting out retribution to any such criminals that fell into their hands.

There is no available count on how many other Germans have silently shared the fate of those the correspondents saw swinging from the balcony in Kiev. Isolated episodes are rare in Russia; most things happen according to plan. One month later, on December 15, a public trial of war criminals opened in Kharkov in the liberated Ukraine. This time the Russians made every effort to publicize the proceedings as widely as possible. The best Soviet writing talent was mobilized to cover the trial, and representatives of the Allied press were flown down to attend the last day's session and witness the executions the following morning.

The defendants were small fry. Chief of the lot was a captain, Wilhelm Langheldt, described as a member of the German Military Intelligence, attached to a prisoner of war camp. The others were Lieutenant Hans Ritz, commander of a special SS detachment; Private Reinhardt Retslau, attached to the 560th Group of the German Secret Field Police; and a Russian traitor, Mikhail Bulanov, who had chauffeured for the Kharkov Gestapo.

The Russians are past masters at *mis en scène,* and the atmosphere of that Kharkov trial room was distinctly reminiscent of the famous Treason Trials of 1936-38. In fact, two of the defense lawyers, Kommodov and Kaznacheyev, had defended some of the figures in the treason trials. Their presence provided an element of direct continuity. This, too, was a military tribunal: judges, prosecutor, and attendants were all in uniform.

The sessions were held in the Kharkov Dramatic Theater, which had somehow miraculously escaped demolition even though the city had changed hands four times. As at the Treason Trials, admission tickets valid for one session only were distributed to factory workers and office employees through their trade union organizations, so that the audience kept rotating. The massed faces of these Kharkov civilians who had lived through two years of Nazi occupation—mostly young girls and older men and women— were charged with a breathless tenseness that never once relaxed through the long hours of the interrogation.

During the recesses, I discovered that many of the people in the audience had personal knowledge or experience of the events and atrocities described, and had seen or known the defendants during the German occupation. Several times during more gruesome bits of evidence there were stifled sobs from some woman—not out of pity for the defendants. For the most part the proceedings took place against a background of concentrated silence.

The theatrical setting of the trial was enhanced by the blaze of klieg lights as whole batteries of cameramen filmed every minute of the proceedings from all possible angles.

As in the Moscow Treason Trials all legal niceties were observed to a fault. The defendants and their counsel had full latitude to speak or interpolate, and every comma of what was said was translated into German for their benefit.

Another interesting parallel with the Treason Trials was the apparent eagerness of the defendants to confess to their crimes. They almost seemed to revel in their wickedness, gratuitously filling in all the lurid details.

Thus stocky, red-headed, beefy-faced Wilhelm Langheldt, whose carriage, heel-clicking, and rows of ribbons proclaimed a German soldier of the old school, calmly described how he trumped up charges against Soviet war prisoners when he was in command of a prisoner of war camp.

"My immediate superior, Major Lulai, upbraided me for not shooting enough people. I excused myself by saying that I had only been at the camp a short time and had not yet had an opportunity to show my diligence."

Langheldt then went on to show how he made up for his early laxity. When prisoners refused to sign faked testimony, he simply had his translator forge their signatures. When Ukrainian peasant women from near-by came to the camp looking for relatives, he had them arrested on charges of helping to establish contact between prisoners and Partisan groups. They were beaten and then shot, together with children whom they had brought along with them.

When the prosecutor asked Langheldt whether the German High Command ever punished its soldiers or officers for ill treatment of civilians, he pondered a moment, rocking slightly back and forth on his toes and heels, and then answered, in the same quiet, measured voice in which his entire testimony had been delivered, that on the contrary such treatment was deliberately encouraged and rewarded. At each conclusion of his testimony, Langheldt saluted smartly, turned on his heels, and strode back to his seat in the prisoners' box.

A Nazi horse of a different color from the hard-bitten Langheldt was the next on the stand, Hans Ritz, a baby-faced youth of twenty-four, with a tender little mustache. The son of a Koenigsberg professor, he testified that before being drafted for service on the Eastern Front he had studied music. Ritz had commanded an SS punitive expedition at Taganrog and admitted personally issuing orders for the shooting of between two and three thousand civilians. He had herded other thousands into *Gasenwagens*. This bit of Nazi deviltry is a sealed truck into which the exhaust fumes are diverted. The victims are simply loaded into this portable lethal chamber and are ready for burial by the time the truck arrives at the mass burial pits, usually located on the edge of town. The *Gasenwagen,* Ritz stated, had been used extensively in Warsaw, Riga, Kiev, Poltava, and Smolensk—as well as in Kharkov and Taganrog.

Ritz, like his co-defendants, made no effort to hide his crimes. He even told of having himself used a tommy gun on civilians on the orders of a superior officer who was trying to "test his nerve." But, unlike the others, he was university-bred. At one point in his brief and about-to-be-terminated career he had studied law, which he now proceeded to quote to his accusers.

Thus he sought to place the blame for his own misdeeds and those of others like him on the shoulders of his superiors. He cited Hitler's direct orders for the inculcation of systematic cruelty and the doctrine of German race superiority, whence followed the advisability for exterminating inferior races, including the Russians. He also quoted Himmler, the Gestapo Chief, as having declared that in imposing capital penalty one needn't consult the statutes, but only one's Aryan instincts.

He ended with what was intended as a moving plea for himself and others like him who had grown up under Nazism and had never had a chance to know anything different. If only his life were spared—if only the court gave him another chance, he would devote his entire energies to the destruction of Nazism. When the time came, he said, he would gladly give evidence against the Fuehrer himself. But his words thawed none of the ice in the court. Every face in that room outside the prisoners' box wore the same expression of hatred and contempt that signified too clearly "thumbs down!"

The court and the people watching knew what was coming. Most of them had seen the four gallows-trees being erected in the center of the market place. But even though the defendants must have sensed the hostility around them, I wonder if they appreciated the full hopelessness of their position. After all, they doubtless told themselves, they had merely acted on orders from higher up. Had they refused, they would have been subject to court martial. They probably expected they would now be let off with a prison sentence that would be commuted when the war had ended and its animosities had had time to cool off. The very decorum of the court strengthened such optimism. After all, they probably figured, if the Russians intended to execute them, they could have simply lined them up against a stone wall.

It should be added that the one Russian in the prisoners' box, Bulanov, did not share the illusions of his German co-defendants. From the very start the quaking fear that convulsed his frame and the wild horror in his eyes showed he knew full well the shadow of the gallows was upon him. Of course he doubtless realized, as did the Germans sitting alongside him, that he was in a separate category—a traitor who could therefore expect no clemency.

The readiness of the defendants in the Treason Trials to testify against themselves has been a source of endless speculation. It has been the subject of several books, including one novel. The explanations have ranged all the way from dark references to Dostoyevsky and the mysterious, unfathomable Russian soul, to fantastic theories about a "truth serum" or some form of hypnosis, to subtle psychological inquiries such as that conducted by Arthur Koestler in *Darkness at Noon.*

The fact that these Germans behaved in an almost identical manner seems to dispose of the Russian soul theory, as well as of Koestler's ingenious argument that pangs of conscience led the old Bolshevik revolutionaries to accuse themselves of crimes they had never committed.

The Kharkov trial parallel suggests that the similarity of behavior proceeds, not from any peculiar Russian national trait, but from a similarity of methods employed by the prosecution in both cases. During 1937-38 when Stalin, sensing the approach of war, cleaned house, not all the people who faced firing squads or were put away for an indefinite period were given a public trial. With a wide variety of defendants to choose from, it was inevitable that some would be found who were willing to confess publicly. The lines, however, were not put in their mouths for them. Subsequent events have proved that the charges and admissions at the Treason Trials, fantastic as they may have seemed at the time, were not fiction.

Similarly, not all the Germans whom the Russians decided to hang for crimes and atrocities against the population were given a public trial. The Germans swinging from the balcony in Kiev were proof enough of that. From the hundreds undoubtedly available they presumably chose those three most pliant to their purpose. Perhaps, these Germans thought that by playing their parts as fully and convincingly as possible they would be rewarded with mercy.

But there was no room for mercy in that surcharged courtroom; it was crowded out by the unseen audience of uncounted thousands of tortured and massacred Ukrainian men, women, and children whose blood the defendants and others like them had shed.

The sentence of hanging was read by the chief judge around midnight in a final blaze of klieg projectors. As he heard the sentence, Bulanov sagged and had to be supported. But the Germans stood stolid and unconcerned, first through the original reading and then through the painfully slow translation. Apparently the illusion still persisted. Wasn't it an old Russian trick to lead a presumably condemned man to the scaffold before finally revealing that it was all a bluff? Not till the following morning when they were hustled out of a Black Maria and saw the four newly erected gallows-trees stark against the gray December sky, saw the close-packed crowd that thronged the market place, surging against the cordon of soldiers struggling to keep the space around the gallows clear—not till that moment did they realize the jig was indeed up.

We, too, witnessed the hanging. It was all over in a few moments. The defendants were hoisted into the back of four open trucks and stood on stools. Then the nooses were looped around their necks. There was no blindfolding. During the preliminaries three of the four prisoners had to be propped up. Bulanov had fainted; Ritz and Retslau had turned a pasty white; they drooled at the mouths and their knees gave way. Only Langheldt, the old soldier, remained stiff as a ramrod throughout, never once flinching. Once the nooses had been adjusted, at a signal the trucks pulled away and the four were left dangling and kicking in mid air.

Throughout all this, the crowd of more than a hundred thousand watched in complete silence. There was no sign of emotion—no pleasure, no revulsion, no sympathy—at the spectacle of men being hanged; only natural curiosity, like that of people watching a steam excavator somewhere in Manhattan. Strangely enough, this attitude was contagious and none of our group of British and American correspondents—which included two women—felt any untoward emotion. At first I was baffled for an explanation. Then I realized that in the past two years these people had lived in such constant daily contact with this sort of thing that they had become hardened to it. It was as though their cup of feeling and emotion had evaporated. From now on nothing could phase them.

Throughout the Soviet press the Kharkov executions were hailed as the "first realization" of the Stalin-Roosevelt-Churchill declaration on war criminals. Wrote the English-language *Moscow News*: "The long arms of the freedom-loving peoples will pursue those guilty to the ends of the earth and will deliver them to be judged and punished in the places where they committed their crimes; they will be tried according to the laws of the countries whose citizens fell victims to the Hitlerite terror." And the editorial concluded significantly: "Irrefutable documents leave no doubt that all these crimes are being committed by the Hitlerites at direct instructions of the German Government and the High Command of the German Army."

Thus the ink was hardly dry on the signatures under one of the Teheran documents before the Russians were acting upon it. To be sure, the defendants in this first public atrocities trial were nonentities, but it was hinted in the indictment that there were other and bigger fish to fry. The Kharkov trial balloon was to test reaction to this sort of procedure both at home and abroad, and to draw the attention of world public opinion to the truly monstrous nature of the German crimes. To this end the authorities were naturally eager that the proceedings be widely read abroad. But they fumbled at the start by not arranging for the Allied press representatives to attend. They made a recovery in time to get us down there for the final session of the trial and for the hanging. Later shots of the foreign press were included in the extensive newsreels of the trial that were shown throughout the Soviet Union and in Britain and America.

But apparently they were not altogether satisfied with the reaction. For the newsreel was soon taken off and to date there have been no more public atrocity trials and executions, though the evidence and the culprits have presumably continued to pile up. This does not necessarily mean, of course, that the Russians are not quietly dealing with whatever Nazi criminals fall into their hands.

The trip to Kharkov gave us more than a sight of the atrocity trials. It was a splendid opportunity to observe the aftermath of Nazi occupation in a big city and the early stages of reconstruction. Physically the town was a ghastly wreck. Almost every building in the center of the city had been gutted by fire and explosives. On the outskirts the blocks of little one-story wooden houses had survived, partly because their destruction would scarcely have been worth the trouble, but also because it enabled the Nazis to claim that they had nothing against the poor folk but were only out to destroy the buildings used by Party and Government people.

They had naturally done their best to wreck the city's big enterprises. But already the Soviet authorities had made considerable headway toward the restoration of the great tractor plant, the electrical equipment factory, and the mining machinery plant whose output was so urgently needed for the reconditioning of the Donets Basin coal mines.

And through the main thoroughfares flanked by charred ruins of what had been one of the Soviet Union's most modern cities, the streetcars were already proudly running.

But the reconstruction of buildings and factories, of watermains and gasmains, was not the only or even the major task facing the Soviet authorities in Kharkov and other liberated cities. Far more serious than this damage to material equipment was the destruction of human capital. Besides the millions of soldiers, flower of the country's manhood, who had perished on the battlefields, additional millions of civilians had been executed by the Nazis or else had perished by starvation. There was also damage of a less tangible character—injury that could not be gauged in terms of money or vital statistics, but was all the more insidious. This was the spiritual and moral damage inflicted on the surviving population by two years of Nazi rule. Aside from the actual traitors and collaborators who were beyond hope of recovery, hundreds of thousands of ordinary citizens had been exposed to the Nazi virus and would have to be re-educated and mentally disinfected before they would again be healthy cells of the Soviet body politic.

From the watchman at the Kharkov Dramatic Theater, with whom I chatted during the recesses at the trial, I got some colorful sidelights on life and customs in Kharkov under the Nazis. He was a rosy old man with a luxuriant walrus mustache worthy of some old Ukrainian hetman and yellowed by tobacco to the shade of old ivory. He spoke Russian with a soft Ukrainian slur. The old man had been on this same job since long before the Revolution and had stuck to his post through all the comings and goings of governments and armies. This, in fact, had been his second German occupation. The first was in 1918. When the Germans pulled out of Kharkov for the last time at the end of August, 1943, it was this old man who had saved his beloved theater from demolition simply by cutting the wires leading to the explosive charges the sappers had placed in the cellar.

Under the Germans the theater had functioned as the *Operahaus*. Here and there on the boardings, theatrical bills dating from the occupation announced performances of such old favorites as the *Rosenkavalier*, *The Merry Widow*, *Rosemarie*, and the *Swan Lake* ballet.

The company of performers had comprised the moral dregs of the local theatrical world. The leading ladies or ballerinas were obscure extras and chorus girls who had sold their souls to some Nazi devil in exchange for leading parts. Off stage, they had been kept by German officers who had provided them with gowns, silk stockings, and other undreamt-of attributes of chic. There were others, like the ballet master, people of some professional standing, who for a quarter of a century had nursed a secret hatred of the Soviets and therefore had readily collaborated with the Germans. When the Nazis fled, all these campfollowers, kept women, and collaborationists had gone with them.

"And good riddance!" the old man ejaculated. "But," he added with reflective bitterness, "there are other women still around who slept with Nazis." "German sheepdog bitches" was the local term for them. Not all of them, he added, deserved the same degree of condemnation. It was all very well to prate about "dishonor being worse than death," but if you were a mother with hungry children to feed, and the only way to get food for them was. . . .? All through the Ukraine, he concluded, the retreating *Wehrmacht* had left little Fritzes in its wake.

Before the war the venereal disease rate in the Soviet Union had been one of the lowest in Europe, vying with that in the Scandinavian countries. But now it had risen to epidemic proportions throughout the areas of German occupation.

From the Soviet ideological standpoint, a far worse evil than prostitution or venereal disease was the private trade which the Nazis had encouraged everywhere as a means of corrupting the people and weaning them away from the principles of socialist economy.

In Kharkov, at the time of our trip, the authorities had not yet made any move to curb private trade, which was going full-blast and was regulated only by the laws of competition. I visited the market some hours after the hanging. The bodies were still dangling there, but the grim presence had no chilling effect on the traders and the customers who swarmed about them. Not ten feet away an old crone had laid out her stock of Christmas tree ornaments and artificial flowers.

Everywhere motley assortments of shabby merchandise were spread on the ground on rugs or cloths, Oriental bazaar fashion. Second-hand furniture, old clothing, and crockery were for sale at prices that defied the wildest fancy. For sixty rubles—twelve dollars by the official exchange rate—I bought a small china teapot for use on the trip back to Moscow. There was one woman offering a pair of almost new lady's galoshes for eight thousand rubles—sixteen hundred dollars in American money. For the equivalent of two hundred dollars one could buy a small bottle of French perfume.

Even though the Germans had been gone many months, most of the merchandise bore witness to their visit. Thus a considerable area of the market was given over to assortments of empty bottles of every conceivable size and shape; these found ready buyers at prices averaging between five and six dollars. For seven dollars one could purchase a genuine *Cordon Rouge* champagne bottle, whose frothy contents had long since irrigated some German gullet.

From the other end of Europe the Germans had brought in trainloads of luxury loot. Though such things as champagne were meant for the exclusive use of the master race, German officers were often quite prodigal toward local women who shared their favors. The collaborationists also got a few crumbs. Inevitably some of the loot trickled into the open market; and thus, while the mass of the population lived on starvation rations of less than half a pound of bread per day, anyone with enough occupation marks or rubles could buy the finest French champagne or vintage wines, *Chanel* perfumes, the best-grade silk stockings, the loveliest fabrics, and quantities of other finery.

The Germans encouraged private trade, and anyone with anything to sell was free to dispose of it on the market or to open a small shop. In the early days a brisk business was done in clothing, furniture, and every variety of household appurtenance by house servants who had stayed behind when their employers evacuated. These people lived in luxury for a while by selling their employers' effects. In the early days of the occupation, in fact, Kharkov must have been a sort of housemaids' paradise, with servant girls dressed up and strutting about in their mistress' clothes. The comely ones conducted flirtations with German petty officers and privates who were in a position to buy, steal, or smuggle merchandise from the military stocks. This the servant girls would dispose of in the market at a handsome profit.

Today the Russians generally agree that of all categories of the population domestic servants behaved the worst under the Germans, betraying an appalling lack of integrity, morals, and loyalty.

But though the Germans brought in quantities of luxury articles, there was no effort to supply necessities to the population, and most of the newly opened commercial enterprises were soon reduced to selling and reselling an ever dwindling stock of second-hand goods at ever rising prices.

In the wake of the German Army came German commercial travelers, representatives of such notorious robber concerns as the Hermann Goering Steel Works, and others on the prowl for profitable concessions. Many of these opened up regular branch offices in Kharkov. And in the summer of 1942, when the entire Ukraine seemed firmly in the Nazi grip, with the *Wehrmacht* advancing toward the Volga and Kharkov far behind the lines, many of these burghers sent for their families. The peace and quiet of Kharkov or Kiev was doubtless a relief after the hideous bomb-shattered nights in the Reich.

These German menages made themselves at home in those of Kharkov's modern apartment houses that were still habitable. A certain amount of repair work was done for their benefit. Among the buildings that escaped the demolition squads in Kharkov, Kiev, Dniepropetrovsk, and other Ukrainian towns, are some equipped with the best German plumbing, which is technically ahead of the Russian. In Kiev a big new block of apartments for employees of the Ukrainian motion picture industry was in an advanced stage of construction when the Germans invaded. The Germans actually completed the work, made bathroom installations, and then furnished the entire block with Czechoslovakian modern furniture, complete with carpets and electric household appliances.

In the haste of the evacuation the demolition squad overlooked this block; the Russians recaptured it intact, furniture and all. The beneficiaries from this windfall were the directors, actors, and cameramen of the Kiev motion picture trust.

Besides comfortable living quarters, these Germans who settled in the new *Lebensraum* in the East had their own special stores which no Russian or Ukrainian could enter, and which stocked everything to delight the German *hausfrau*. They also had their own clubs and restaurants, where night after night the walls resounded to drunken revelry as the Nazi carpetbaggers toasted *der Führer's* health.

But though the members of the *Herrenvolk* danced like Valkyries on the bloodsoaked soil of the enslaved Ukraine, they derived scant economic benefit from their rich prize. In agriculture they made the fatal blunder (from their standpoint) of trying to retain the collective farms, believing that such large-scale agriculture would serve their purposes better than a return to small farming. But the collectives, under German-appointed managers, showed no enthusiasm whatsoever to produce food for the *Wehrmacht*. Added to this was the fact that the war had played havoc with the tractors, harvesters, and other modern farm machinery on which collective farming had become completely dependent.

But in practically every village there were families that had harbored grievances against the Soviets ever since the time of mass collectivization and the expropriation of the well-to-do peasants. Had the Germans restored to such elements their former lands and possessions, they would have gained a certain political and economic foothold in the countryside. As it was, their agrarian policy was a flop.

The Germans fared no better in their efforts to reorganize Ukrainian industry, for all their renowned technical efficiency. Thus in the coal-rich Donets Basin, industrial core of the Ukraine, they failed to get a single major plant back on its feet and operating. Before the war the vast Ordjonikidze Iron and Steel works at Yenakievo had produced 3000 tons of pig iron and 2500 tons of steel daily. But in two years of trying, the Hermann Goering Steel Trust, to which this plant was turned over as a concession, failed to produce a single ton of steel. They had no more luck with the neighboring Makeyevka plant. The prewar output of the Donets coal mines had varied between 200,000 and 250,000 tons daily, but the best the Germans could extract was 10,000 tons daily. Unable to use the highly mechanized mining methods the Russians had installed, they were forced to go back to the manual methods of fifty years ago. The best the German concessionaires could do with the Kharkov Tractor Plant was to manufacture cigarette lighters and kitchenware.

This German inability to harness the vast industrial resources of the Ukraine to their war chariot was one of the central causes for their subsequent military reverses.

The reason for this colossal German failure was not lack of equipment. All of the industrial giants which the Soviets had reared in the Ukraine during three five-year plans were not dismantled before the Germans got there. There wasn't time enough for that, especially since some of the plants had continued production right up to the time of the Germans' arrival. The explanation lay primarily in the passive resistance of the working population. The urban middle classes had provided the Germans with a small quota of fifth columnists and collaborationists in the shape of unregenerate intellectuals and former shopkeepers who had prospered briefly under Lenin's New Economic Policy and who longed for the opportunity to reopen their own private businesses. In the villages there were also former *kulaks* and others who for various reasons bore grudges against the Soviet regime and were therefore willing to help and serve the new masters. But the workers were solidly against the invaders. Against the blank wall of their resistance the Nazis were stumped. All attempts at suasion or coercion proved unavailing, and the Germans were forced to give it up.

Conversely, once the Germans were chased out, it was these same workers who flung themselves with tremendous enthusiasm into the work of reconstruction; so that today, despite the appalling demolitions which the Nazis carried out before leaving the Donets Basin, production is steadily being restored both in the mines and plants. In reconstruction, human skill and human labor are far more important than buildings and machines, however costly.

Kharkov furnishes striking evidence that the Russians can make good their losses in fixed capital with amazing swiftness if their human capital is still intact. It also indicates that the working class was more immune to the Nazi mental poison than any other section of Soviet society.

It was against the intellectuals that the Nazis directed their main efforts. In the cultural fields their policy may best be defined as a deliberate reversion to the dark ages. Colleges and universities ceased functioning. Their libraries were either destroyed or carted off to Germany, their buildings burned. Museums and scientific research laboratories were plundered and dismantled.

A week after they entered Kharkov, the Germans ordered the city's many institutions of higher learning and research to prepare for resumption of their activities. But this was only a hoax to trap the personnel into bringing their libraries, valuable collections and exhibits, and scientific apparatus out of concealment, and thereby to expedite the Nazi plundering which began immediately. A German *Kommissar* with absolute powers was assigned to each institution. Usually he was a semi-literate non-commissioned officer. In some cases German professors and scientists were brought in to go through the files and inventory, and set aside for shipment to Germany whatever they considered useful or valuable. Whole libraries were sent to the Reich; great quantities of scientific apparatus, including a large and expensive unit for cracking the atom from the Kharkov Physics Institute, were sent. For this dismantlement the Germans offered their stock excuse that such learned and scientific pursuits were not for the slave races.

Russian professors and scientific workers, with the exception of a small handful who agreed to work for the conqueror and were sent to Germany, were barred from continued work in their special fields. Many perished by starvation or at the hands of the Gestapo. The remainder eked out a miserable existence by peddling matches or shoestrings in the open market, or by making soap or shoe polish. One renowned elderly physicist kept himself and his wife alive by making candles, which he bartered with the peasants for food.

Elementary education fared little better. For though the Germans went through the motions of reopening the schools, there was a shortage of teachers and books, and attendance soon fell off. A few more years of German occupation would have produced a new crop of illiterates in a land where under the Soviet education policy illiteracy had been virtually stamped out. Deprived of books, magazines, and newspapers—during their occupation of Kharkov the Germans did not open a single bookstore even for the dissemination of their own literature—many people suffered intellectual stagnation. They indulged in no brain effort beyond the minimum required to satisfy their barest physical needs. At the same time, the Germans executed every member of the Communist Party and of the Communist Youth Organization whom they could identify. Thus they killed off the most intelligent and enterprising section of the population.

Having destroyed the economic and cultural life of the area, having shot the intellectual and political leaders, the Germans proceeded to offer anti-Semitism as a panacea. Their extermination of the Jews was everywhere systematic and thorough. This in turn contributed to the general cultural degradation, for the Jewish minority had been among the most progressive and mentally alert elements of the community, often providing a much-needed intellectual leaven.

Kharkov, like all the other cities of the Ukraine, was now a city without Jews, though its prewar Jewish community had numbered over thirty thousand.

Their extermination had started in mid-December, 1941. At that time the German commandant of the city ordered all Jews to vacate their houses and apartments inside the city and to move to the grounds of the Kharkov Tractor Plant within three days. Carrying or hauling as much as they could of their worldly goods, these hapless people set forth. Many never reached the Tractor Plant; they were shot en route by the German soldiery, who regarded them as fair game. About four hundred stragglers, mostly the old and infirm, were rounded up by the Gestapo and locked inside the Kharkov Synagogue without food or fuel. Some seventeen thousand Jews actually got as far as the Tractor Plant where they, too, were locked inside some barrack buildings. Those who tried to venture forth in search of food or water were shot by the sentries. Between January 7 and 10, all the survivors were taken off in truckloads and executed.

The Germans made every effort to involve the non-Jewish population in their persecution of the Jews, disseminating translations of Dr. Alfred Rosenberg's treatises and, of course, the inevitable *Protocols of Zion*. They also used their "Ukrainian Police" and "Russian Police," composed of fifth column and criminal elements, for pogroms. It is hard to gauge the effect of such a campaign, but I have seen indications that their seeds took root among some of the more backward sections of the population, especially in places where a latent tradition of anti-Semitism had lingered from Tsarist times. Here, too, the Soviets face a big task of re-education.

But Jews were by no means the only victims of the Nazi firing squads, *Gasenwagens,* and corpse factories, or of the famine and disease brought by the Nazis. The plight of the Ukrainian inhabitants steadily deteriorated under the Germans.

In the beginning the Nazis had made some pretense of setting up an autonomous Ukrainian state with its capital at Kharkov. To that end they imported followers of the Ukrainian fascist and terrorist, Stepan Bandera; members of the U.N.O., the Western Ukrainian fascist terrorist organization; and sundry denizens of the Nazi political zoo whom the Germans had been feeding for years against the day when they might serve some useful purpose. But soon the Nazi policy of plunder, enslavement, and extermination proved too cynical and ruthless even for these puppets, and early in 1942 the "Ukrainian National Government" was suppressed and its members executed. Thereafter the Ukraine was ruled openly and exclusively by the SS and the Gestapo, under the supreme direction of *Reichskommissar* for the Ukraine Koch, with headquarters in Rovno, conveniently closer to Germany, but, as it proved, not close enough.

At a meeting of his district *Kommissars* in August, 1943, Koch is quoted as having said: "Extermination of the maximum number of citizens of Soviet Russia can but benefit Germany because it weakens Russia."

Such directives were carried out with German thoroughness. Before the war, Kharkov had been a flourishing industrial city of 925,000 inhabitants. When the Germans arrived, there were still 450,000 people in Kharkov. According to the Germans' own statistics, by the summer of 1943 this number had been reduced to 135,000. Famine had accounted for 100,000; an additional 100,000, including the most physically fit, were deported to Germany for forced labor.

The fate of Kharkov and its inhabitants under the Germans was typical of what had happened in all the Nazi-occupied areas. For though the degree of devastation and of persecution might vary with the zeal of the individual German commandant and the duration of the German occupation in a given district, the basic policies and directives were everywhere the same.

Close in the wake of the advancing Red Armies came the police and civil administration. The Soviet intelligence system had functioned efficiently throughout the occupation period, and the reinstalled Soviet authorities had not only exhaustive lists of the Germans responsible for crimes and atrocities, but also complete dossiers on the local inhabitants. They knew just who had collaborated with the Germans and to what extent. They knew who had been neutral or simply passive, and of course they knew who had worked against the Germans, either by joining or secretly aiding the Partisans, or by gathering and transmitting information for the Soviets.

Statistically, a very sizable portion of the population fell in the neutral or passive group. These were the people who had simply tried to mind their own business and stay alive by keeping out of trouble. It was from this element that the Nazis had sought to recruit agents and collaborators. The familiar technique was to force them to incur some small obligation, quite innocent in itself, and then to use that as a lever for further enticement or intimidation, until the victim was completely enmeshed in their toils. There were, in addition, some traitors and collaborators who had volunteered to serve the Germans out of hatred for the Soviet regime.

Yet there was no attempt by the reconstituted Soviet administration to institute a drastic purge of everyone who had been the least bit tainted by contact with the Nazis. Aside from any humanitarian considerations, the regime could not afford any further reduction of a population that had already been decimated. And so, while there could be no lenience for traitors, the policy now was to treat the average citizen who bore the mental scars of the Nazi occupation as a patient to be healed rather than as a criminal to be punished.

The most effective way to rehabilitate both the country and the people was to return that portion of the population which had been evacuated before the German occupation—a portion that included many of the best elements.

But this ran directly counter to another Government policy, which was to leave the populations transferred from western Russia and the Ukraine to Siberia and Central Asia permanently in their new location, along with the plants, factories, and sundry institutions that had been carted off piecemeal and reassembled. And so, since young people are easier to reallocate than their elders, the Komsomol, or Communist Youth Organization—just as it had done in the early heroic period of the First Five-Year Plan, when populations were required for the new industrial cities then being pioneered—called for youthful volunteers to help rebuild and settle the devastated cities and areas, and to infuse the local populace with some of their fiery enthusiasm and faith in the future.

Fifteen thousand had flocked to Stalingrad from all parts of the Soviet Union in response to such a call. They lived among the ruins—in dugouts, caves, and tents—with none of the comforts of home. Food was scarce and bad. Even water had to be hauled from the Volga. But this was no deterrent. The Stalingrad example was later followed in the Donbas and at the historic naval base of Sevastopol, where a Komsomol Brigade from Irkutsk in Eastern Siberia arrived ten days after the city's liberation.

One of the most serious tasks of Soviet reconstruction was the re-establishment of the Communist Party organization in the devastated regions. In some places the Nazis had succeeded with diabolic thoroughness in exterminating both the Party membership and the Party sympathizers. To fill this vacuum, the Party Central Committee combed the Army for dependable Party members who had originally come from such localities. They were promptly demobilized and sent home to live and work among the local population and to serve as a nucleus for the new Party organization.

All available Party instructors, organizers, and propagandists were sent to the liberated areas. Their job was to go the rounds of the village and cities, helping to rebuild the Party units and to form Party sympathizers' groups. At the same time, they spoke and lectured on everything from Party history to world politics and current events, always emphasizing the fundamentals of Marxism-

Leninism. One of their main assignments was to combat anti-Semitism and any other forms of race hatred sown in his wake by the retreating Hun. Speeches and lectures were supplemented by millions of pamphlets and textbooks. This intensive propaganda campaign of re-Sovietization was strongly reminiscent of the early days of collectivization and the launching of the First Five-Year Plan, when Bolshevism, after the lull of the New Economic Policy, resumed its internal offensive. But now the emphasis was far more on persuasion and far less on strong-arm methods.

The maximum use was made of the motion picture as a propaganda medium. Traveling movies made the rounds of the villages and towns where no regular movie theater existed. Pictures were selected for their propaganda value, with an emphasis on the realistic portrayal of German atrocities—films like *Rainbow,* based on a novel by Wanda Wasilewska.

Along with the campaign of mental rehabilitation, strenuous steps were taken to restore economic life. People throughout those regions of the Soviet Union which had been spared the blight of invasion were urged to share their possessions with those less fortunate. The response was tremendous. Millions of parcels of clothing, toys, cooking utensils, and household sundries were sent for distribution in the devastated areas.

In a similar spirit, collective farms shipped cattle, horses, sheep, and other livestock to collective farms in the liberated regions. Tractors, harvester combines, and other farming machinery have also been distributed. Aside from greatly speeding the reconstruction process, this sharing has strengthened the feeling of national solidarity and cemented the loyalty of people in the formerly occupied regions.

While engrossed in other reconstruction problems, the Russians did little with the legacy of private trade left them by the Germans. Not that they did not regard its elimination and a return to a socialist system of distribution as essential. But they were anxious to avoid the use of repressive measures. When the war ended, they predicted, the flow of consumer goods to State stores at reasonable prices would automatically eliminate private channels of distribution.

DIALOGUE ON A TRAIN

☆ ☆ ☆ ☆ ☆ ☆ ☆ ☆ ☆ ☆ ☆ ☆ ☆ ☆ ☆

THE flight from Moscow to Kharkov had taken us about three hours. We made the return journey by train in just under forty-eight hours. Though the distance by rail was not more than six hundred miles, there was only the temporary single-track line, laid down in haste by the military engineers close in the wake of the retreating Germans. The bumpy uneven roadbed held us down to something less than twenty miles an hour, and often we were shunted onto sidings to make way for south-bound trains.

But the slow journey had its compensations. We had been given space in a car reserved by the Union of Soviet Writers for the benefit of its top-flight members who had been sent down to cover the trial. Our traveling companions included such literary celebrities as the noted journalist and pamphleteer, Ilya Ehrenburg; the distinguished historical novelist, Alexei Tolstoi; and the young poet and playwright, Constantine Simonov, leader of the young generation of Soviet romanticists who first achieved recognition in wartime.

The conversation was completely dominated by Ehrenburg and Tolstoi, both of them born raconteurs and both of them used to doing most of the talking in any gathering. Both were in cracking form, each trying to out-epigram the other. The conversation, however, was mostly of a serious nature, revolving around impressions of the trial and of Kharkov. It seemed that the trial had originally been scheduled earlier, and the Russian writers, having gone down to Kharkov in time for the slated opening, had had fully ten days in which to cool their heels and wander about the dreary, desolate city. Being of an inquisitive turn of mind and forever in search of human interest for their books and articles, they had improved their time by talking to as many of the local inhabitants as possible.

Even for such Soviet celebrities, whose position entitled them to the best of everything available, living accommodations were none too comfortable. They were put up, as we were, in the city's sole surviving hotel, an institution which in peacetime had been run by Intourist for the benefit of those clients who had booked third-category tours. There was no heat and the plumbing was out of order. But Alexei Tolstoi had a faculty, doubtless inherited from generations of titled ancestors, for making himself comfortable wherever he happened to be. He had, so Ehrenburg declared, cornered the only three electric heaters in the whole of Kharkov. And he held court in his hotel room, snugly fitted into a tattered upholstered armchair that had once accommodated the equally capacious fanny of some German senior officer—the hotel had been used as a billet during the occupation—toasting in the concentrated warmth of his three electric heaters and with a bottle of the best Armenian cognac on a stand within easy reach. The others might wander about the town in search of information. Tolstoi let the information come to him. And such was his popularity that more people flocked to see him than he could ever have coped with had he remained in Kharkov ten months.

Tolstoi and Ehrenburg were a study in contrasts. Like his senior contemporary, Ilya Grigorievich Ehrenburg had come to the Revolution *a posteriori*. Like Tolstoi, he had started his literary career under the old regime. Long years of residence in western Europe and absorption of its culture had profoundly influenced the thinking and writing of both men. From the Russian standpoint they were both *zapadniki*—"westerners." But with that the similarity ended. Whereas Tolstoi was Russian to the marrow, Ehrenburg, for all his cosmopolitanism, was the eternal questing Jewish intellectual, a citizen of the world and a stranger in any one country. Thus despite his magnificently powerful command of the Russian language, whenever he visited a collective farm the local peasants invariably mistook him for a foreigner.

If there was one place on earth where Ehrenburg felt more completely at home than anywhere else, it was Paris. Yet no one, no matter how ignorant, could ever have taken him for a Frenchman. His French, while fluent, had never lost a thickness of flavor, even though before the war he had lived in Paris almost continuously for years, coming to Moscow only for occasional brief trips.

Ehrenburg had been in Paris in the fateful days of June, 1940. He had watched the brown and gray flood submerge the city of light and liberty and had loathed every minute of it with all his being. But those were the days of the Great Poker Game when Russia and Germany pretended to be friends, and so Ehrenburg could not vent his feelings publicly. His spirit writhing with pent-up bitterness and rage, he returned to Moscow via Berlin. Going into almost complete seclusion, he committed his thoughts to paper. The resulting manuscript was his novel, *The Fall of Paris,* not published until after the Nazi attack on the Soviet Union, when it won the Stalin Literary Award.

But even before the Hitler invasion, as relations with the Reich cooled off, the Soviet attitude toward embattled Britain slowly changed for the better. Ehrenburg was permitted to publish small pieces praising the courage and fortitude of London under the blitz. Not that Ehrenburg had ever been pro-Anglo-Saxon. But he was *ipso facto* in favor of anyone who was against the Germans.

Ehrenburg usually tended to look at both Britain and America through the somewhat jaundiced eyes of the inveterate Francophile. Though he understood and read English easily, he rather prided himself on not speaking it.

"I couldn't speak English if my life depended on it," he once told me. "And at one time it almost did. That was back in the first World War. I was a correspondent for a big Petrograd daily, accredited to the British Army on the Somme Front. We had plenty of freedom, I must say, to go about wherever we wanted and see anything we wanted, though the censorship was a bit strict on what we wrote. It was a tough sector, with heavy fighting at close quarters, and several Germans had been caught trying to worm their way into the British positions. So the Tommies were on the constant lookout for spies, and any stranger who didn't know English and who happened to be challenged by a sentry was liable to have a bad time of it—especially if the sentry happened to be a bit triggery, as some of them were. One French colleague had a most unfortunate experience, his last, in fact. You see, to the ordinary Tommy anyone who could not speak English or who did so very brokenly was necessarily a German. The fact that as a war correspondent accredited to the British Forces I wore a British uniform would have made my position worse instead of better. For there had been plenty of Germans caught masquerading in British uniforms, and my inability to speak English in a British uniform would have seemed doubly queer. Luckily I was never challenged."

Ehrenburg shared the average Frenchman's feeling that somewhere along the line, around about Dunkirk, the British had sold France down the river. And as for the Americans, he violently and aggressively championed General Charles de Gaulle against the State Department, President Roosevelt, and others—all of whom he accused of harboring sinister designs against the territorial and political integrity of France and her colonies.

In the days before the Moscow and Teheran Conferences, Ehrenburg had led the chorus of Soviet criticism of the Allies for delaying the opening of the Second Front. And even after the Conferences, when most of the heat on this subject had been turned off, he continued to drop innuendoes which, as winter passed into spring with nothing new from the West, grew more and more virulent. At the reception tendered by Foreign Commissar Molotov to the diplomatic colony and foreign press on February 23, 1944, Ehrenburg remarked that the promise of the opening of a Second Front had aroused in the Russians first hope, then hatred, and finally laughter.

But that is getting ahead of the story. At the time of our trip from Kharkov, Ehrenburg was still willing to admit for the sake of argument that the Allies would presently land in France. He was deeply gloomy about what they would find when they got there.

"It was bad," he remarked, "very bad, in Kharkov. Worse than I had any concept of. It will take years and years of patient education to rehabilitate those people, to overcome the mental degradation caused by Nazism. If Kharkov is like that after only two years of Nazi occupation, what will Paris be like after twice as long?

Just think, today's young people of eighteen were only fourteen when the Germans arrived. The most formative years of their adolescence have been spent under the corrupting, degenerate influence of the Nazis. They'll have practically forgotten everything else. I tell you, Europe has sunk into a new Dark Ages and it'll take generations to climb out."

Ehrenburg had been visibly shaken by some of the things he had heard and seen in Kharkov. What distressed him most was the evidence he had unearthed that the Germans had succeeded in involving some of the Ukrainians in their anti-Jewish campaign. There were also some ugly rumors about the doings of Vlasov's Cossacks. (Vlasov was the renegade Red Army general who deserted to the Germans, opening a whole sector of the front by his treason.) In some places the Germans had also brought in White émigrés to work as translators and investigators for the Gestapo.

While in Kharkov, Ehrenburg had been particularly interested in gathering data on the atrocities committed against the Jews. He would sit for hours recounting the details of the most ghastly crimes—crimes he had duly documented and authenticated. There was a story told by a woman who had watched a crowd of Jews being goaded along the street toward the mass grave pits outside the town. A Jewish woman came abreast of her carrying a lovely, curly-headed child of two. Thrusting the child toward her, the Jewish woman pleaded with her to take it and save its life. But at that moment one of the Nazi guards came up. "Keep moving, you Yiddish sow!" he yelled, striking a heavy blow with his rubber truncheon that left the child's face a welt of bleeding flesh. Mother and child moved on, shrieking.

There was the story of a Ukrainian with a Jewish wife. She had vanished during one of the early pogroms, leaving him with a baby to care for. One day, three months later, with the child in his arms he opened the door in answer to a knock. He was confronted by three SS men. Producing a typewritten list, one of them asked him sharply if he was so-and-so and if that was his child named so-and-so, aged five months. The man nodded a bewildered affirmative, whereupon without further ado one of the SS men grabbed the baby from his arms, bashed its brains in against the housewall, handed him back the limp, bleeding little body, and informed the man that they were members of a commission enforcing race purity.

Ehrenburg's hatred for the Germans was now a double-strength combination of the implacable Gallic hatred for the Boche, which he had absorbed in France, and the bitterness of the Russian Jew whose kinsmen had been murdered by the Nazis. For the first time the war had wakened in Ehrenburg a strong feeling of race-consciousness. And nothing could alter his conviction that Nazi cruelty was an atavism of a people who had always been barbarians.

"I once knew a good German," Ehrenburg remarked between puffs of his pipe, "but I lost track of him many years ago. I don't even know if he's still alive—I seriously doubt it."

"If only you realized," he added, "how sick and tired I am of Germans, Germans, Germans! When in the name of heaven will we have time to think and talk of something besides Germans? After all the suffering they've caused, after all the towns they've destroyed, no punishment ever devised would be severe enough. The trouble is that our Russians are too kind-hearted. Even if you tried, you couldn't order our Russian soldiers to do any of the things to German civilians that the German soldiers have done to ours. It's a pity in a way."

Only the permanent removal of the Germans as a political factor in Europe, he declared, could guarantee the future peace. The distinction sometimes drawn between the German people and the Nazi Party he ridiculed as a sentimental fiction. The German people and the Nazi Party were one and the same thing.

I objected for the sake of argument: "But suppose the Germans overthrew Hitler of their own free will and welcomed the advancing Red Army by getting out the old red flags and singing the *Internationale?*"

"Those," said Ehrenburg, "would be the first people we should shoot."

Ehrenburg had interviewed lots of German prisoners on different fronts—so many, he declared, that he was utterly fed up with them and never wanted to see another one.

"If there is anything I despise more than the haughty, unrepentant Fritz," he declared, "it's the sniveling, groveling kind who, when he's captured, bleats: '*Hitler kaput,*' and goes on to assure you that he's an anti-Nazi from way back, a Communist, in fact. And then when you look into the magazine of his rifle you find that he's fired off his last cartridge.

"And when you question him as to what induced him to fight for *der Führer,* if he was such an anti-Nazi, all the meanness of his nasty, greedy German soul comes out into the open. You find that he, like thousands of other Fritzes, had watered at the mouth at the prospect of getting a piece of our rich, juicy Ukrainian soil— the swine!"

"I can see," I suggested, "that if the Allies want to be really severe with the Germans, they ought to appoint Ilya Grigorich chief commissar for the Reich after the war."

"Bah!" snorted Tolstoi, "our friend Ehrenburg, he talks tough and writes tough. But it's all on the surface. Underneath he's as soft-hearted and sentimental as a schoolgirl. Why, he couldn't harm a fly! He can't bear to see anyone suffer, I don't care who it is. The reason he's so worked up about the Germans is because of the cruel things they've done. But the first time he saw a German woman or child cry, he'd feel sorry for them."

Tolstoi had mumbled all this in a deep, lazy voice, with a mischievous glint just visible in his half-closed eyes. Ehrenburg was about to rise to the bait like a trout, but suddenly he checked himself with a grin.

"So that's what you think, Count? Well, it's beside the point anyway. There's about as much chance of my being appointed to rule the Reich as there is of your becoming Tsar."

"And why not?" said Tolstoi, with mock seriousness. "I guess my family had more of a claim to the throne than those upstart Romanovs."

Alexei Tolstoi, heir to one of the oldest Russian titles, was one of the very few scions of the nobility that had made his peace with the Soviet regime, which had rewarded his literary genius with honors and riches. His eminence as an author had earned him a unique position in the present scheme of things as a sort of link between the old and the new. As Tolstoi, he was above criticism, and thus was himself free to criticize and to play the non-conformist, often going to lengths that horrified his more discreet colleagues. But his unquestioned patriotism, honesty, and sincerity shielded him from all attack, though it was often said in jest that the Count didn't even know there had been a Revolution.

This was, of course, an overstatement. Though his friends still called him "Count," he had long ago dropped the title as a concession to the times. But he had not permitted the Revolution to interfere with his personal habits and mode of life beyond an unavoidable minimum. His country-place outside Moscow, modestly called a *dacha*—summer cottage, was more like a chateau. He had, in addition, an estate near Leningrad which he generously lent to his writer colleagues when he was not using it himself. His income from royalties on his books and plays and his special food and clothing allowances exempted him utterly from any material pinch even in these trying days. He was generous to a fault with his needier friends.

One of the most colorful anachronisms of the Tolstoi household was an old retainer who had been born into the service of the Tolstoi family, his parents having been serfs of theirs. If Tolstoi himself kept the Revolution in its place, this old servant ignored it completely. He still addressed his employer as "Your Grace," and one story current around Moscow told how a friend had phoned Tolstoi and had been told by this retainer that "His Grace the Count" was at the meeting of the Party Central Committee.

There was one point on which Tolstoi remained utterly and openly at odds with the new regime. And that was the practice of renaming old historical towns and places in honor of some latter-day celebrity. Thus once I told Tolstoi of having made a trip to the town of Kalinin (named after the present Chairman of the Presidium of the Supreme Soviet of the USSR, Mikhail Kalinin). Tolstoi pretended not to understand me.

"To where?" he inquired.

"To Kalinin," I repeated. "Don't tell me you don't know that important city on the road to Leningrad, Alexei Nikolaievich. Tver, it was called in Tsarist times."

"If you meant Tver, why didn't you say so?" he said.

"But it's Kalinin now," I insisted.

"Not to me it isn't," he countered. "I don't recognize those new names. The sooner we forget 'em and go back to the old historic names, the better."

It should be noted that Tolstoi did not quarrel with the name of Leningrad for old St. Petersburg. After all, Lenin was Lenin, and his name had somehow fitted the city from the outset, so that today to every Russian, Alexei Tolstoi included, Leningrad is never known by any other name.

Scores of other new labels imposed in that eagerness to obliterate the past—so typical of the early days of the Revolution—had never been accepted in popular usage, and with time they tended to be dropped completely. And so in his campaign for restoration of the old names Tolstoi was fighting a winning battle. Soviet Government policy took cognizance of this popular trend. And in many instances, without any official restoration of the old name being announced, the press and radio would gradually drop the new name in favor of the old. This was especially noticeable in war communiqués announcing the liberation of certain towns. Thus the historic town of Gatchina, some twenty-five miles from Leningrad, where the Tsar had his favorite palace, had been rechristened Krassnogvardeisk in honor of the Red Guard. But from the moment of its reoccupation in January, 1944, it was officially referred to as Gachina, to the immense delight of Alexei Tolstoi.

Tolstoi shared none of Ehrenburg's professed antipathy to the Anglo-Saxons nor his caustic views on the subject of the Second Front. His whole personality, in fact, seemed to radiate conviviality and benevolence toward his fellow-man—and regard for his own blood pressure.

"Of course our Allies will land in France at the proper time," he said. "To doubt that is to doubt the intelligence and integrity of the three chiefs who met at Teheran."

"At the proper time," echoed Ehrenburg sarcastically. "When our Red Armies have been bled white—a color more to the liking of some of our Allies; when the Germans have had time to complete the extermination of the Jews and to destroy France beyond hope of its recovery as a first-class power for years to come. Then perhaps the Allies will invade!"

"At least I hope the Germans haven't killed off all the French cooks and thus destroyed culinary art at its fountainhead," replied Tolstoi, deftly veering the conversation from the ominous course it had taken. "That would be the unpardonable crime! Or destroyed the French vineyards and killed the wine growers. Thank Heaven the Germans never got to our Southern Caucasus, not only on account of the oil, but for the sake of our Georgian and Armenian wines."

"Mouthwash!" Ehrenburg exploded with a wry face. "No bouquet, no taste, no body. The only wines worthy to be called wines are French wines. To apply the term to anything else is blasphemy!"

"Didn't our winegrowers," Tolstoi insisted, "import the best grapevine shoots from France together with French winegrowers?"

"But they couldn't import the French sunshine, the French soil, the French rainfall, the springs in the French hillsides, the waters of the Loire or the Rhone! You may laugh, but I tell you without those ingredients, the vine shoots were valueless. Wine is more than fermented grapejuice. It is a symphonic poem of nature in all its finer nuances, delicately blended. And only in the French countryside are these elements present in the proper proportions."

It was Tolstoi's turn to be indignant.

"And what's wrong with our Caucasian, or for that matter Crimean, sunshine, soil, or springs? Are they inferior to the French? Didn't the elements of nature in the Caucasus inspire the incomparable poetry of Lermontov? I guess if they could do that, they could equal your symphonic wines."

"All right," said Ehrenburg, "if you're so positive about it, just name one Caucasian wine you consider up to French standards."

"What a question!" Tolstoi snorted disgustedly. " 'Name one wine.' What would you like, Ilya Grigorich, a red wine or a white wine, a dry wine or a sweet wine, a strong wine or a light wine, a wine to go with soup, fish, fowl, meat; and once you have settled that point, with what kind of soup—Ukrainian borshch, cold borshch, hot borshch, fresh cabbage *shchi,* sour cabbage *shchi, okroshka, kvass* soup, pea soup, carrot soup, onion soup, fish soup; or with what kind of fish—lake trout, mackerel, bass, pickerel, sole, sturgeon, whitefish; and how will your fish be cooked—boiled, fried, baked in the oven; or with what kind of fowl—juicy tender grouse roasted on a spit over a slow fire. In the stuffing I would suggest—"

"Stop it, stop it," cried Ehrenburg, laughing. "I give up. You're taking unfair advantage of an empty stomach and of the fact that we haven't had a decent meal in two weeks. That's really unfair—hitting below the belt."

At this point, the *praw-vawdnéetsah*—lady porter—made a perfectly timed entrance with a steaming samovar, followed immediately by a teapot and a tray of glasses. Ehrenburg poured, Tolstoi carved up a loaf of bread and a length of sausage into chunks of equal size, and the company fell to. Jean Champenois, correspondent of the Free French Agency, who had been dozing throughout on the upper shelf, woke up just in time to be handed his share.

Outside the grimy double window of the car, the shattered countryside of Southern Russia crawled slowly by. A thin mantle of fresh-fallen snow failed to soften or conceal the tortured miles of desolation and destruction. Twisted rails, burned freight and passenger cars, lined the track. Even the trees planted as a windbreak along the right of way had been cut down or mutilated by shellfire, testifying to the terrific battle which had taken place along here in July, 1943, when the Germans launched their unsuccessful Kursk offensive.

Constantine Simonov had covered the Kursk offensive for the Red Army newspaper *Krassnaya Zvezda—Red Star*. He had been over every inch of this ground and gave me a running explanation of the battle. At one place, a near-by field was littered with scores of derelict German Tiger and Panther tanks. They were all headed eastward, their long-nosed heavy guns tilted at crazy elevations.

"Those tanks over there," said Simonov, "mark the farthest point of the Nazi advance. A *Panzer* column had driven a wedge some twenty kilometers into our lines. We let them come this far, and then our anti-tank guns let them have it from three sides."

Simonov had also covered the long battle for Stalingrad. He was, he said, at present finishing a novel about it—his first novel. His career had been meteoric. He had made his debut as a war correspondent by covering the undeclared Soviet-Japanese war at Halkingol on the Outer Mongolian border. The Japs had sent an army to invade the Mongolian People's Republic, bound to the Soviet Union by a close military and political alliance, but they had been knocked back on their ear with casualties over the hundred thousand mark. That lesson had probably kept the Mikado's militarists from attacking the Russians in the Far East in December, 1941, when they jumped the United States at Pearl Harbor.

Later Simonov had done a spell on the Finnish front during the Soviet-Finnish winter war. But it was as a poet rather than as a journalist that he first achieved fame. In the tragic middle months of 1942, when Russia's military fortunes and those of her Western Allies were at their lowest ebb, Simonov, still comparatively unknown, published a little poem entitled "Wait for Me." It was addressed to Simonov's wife, Valentina Vassilyevna Serova, but its simple touching lines struck a responsive chord in the heart of the Russian soldier, apparently voicing the message of millions of men at the fighting fronts to their wives and sweethearts back home.

Since the Revolution, Soviet poets had scorned lyricism and the love motif as bourgeois sentimentality, whereas their task was to sing about the Revolution. Had not Vladimir Mayakovsky, posthumously acclaimed by Stalin as "the most talented poet of the Soviet era," boasted in this connection:

> I subdued myself, stepping on
> The throat of my own song. . . .

Not that Mayakovsky had himself been immune from affairs of the heart. On the contrary, in 1940 he had taken his own life, leaving behind him his only scrap of lyric poetry, the lines:

> The loveboat was wrecked
> On the shoals of life. . . .

Before and after his tragic death, Mayakovsky and his poetry were storm centers of controversy. His opponents argued that his language was difficult, his meaning obscure, his sound effects and meters intricate beyond the possibilities of ordinary recitation. Then had come Stalin's public expression of opinion and all dispute ceased. Streets and squares were named after Mayakovsky. A Mayakovsky Museum was established where the poet's manuscripts, scratch-pads, and personal effects were placed on permanent exhibit.

But despite such canonization, Mayakovsky's poetry remained too complex for mass appeal. Also people were surfeited with political propaganda and eager for a different note. Yet it was not until the war brought a widespread revival of many older values that poets and writers ventured back to romantic forms. "Wait for Me" took the country by storm, and over night Simonov was raised to the topmost pinnacle of fame and popularity.

Recognition or acclamation, when it does come in the Soviet Union, is so complete as almost to overwhelm the individual, for it has all the force of an organized, centralized, and all-inclusive State behind it. Few critics would venture to disagree with such official approval; and if they did, they would be drowned out in the general chorus.

Only the greatest human natures are proof against the flattery that breeds conceit and self-complacency. The young are especially susceptible. The unfettered exchange of ideas and the searchlight ray of criticism focused on their defects and shortcomings are essential to the progress of young authors, however talented. Otherwise their growing pains become chronic ailments and their literary development is paralyzed.

As part of its policy of encouraging the arts, the Soviet Government lavished money and privileges on all successful writers. At the age of twenty-seven Simonov had a Chrysler car and a luxurious apartment, and was otherwise almost as materially blessed as Alexei Tolstoi.

He had also acquired something that the older man notably lacked—an air of subdued arrogance and easy superiority that told the world he was pretty darn good and he knew it. But sometimes in the heat of narrative, he would become completely absorbed and forget for the time being that he was Simonov. At such times an engaging expression of earnestness and boyish enthusiasm would come into his handsome face. And one realized that here was a man capable of great achievement if given the chance.

CHRISTMAS IN MOSCOW

☆ ☆ ☆ ☆ ☆ ☆ ☆ ☆ ☆ ☆ ☆ ☆ ☆

BACK IN Moscow the Christmas holiday season was on. Not for the Russians, who in matters of such observances still clung to the old Orthodox calendar. But for the foreign colony, whose social life revolved in circles around the embassies and legations, it was the excuse for a continuous whirl of parties, with too much to eat and too much to drink.

Not the least lavish of these were staged at Spasso House, once the palatial mansion of a Moscow merchant prince and now, its grandeur only slightly faded, the residence of the American Ambassador. The newly arrived incumbent, Averell Harriman, was making his Moscow debut by entertaining batches of guests—graded according to importance—at elaborate buffet suppers followed by professional entertainers who were secured through the good offices of the Protocol Department of the Foreign Commissariat.

Harriman was a gracious and amiable host; he never ran out of *savoire faire*. When the occasion required, he could handle an intoxicated and pugnacious fur buyer with the gentle firmness and consummate tact of a bouncer at the Stork Club. During some of the Christmas parties he found plenty of play for his talents as planeloads of thirsty airforce pilots kept coming in out of the blue. After the other guests had made their separate exits, some of the Americans, usually including the correspondents, would adjourn to the cozy atmosphere of a small back room for a session of Gypsy accordion and balalaika music with some of the entertainers. The Ambassador himself invariably remained on deck till the final encore.

A lovely complement to the Ambassador's hospitality was his daughter Kathy, who, as the only American girl for thousands and thousands of miles, looked pretty good to the homesick members of the all-male American colony. Father and daughter were indeed an unbeatable social combination. The ambassador's youthful appearance, which totally belied his fifty years, made the two of them seem more like brother and sister than father and daughter.

Kathy's popularity among the Russians was instantaneous. To them she embodied the typical American girl—intelligent, attractive, a bit too skinny for Russian taste (but that was understandable), tastefully dressed, and a *sportsmenka* who while in Moscow won several prizes in skiing contests.

Kathy was one of the reasons why under the Harriman regime more Russians showed up at Spasso House than ever before. The Harrimans proceeded to cultivate socially as many Russians as they possibly could. They set out powerful bait in the form of lavish buffet suppers and showings of the most recently received American films—Russians have a tremendous curiosity over Hollywood productions, which nowadays seldom reach the screens of Russian movie houses.

Hitherto, Embassy contacts with the Russians had been pretty much confined to the same small group of Soviet celebrities who were invited to official functions. But now people who had never before spoken to foreigners flocked to Spasso House by the dozens. It was still a select group. The entrance to Spasso House was guarded night and day by police and plain-clothes men who peered intently into the face of every visitor. And no Soviet citizen would ordinarily run this gauntlet without some special authorization. Obviously the influx meant that the old quarantine had been relaxed to a degree.

The cream of the Soviet motion picture, theatrical, and literary worlds came to the Harrimans' parties. There was also a liberal sprinkling of uniforms, generals and admirals predominating. A frequent guest was General Ignatyev, a majestic oldster resplendent in gold epaulettes and red-striped breeches. As Colonel Ignatyev of the Imperial Russian Army, he had been military attaché to the Russian Embassy in Paris during the first World War, and at the time of the Revolution had been instrumental in saving large funds and important files for the new Soviet Government. As a reward for his diligence, he had been admitted to the Red Army with retention of his rank. The Ignatyevs had been one of the leading families of the Russian nobility and once at a party General Ignatyev and Alexei Tolstoi had toasted each other as the two Soviet counts. Tolstoi and his charming young wife became friends of the Harriman family, and even Ehrenburg turned up at Spasso parties to sample the refreshments and grouse.

Harriman's crowning social success came some months later on the Fourth of July, when he entertained Molotov at lunch.

Not only did Harriman go out of his way to entertain the Russians socially, but also in his official relations he exercised the maximum tact, taking care never to wound their sensibilities. Strong-arm methods, he once remarked, might gain individual objectives—but only to the detriment of your long-term relations, so that you won in small things only to lose out in big things. On this basis Harriman refused to exert any pressure on behalf of the members of the Embassy staff or the Military Mission with Russian wives whom they wanted to take out of the country with them. Shortly before Harriman's successor, Admiral Standley, left Moscow for the last time, he had gone to bat for the Russian wives of two Embassy clerks, taking up the matter of their exit visas with Molotov. Molotov had answered that the visas would probably be granted eventually, but that it would take some time. Whereupon the old Admiral had countered that applications for visas to America filed by several wives of Soviet Trade Delegation members would also take a long time to arrange. The exit permits for the clerks' wives were forthcoming within the week.

Both the Embassy and the Military Mission made every possible effort to discourage their members from marrying Russians. To this end a ruling was passed that any Army or Navy man who married a Russian would be immediately transferred. But even this drastic measure did not prevent such marriages altogether. Two such cases arose in the first months of Harriman's ambassadorship. For a while the ruling about immediate transfer was held in abeyance, but eventually the husbands had to leave and the wives remained behind. Harriman would not intervene with the Soviet authorities. He had, he said, too many requests of major military and political importance to make to use up his influence on trivial personal cases.

Save for Kathy, the American colony in Moscow was entirely male. A hard and fast State Department policy had prevented all the married men—even those stationed there on a long assignment —from bringing their wives with them. The practice had been instituted in the early days of the war to keep American nationals out of danger areas where they might become a burden and source of embarrassment to the Government. In Moscow, however, this argument had lost all validity. For by the end of 1943 few cities in the world were as secure from the threat of enemy attack as the Soviet capital. But the State Department is loath to alter its precedents. And without enormous influence it was impossible to get one's wife —let alone one's daughter—past Mrs. Ruth Shipley, the adamant boss of the Passport Division. Mr. Harriman took boyish pride in the fact that he had swung the trick with Kathy. He cited his achievement as proof that there were ways of circumventing Mrs. Shipley. But none of the other members of the Embassy staff had been able to duplicate his feat. Some of them had been away from their wives and families for a steady four or five years. Small wonder that many homes had been wrecked by such separations and that some lonely husbands sought and found consolation locally. But there was one American wife back home whose pioneer blood rebelled at the news that her husband was caught in the wiles of a dancing Russian. Determined to fight for her man, she planned her campaign. Love found a way. With neither Harriman's millions nor the President's ear, this plucky gal managed to evade the vigilant Mrs. Shipley and as an employee of a Government wartime agency wangled her way first to North Africa, then to Teheran, and finally to Moscow.

Her unheralded arrival really put her husband on the spot. Unable to bring himself to break with either his wife or his new love, he was kept busy explaining to each in turn that the other woman really meant nothing to him. The eternal triangle was abruptly terminated when the husband was ordered home, accompanied by his triumphant wife—a perfect ending for everybody but the dancer, who was suddenly transferred out of Moscow to a ballet troupe somewhere in Central Asia.

As a genuflection to the rule that Americans of either sex could only be out of the country if they were thereby aiding the war effort, Kathy was assigned to the Office of War Information, without salary, as a volunteer. Day after day she sorted out vast piles of U.S. war photographs for distribution to various Soviet agencies in the hopes that some of them would eventually be published somewhere. It was about a thousand-to-one shot; and if the pictures dealt with the war against Japan, the odds simply weren't even open. However, it was part of Harriman's boring-from-within tactics to include news reels of the fighting in the Pacific in some of his motion picture showings for the Russians.

An important change had come over Harriman since the summer of 1942 when he accompanied Churchill to Moscow. He was still the same thoughtful, unassuming, even-tempered, and likeable person. But a new firmness had come into his still slightly halting speech. In 1942 his reserve had largely been a front for a shyness and an uncertainty that were due partly to inexperience and partly to the ambiguity of his status as President Roosevelt's representative without portfolio, clinging to the seams of Churchill's siren suit. Now, in his new role, his manner was still reserved, but it was no longer a defense, and it often fell away completely to reveal his human nature. He had acquired a new self-assurance and the purposefulness of a man who knows what he wants and is sure of his position. As the months accumulated and the success of his mission was demonstrated in tangible results, even his sharpest critics, who were possibly the members of the press corps, were bound to admit that, regardless of what one thought of Harriman personally, as Ambassador he was a happy choice.

As for Kathy, there was no division of opinion about her among the correspondents. Some of them had known her from the days when, having accompanied Averell to London on his Lend-Lease assignment, she had held her own with the keenest newshounds as a reporter for I.N.S. She often asked the boys from the Hotel Metropole up to Spasso for a cozy evening of supper and bridge, and she was invariably present at every correspondents' party. She submitted goodnaturedly to any amount of kidding, some of it pretty rough, and was unanimously voted a good egg.

Harriman, too, was friendly towards the press. He played no favorites and was not considered much of a news source. He held frequent but not very informative press conferences. When we compared notes afterwards, we usually discovered that he had done most of the questioning and the correspondents most of the answering. Harriman had before him the example of other diplomats who had talked too much or out of turn, and he did not intend to repeat their mistakes. If he erred, it would be on the side of caution.

This fondness for secrecy, while it helped endear Harriman to the Russians, did not make news-gathering any easier in a country where scoops were few and far between. Furthermore, the Soviet censorship worked hand-in-glove with the Embassy whenever the Ambassador wished to prevent something from leaking out. Most of the time this was an unnecessary precaution, for the correspondents seldom violated a confidence or an express wish.

Six weeks after his arrival as Ambassador, Harriman's reticence had become so proverbial that it became the subject of a skit staged by the correspondents at their annual Christmas party. This party, which since the war had become a Moscow tradition, was organized by the Anglo-American Press Association for the purpose of paying off their social obligations and settling some other scores. The Metropole management supplied the room and lavish refreshments for the occasion, at a price which divided up to about seventy dollars per correspondent. Each correspondent invited four guests from among the members of the Anglo-American diplomatic colony, which now included a Canadian Embassy and an Australian Legation (to which a New Zealand Legation was soon to be added).

The correspondents' party was quite the event of the season. Everyone who was invited came, and those who weren't asked called up indignantly to find out why. One end of the spacious upstairs dining room assigned by the Hotel was curtained off as an impromptu stage.

The walls of the room were decorated with humorous posters and facetious wall newspapers, spiced with plenty of malice. As nearly as I can recall, one poster read: "Bring your secrets to the British Embassy Spy Section. We pay highest rates for treaties, texts, stolen documents, or bulk contents of wastepaper baskets. All transactions strictly cash and no questions asked. See Colonel So-and-so. Office hours 10:00 A.M. to 12:00 M. daily, or phone for appointment."

Another announcement: "Coronation of the Tsar. Time: any day now. Reserve your seats through Intourist Service Bureau." There were also quips on the Union Pacific Railway for Harriman's benefit, and one poster declared: "Sun Valley was never like this!"

Down the long center of the room stretched the festive board, groaning with roast turkey, huge bowls of tempting, beady-black caviar, twenty-odd varieties of smoked sausage, and twice as many kinds of smoked fish—not to mention sundry salads decorated with such intricate patterns of sliced boiled egg on mayonnaise that it was vandalism to jab them with a fork. Also vodka, wines, fruit drinks, and mineral waters galore. As there obviously wasn't elbow room enough for all of the hundred-odd guests to be seated, everyone simply helped himself to what caught his eye and navigated about the room chewing, nodding to friends, conversing—all the while juggling a plate and a glass.

When the food had been completely sacked and plundered, the rubble was cleared, the table hauled away, and folding chairs brought in. And as soon as everyone was seated and the tumult had subsided, the correspondents began their routine. The skits had been hastily written and even more hastily rehearsed, and there was plenty of ad-libbing when people forgot their lines. But since the people whom the skits lampooned were present in the audience and the refreshments had put everyone in the proper mood for entertainment, hilarious success was assured.

This time the *pièce de résistance* was a parody on a press conference at Spasso House. The correspondents were interviewing Ambassador Harriman on his opinion of the Moscow weather. With his usual caution, the Ambassador refused to commit himself to any outright opinions. Asked whether he considered Moscow weather too warm or too cold, he answered yes and no. Finally in the tone of one imparting the most momentous information, he agreed to give the day's temperature as recorded by the Embassy's newly installed thermometer and duly cleared by cable with the State Department. The correspondents pulled out their pads and scribbled frantically.

"Hold on a bit," the Ambassador cautioned them. "I want you to remember all this is strictly off the record."

There was a chorus of groans, and one reporter, Bill Lawrence of the New York *Times,* pulled out a revolver, pressed its muzzle to his temple, and shot himself. Lights out. Curtain. Then the master of ceremonies, Bill Downs of CBS, rushed out in front and announced: "Ladies and gentlemen, there has been a terrible mistake!" Voice from the rear: "You tellin' I! They shot the wrong damn guy!"

Harriman, who was present, enjoyed the satire thoroughly and afterwards complimented Dick Lauterbach of *Time* and *Life,* who had played the Ambassador, for his performance. For costume he had worn a jacket of Harriman's, borrowed through Kathy.

Save for a small sprinkling of Russian wives and one or two correspondents' secretaries, no Russians were invited to the party. This was merely because they would not have understood our Anglo-Saxon humor. The program included no jibes at the Soviet.

The Moscow foreign colony ended the holiday season in a whirl of New Year's parties. The Russians also celebrated. For the first time since the war the Government, as a concession to popular feeling and the progress on all the fronts, declared New Year's Day a legal holiday. For once, the one-o'clock curfew was relaxed—which mattered little because most parties continued till morning. The authorities decided to keep celebration within certain bounds. It was all very well for people to feel elated over recent victories. But they must not forget that there was still a war to win. At the last moment an order was issued banning all large social gatherings. Consequently elaborate jamborees on a peacetime scale, which had been scheduled at the House of the Actor, House of the Cinema, Writer's House, and other Moscow clubs, had to be canceled. Russians still had their parties, but on a smaller scale, in private homes. The refreshments, too, necessarily conformed to wartime frugality.

We had a party at our house—a mixed Russian-American gathering. Our guests included two officials of the Press Department, several Russian journalists, some American correspondents, and Kathy Harriman. A good time was had by all despite the language barrier, thanks largely to the joviality of Eddy Gilmore, who, in addition to his Russian child-wife Tamara, brought along his portable phonograph and some new American records.

Most Russians are mad about American popular music, which they rarely have a chance to hear now that they had had to turn in all their radio sets. Moscow has several jazz orchestras that try to reproduce the American technique. The leading one is the band of Leonid Utyosov, a sort of Soviet Rudy Valee. Utyosov enjoys tremendous popularity with Russian audiences, but he has received little encouragement from the Government's all-powerful Committee on Affairs of Art. He once complained that he was the only musician or entertainer of note who had not received some sort of decoration or title—such as Honored Artist of the Republic. Recently, however, he has attained his wish.

Far superior to Utyosov in technique and interpretation was a former Warsaw band which had happened to be in what was then Eastern Poland—in Bialystok or Grodno—at the time the Russians moved in there in September, 1939. Several of its members, including the leader, had been in America. They knew their stuff. Their success with Russian audiences was electric and instantaneous, and they soon eclipsed the local talent. Officially they were billed as a White-Russian orchestra, and once or twice they had been told off by the powers that be for not including enough of their "national" music in their repertoire. Nevertheless they toured the USSR from end to end. In Vladivostok the American Consul, Angus Ward, had hired them to play at the Consulate for the exclusive benefit of Ward and his wife and his American staff of two.

Rationing made entertaining at home a problem in Moscow, just as it does everywhere. Most of the foreign colony got around it by simply inviting people in for tea or cocktails and serving plates of tiny little sandwiches. But my mother-in-law regarded this as an insult to the guests and a reflection on the host. True to the old tradition of Russian hospitality, she insisted that no one leave the house hungry. In wartime Moscow this was a very large order. The guests did ample justice to her three-course, sit-down dinners or her groaning sideboards of buffet suppers. No wonder our parties were a success and people were glad to come again and again! But the pay-off came after the party, when for weeks, until the first of the month, we had to live on practically nothing but bread, cabbage, and potatoes. For our party before New Year's *Mamasha* went out and bought two kilos of lamb on the open market. A great bargain, she told me, at 350 rubles—nearly thirty dollars—a kilo.

Since there was no way of altering *Mamasha's* scale of values or way of doing things, and since Russian friends, whose resources were immeasurably more slender than ours, insisted on trying to repay in kind, we had to give up entertaining, except on the rarest occasions.

TEHERAN AND AFTERMATH

NEWS OF the Stalin-Roosevelt-Churchill meeting at Teheran thrilled the Russian people as no other diplomatic news had ever done before. And, even more than the momentous nature of the decisions reached, it was the symbolic aspect of the meeting that appealed to the Russian imagination.

First, there was the sensational fact that Stalin had actually gone out of the country to attend the meeting. As distinct from Prime Minister Churchill or even President Roosevelt, Stalin is a home-body. Seldom in the past twenty years has he left Moscow. And the only other time in his life that he had ever been out of Russia was long before the Revolution, when he went to Tammerfors in Finland to attend an illegal revolutionary conference.

And now, in time of war, Stalin had actually made a trip out of the country! Even though Teheran was not so far from the Soviet border, to the Russians it was nevertheless "abroad." It was that, rather than the geographic distance, that counted. For, to the average Russian, any place beyond the Soviet border—be it Warsaw, Helsinki, New York, or Rio de Janeiro—is equally remote and inaccessible.

Stalin's trip to Teheran put the Soviet public in mood to believe almost anything, and the reaction to the conference was intensest optimism, encouraged for a time by glowing press editorials on the subject of Allied unity.

Again, as at the time of the Moscow Conference, the Russian commentators stressed the military rather than the political aspects of the Conference. To them the all important point was that agreement had been reached on combined offensive strategy, that plans and timetables for attack on Germany from the West as well as the East had been agreed upon.

One consequence of the Teheran Conference was a tremendous boost to President Roosevelt's popularity among the Russians. It was, they decided, in deference to the American Chief Executive that Stalin had agreed to make the trip. Clearly, they concluded, he would never have done it for the sake of Churchill, but would have suffered the British Prime Minister to come to him in Moscow like Mohammed to the mountain, continuing the already established precedent. Also, when it got noised about that Roosevelt had stayed at the Soviet Embassy while in Teheran, the Russians were deeply touched. They set great store by their tradition of hospitality, and to them this little detail was disarming proof of the President's sincerity and good faith.

The friendship with the Western democracies which Teheran had come to symbolize was generally regarded as the dawn of a new day—the end of all threats of capitalist encirclement. In Russia, as in America, Teheran was a victory for the internationalist over the isolationist who believed that Russia must play a lone hand and who regarded the wartime coalition with the other great powers as a passing contingency.

Contrary to the prevailing impression abroad, the unity of the Soviet State and the Communist Party does not preclude a wide range of opinion on matters of policy inside the Government and Party. And even after Teheran, the isolationist wing in Russia continued to make their voices heard both in Party councils and even in the press. And at the lower levels the new "turn" in the "line" was less noticeable than at the very top.

Thus the prevailing attitude toward foreigners, though gradually changing for the better, was still mainly one of polite but suspicious reserve, verging on quarantine.

The diplomatic colony, which was actually the only foreign colony (various Comintern remnants had long since merged into the landscape), continued to live a caged life of its own. True, a few more Russians did turn up at embassy functions and parties, more at the American than anywhere else, largely because of the tireless efforts of Ambassador Harriman and Kathy. But the old reserve remained.

By comparison with the diplomatic, the correspondents enjoyed remarkable freedom to move and mingle. Yet even they, with the exception of two or three of us who had apartments or houses, lived a cloistered existence in the Metropole Hotel, eating the same food in the same dining room, sharing their translators and couriers. For the correspondents, life was a dull routine of going through a dozen Moscow newspapers each morning—all of which published news items and editorials that differed in phrase, but seldom in content.

None were free to travel out of Moscow save on specially conducted excursions that were arranged whenever there was a story which the Russians wanted played up abroad. The so-called "front trips" were strictly in the nature of post-mortems. The foreign correspondents were never allowed near any battlefield until it had been de-mined and otherwise made presentable. In this connection never shall I forget our trip to the Crimea, following the end of military operations there. The Red Army Chief of Staff, whom we interviewed, berated us for not coming sooner—this after we had been pleading with the Foreign Office for days!

To do them justice, I must say that our hosts on these trips tried to make up for the lack of hot war news in other ways. The accommodations were always the best available. Huge banquets were spread for our delectation in remote places at goodness knows what expenditure of thought and effort. Indeed, on some of our trips our progress was literally from banquet to banquet.

This, however, in no way improved the trips from the standpoint of newsgathering. It underscored the fact that they were conceived, organized, and executed as publicity junkets rather than as serious fact-finding expeditions.

One of the reasons the foreign press was kept well away from the fighting was a genuine concern for their safety. In the Soviet Union responsibility is highly personalized. On these trips the Red Army officer and the Foreign Office functionary assigned to conduct us were directly and personally responsible for the welfare of each one of us. And if anything untoward happened, even as a result of enemy action, it would fare hard with them. One such Red Army officer once told me in good faith that should anything happen to a correspondent, it might cause international complications. The result was that the only guns most foreign pressmen ever heard during their assignments to Russia were the Moscow victory cannon.

But concern for our safety was only half the story. The other half was their long-standing distrust of the capitalist press, based on unfortunate experiences. And against this unavowed objection all pleas and protests of the correspondents were unavailang. Many times the Anglo-American Press Association had written letters and appeals to the head of the press department and over its head to Vyshinsky and Molotov. The letters remained unanswered. Sometimes they brought some temporary result in the form of a press conference. But the basic policy remained unalterably the same.

For the foreign correspondents there was nothing more demoralizing than the deep sense of frustration at sitting in a Moscow hotel room culling from the Soviet press while one of the greatest news stories in history lay just beyond their reach. No wonder if many of them became slightly unbalanced or had nervous breakdowns. But though individual members of the correspondents' corps might go under or get discouraged and leave, the good fight continued in the hope that someday, when the spirit of Teheran percolated down to the level of the Press Department, the line would change. For this reason we were keenly attuned to every nuance in the international political atmosphere.

But in the weeks immediately following Teheran, the political situation, instead of improving, had taken a turn for the worse. The cause was Poland.

Both the Moscow Conference of foreign ministers and the Teheran meeting of the Big Three had left the Polish problem as one of the outstanding differences between the major powers—a chronic source of discord and irritation. In Britain and America the Soviet-Polish dispute was widely publicized by those elements who, with no particular interest in the fate of Poland as such, were ready to champion any cause that could be turned aginst the Soviets. These elements were the unwitting counterparts of those circles in the Soviet Union who also sought to use differences over Poland to divide Russia from the Western Powers, arguing in favor of unilateral action by the Soviet regardless of the Allies.

The factor that brought the Polish issue to the fore in the weeks after Teheran was the spectacular momentum of the Soviet winter offensive that was carrying the Red Army toward Poland ahead of schedule.

The German counter-attacks which in November had forced the Russians to relinquish newly liberated Zhitomir and to retreat almost halfway to Kiev had been bled to a standstill. In the latter part of December the Russians struck blows that sent the Germans reeling back with heavy losses along their recent line of advance. The Russians took Korosten, north of Berdichev, cutting the railway that had served the Germans as their main lateral artery for shifting their forces from one sector of the front to another. Korosten was less than sixty miles from the old Polish-Soviet frontier; and from that moment on, the world waited with eager expectancy for the news that the Red Army had crossed into Poland. We in Moscow scanned the communiqués avidly for the first indication of this new phase of the war. The news agencies in their eagerness for a scoop jumped the gun several times. Reuter's correspondent Harold King had Cossacks galloping across the frontier well in advance of his competitors and, as it proved, of the Red Army. In fact, he got so far out in front that he was in imminent danger of being cut off and had to make a hasty withdrawal. Thereafter, "King's Horses and King's Men" became a byword of the correspondents' corps. On January 13 came word of the capture of Sarny, an ancient fortress town just across the line. That was indisputable proof, although it was impossible to ascertain whether the Russians had crossed the frontier prior to that. The fact was that the Soviet press no longer made any reference whatever to the old boundary. All that was part of a forgotten past so far as they were concerned. And the powers of the Kremlin were doubtless slightly taken aback when they heard that newspapers in Britain and America had carried headlines announcing that the Red Army had entered Poland.

The result was that the censorship immediately clamped down on all mention of the old border in our stories, either directly or indirectly. Henceforth the best we could do was to say that the Red Army was operating in the Western Urkaine.

Prompted undoubtedly by the rush of interest and widespread discussion which this latest Red Army advance had occasioned, the Russians came forward at this time with their public offer to the London Poles to settle the boundary dispute on the basis of the Curzon line, proposed by the Allies in 1920, with certain modifications in Poland's favor, and with the added proviso of territorial compensation in the west at Germany's expense.

The Polish Government in London, instead of promptly accepting the Soviet offer, made public a rather vague general statement. (In the absence of diplomatic relations between Moscow and the Polish Government, public utterances were the medium of exchange.) This the Soviet Government chose to construe as a rejection of the proposal. Whereupon the Russians felt deeply incensed at the offhand and cavalier treatment of what they considered a very magnanimous offer on their part. Their animus was not confined to the Polish Government. They thought they saw behind the Poles and backing them up the hand of Britain. This suspicion was confirmed by the tone of much of the British press and, for that matter, American press comment, sharply critical of Soviet policy and full of misgivings as to its aims. The Russians, stung by these attacks, decided to have some misgivings of their own.

Such was the background of the famous "Cairo rumor," a brief item published on the back page of *Pravda,* January 17, 1944, under a Cairo dateline and purporting to be from *Pravda's* "own correspondent." It stated that according to usually well-informed circles British representatives and Nazi Foreign Minister Ribbentrop had met in some seaport town of the Pyrenees Peninsula to discuss separate peace terms, and that negotiations were already in an advanced stage.

For once, *Pravda* had "scooped" *Izvestia* and all the other papers of that same day. None of them carried the story. But the Cairo rumor was subsequently reprinted by the provincial press throughout the length and breadth of the land. One week later, in the ruined town of Smolensk, I discovered that the local authorities had evidently thought the rumor story of sufficient importance to reprint it in their tiny quarto-sheet newspaper—one of but two items of foreign news. The other was an announcement of General Eisenhower's arrival in England to direct invasion preparations. One can imagine how confused the Smolensk reading public must have been on the international situation that day!

The effect on Russians everywhere was deeply depressing. They had just been reading the panegyrics of Teheran and the complete accord achieved between the Big Three Powers. And the Russian ordinary citizen had rejoiced in the feeling that at last his country was no longer alone in the world, but closely allied with the other two most powerful nations of the earth. That was tremendous balm to any lingering traces of inferiority complex. And now, this! It was a very rude jolt after a delicious dream.

The Cairo rumor penetrated to all sections of the population. People who never saw a newspaper or followed events heard about it. And it lost nothing in the telling—until it reached the point where many believed the British actually had made peace with Germany and left Russia holding the bag. It's curious how rapidly rumors, even false ones, spread in Russia. I remember one day when the word went around that at a certain time in the afternoon Molotov would make a momentous announcement on the radio. Everybody had heard about it, including the functionaries of the Foreign Office Press department, and believed it to be true. When the time came, there was no announcement; and it later developed that Molotov had never had the slightest intention of making an announcement.

The Cairo rumor caused such alarm among the population that the authorities felt it necessary to administer a sedative. When Anthony Eden in London entered a vigorous denial, it was widely published—in fact, some of the provincial papers carried the denial alongside the original *Pravda* story.

There were doubtless other motives besides pique over the Polish issue involved in the publication of the Cairo rumor story. Every word and sentence in *Pravda,* particularly on matters of international relations, is carefully assayed. The editors must have been aware of the international furor they would cause. Also the provincial press would not have reprinted it without some directive from the center. Perhaps the Government decided that enthusiasm over Teheran had gone too far and it was necessary to remind the

inhabitants that, after all, the Western Powers were not completely
to be trusted. In addition, it doubtless expressed some genuine
uneasiness on the part of the Kremlin as to the various reports of
German peace proposals that were going the rounds at the time,
especially in Ankara. When the denials started flocking in, and
when efforts by newsmen in Cairo to find a *Pravda* correspondent
proved fruitless, and inquiries at the Cairo censor office and at the
cable office disclosed that no such message had ever been tele-
graphed from there, the Russians tried to cover the *Pravda* story
by publishing a lengthy TASS dispatch with a London dateline
under the head: "An English Correspondent on German Peace
Proposals." The dispatch consisted chiefly of quotes from an article
in the *Sunday Times* of January 15, written by that paper's Ankara
correspondent. Discussing reports of new German peace proposals,
the author denies that such were made by the German Ambassador
Franz von Papen, but asserts that proposals had been made to the
Turks two months previously for transmission to the Allies.
Turkey, the correspondent says, had refused to be a go-between,
and subsequently similar proposals were made in Stockholm and
Lisbon. They emanated directly from Hitler himself and were intended to split Britain, America, and Russia. Still quoting the
Sunday Times, the TASS dispatch went on to enumerate the proposals, which included the withdrawal of German troops to the
prewar frontiers and the renunciation of colonial claims, but at the
same time left the Germans a limited freedom of action in the East.
The German Navy, including submarines, would be immediately
handed over or scrapped. The present regime in Germany would
continue until these conditions had been carried out, after which
Hitler and the Nazi Party would place themselves at the mercy
of the Army. The article quoted had appeared in the *Sunday Times*
a full day prior to the publication of the Cairo Rumor story. Presumably the text had reached Moscow in time for the *Pravda*
editors to see it before they released their story. In this connection
it is important to note that the *Sunday Times* article, as quoted
directly, mentions Lisbon as one of the places where the German
proposals were transmitted to the British, which fitted in with the

reference in the *Pravda* item to a seaport town of the Pyrenees Peninsula.

Rightly or wrongly, the Russians suspected that something was going on behind their backs in the diplomatic demimonde of Lisbon, where they had no official representatives. From the reaction to the Cairo rumor they hoped for some indication as to whether their suspicions had any basis.

The Russians doubtless realized that the Cairo rumor story would shock public opinion in Britain and America and that the reaction would not be exactly favorable. They balanced this against the effect the story would doubtless have in the occupied countries of Europe, from the Channel to the Black Sea and from the Arctic to the Mediterranean. It would serve notice to all captive people of all these countries that the Soviet Union was on the job defending their cause against all possible defections by the Western democracies—a role which would be remembered.

DEAD MEN TELL A TALE

☆ ☆ ☆ ☆ ☆ ☆ ☆ ☆ ☆ ☆ ☆ ☆ ☆

WHILE the excitement stirred up by the Cairo rumor was still bubbling, the Russians announced that they had dug up—literally—additional evidence in the Katyn massacre. It will be recalled how in April, 1943, Dr. Goebbels had announced to the world the discovery of the remains of several thousand Polish officers in the Katyn Forest, near the city of Smolensk. The Germans announced that these Poles had been shot by the Russians in the spring of 1940. They had bolstered this claim with the findings of a group of "impartial" medical experts from Nazi-occupied countries, who exhumed and examined some of the bodies. The Polish Government in London swallowed this bait to the extent of issuing a statement through its War Minister Kukiel, declaring that fifteen thousand Polish officers had indeed disappeared without a trace and calling for an investigation of the Nazi charges by the International Red Cross.

The Russians, infuriated by what they regarded as Polish collaboration in Nazi propaganda, took the occasion to sever diplomatic relations with the Polish Government. Dr. Gobbels and the Nazis were jubilant. They had scored a bull's-eye and cracked the wall of allied solidarity.

In September the Russians retook Smolensk, and with it the bodies of the Poles in Katyn Forest passed to their jurisdiction. The world had all but forgotten this gruesome and tragic mystery when, in January, 1944, the Russians suddenly announced that the bodies had again been exhumed, this time by what was described as the "Special Commission to Investigate and Ascertain the Circumstances of the Shooting by German Fascist Invaders of the Polish War Prisoners and Officers in Katyn Forest." The lengthy designation spoke for itself.

Suddenly, in the middle of the night (for some reason the Russians prefer night to daytime), I got a phone call from the Foreign Office: would I like to go on a trip to Katyn Forest? I would. Very well, we would be leaving by car the next evening at nine from the Metropole. We should take along food for two days. Yes, we would be driving all night.

Even this cheerless prospect and the fact that the story itself was pretty dead—in more ways than one, for the offensive that was to destroy the Leningrad siege ring had just opened—did not deter a sizable group of correspondents from signing up for the trip. Somebody mentioned it to Kathy Harriman, and when she half-seriously wished that she could go along too, he called up the Foreign Office. Rather taken aback by the request at first, they made a rapid recovery and approved the plan.

That evening, when we were all steeled for the ordeal of the cold ride of some 250 miles through wintry Russia, word suddenly was received that we wouldn't be leaving that night at all, but instead would start out the following afternoon by train, and that we would not need to take food. We immediately guessed that the Foreign Office had decided to lay out something extra for Miss Ambassador's benefit. Next afternoon at five o'clock, on a track in the White Russian station which was once Moscow's gateway to and from western Europe, we found an extremely spruce little train of two sleepers and a dining car. It was promptly christened the "Union Pacific Special" in Kathy's honor. We also learned that we were to be escorted by Mr. Petrov, Assistant Manager of the Press Department, with a diplomatic rank equivalent to that of lieutenant general in the Army.

The dining car was one of those early twentieth-century dreams of richly carved and polished black walnut and shiny brasswork, reflected in a profusion of mirrors. The aisle was thickly carpeted in red plush. The car was immaculately kept and well stocked with food. At mealtimes, Petrov would play the host to Kathy and John Melby, the Embassy Third Secretary, who had come along as a sort of chaperone.

In view of the fact that most of the British correspondents had declined the invitation to go to Katyn—whether or not as a demonstration, I do not know—the Americans had an overwhelming majority. And considering the grim and gruesome object of our journey, it was quite a jolly little party that boarded the "Union Pacific Special." Our spirits were improved by the news flashes we got at various stations of the brilliant progress of the newly launched, all-out offensive to smash the German blockade of Leningrad. But our joy was not unmitigated by sadness at the thought that instead of our being on our way to Leningrad to report history in the making, we were headed in a different direction, toward Smolensk to see the corpses of some Poles which by all counts had been moldering in the grave for at least two years, and which were now being dug up and exhibited for the second time.

Next morning we pulled into what was left of Smolensk. There wasn't much. Of the railway station not a stone remained. But across the river the skeletons of houses straggled up the hill to where the ancient fortress wall of the Smolensk Kremlin still stood. Smolensk had been the first town in Russia proper reached by the Nazis. And here on the upper Dnieper their spearhead bearing on Moscow had been checked for several weeks during that first summer scramble. The Germans had held the main part of town across the river, but the Russians had clung tenaciously to the railroad side, and there had been heavy shelling back and forth across the river. In September the first Russian counter attack from Yelnya had come within ten miles of retaking Smolensk. At that time the Germans had carried out some demolition, but they completed the job in September, 1943, when they were forced to abandon the city. And now of the city's 7900 prewar buildings only 300 still had roofs. These were for the most part little one-story wooden houses on the outskirts. Almost all the city's public edifices and modern apartment blocks had been reduced to rubbish.

But the battered, red-brick Kremlin wall, built around the old town by Ivan the Terrible, still stood. To the old scars of Napoleon's siege guns were added the fresh gouges from Nazi artillery. A row of tarnished bronze tablets inscribed with the names of regiments that had distinguished themselves in the fighting around Smolensk against Napoleon were imbedded in the wall. They had been placed there in 1912 during the centennial celebration of the Napoleonic War. Directly under them now were inscriptions to the memory of heroes of recent battles over the same ground.

But though the ancient wall had outlasted another invasion, nothing remained but a solitary granite slab to mark the former location of an imposing equestrian statue of General Kutuzov, who commanded the Russian armies that drove Napoleon out. According to the local inhabitants, this monument to Napoleon's Nemesis had suggested a too poignant analogy to the impressionable Fuehrer. It was removed at his orders.

Hitler, like Napoleon, made Smolensk his headquarters during his drive on Moscow. According to a local story, this was where Hitler and Mussolini had conferred together on Russian soil. The same source said the Feuhrer had arrived with Mussolini in the latter's personal plane, with the Duce at the stick.

By a flanking maneuver, the Germans had overrun the main portion of Smolensk so swiftly that there had been little time to evacuate civilians. The prewar population of the town had numbered 180,000, but under the Germans it dwindled to about 30,000. Some had fled to the country, but many thousands of others had either been executed or else had perished of starvation or exposure. It was hard to find shelter among the ruins, and the Germans lost no time in clearing whatever buildings were still habitable for their own use.

I spoke to one woman who could not have been old, but suffering and sorrow had cut the lines in her tired face deeper than time ever would. An old gray shawl, enveloping her entire figure save the old felt boots, seemed to smother all individuality in the uniform of sorrow.

"Americans," she said absently, as though speaking to herself. "How do you like our city? Smolensk, you know, is—or was—the second oldest town in Russia. We had museums. It's too bad you and your party didn't come three years ago. There would have been more to see and do. Not a bad place. Not a center, mind you, not Moscow or Leningrad. But we have, or rather had, our own theater, ballet. And I could have invited you all to my home for a glass of tea, over there."

She pointed to the roofless shell of what had evidently once been an imposing modern apartment house. The Germans had moved her and her family out into the street, taking over her apartment complete with furniture and household goods. Then when the Germans retreated, they had set fire to the house and so she had been unable to recover any of her possessions, though she had poked around in the rubble hoping she might at least turn up an iron skillet.

She and her two sons, aged twelve and fourteen, were at present sharing a moldy one-room cellar with another family. There was no way to keep the rain water from running in.

Thousands of other inhabitants were in a similar or worse predicament, living in the cellars of ruined houses, in dugouts, and in caves. The local paper—the same one that reprinted the Cairo rumor—complained of the total absence of such housekeeping necessities as cups, plates, cooking utensils of all descriptions, buckets, pans—in fact, of practically all the elementary things that people ordinarily take for granted but cannot do without.

Under the German occupation supreme authority in Smolensk had been vested in the German military commandant of the city, General von Schwetz. But much of the administrative detail was performed by a Russian traitor named Menshagin, a lawyer by profession, whom von Schwetz appointed Burgomeister.

A cursory examination of the pages of Menshagin's notebook (it had fallen out of his pocket when he fled Smolensk with the Germans before the Russians retook the town) discloses that he was chiefly concerned with the prosecution of petty thefts of foodstuffs and firewood by the inhabitants from stock earmarked for the *Wehrmacht* and with the operations of the so-called Russian Police Corps, composed of traitors like himself, whose chief function was to spy upon and inform upon the civil population, to keep the Germans advised of the mood of the civilians, and to make denunciations to the Gestapo. It was also evident from the entries that the Germans treated this tool of theirs with thinly veiled contempt, holding him strictly accountable for the execution of their directions and keeping close check on his every move lest he double-cross them. At last his twisted, miserable soul had come to fear the Gestapo almost as much as the retribution of his own people whom he had betrayed—almost, but not quite; for when the time came, he had fled with his German masters rather than stay to face the firing squad or hangman's noose.

But though Menshagin had left, the Deputy Burgomeister had elected to stay behind. In peacetime, Professor Boris Basilyevsky had been director of the local astronomical observatory. A frightened wisp of a little old man, limp and faded as an old rag doll, he was one of the material witnesses in the current investigation of the Katyn massacre. He had, he pleaded, been a victim of circumstance. Originally the Germans had tried to make him assume the post of Burgomeister. When he refused, they had forced him on pain of death to serve as Deputy Burgomeister. In this official capacity, he told us, he had tried to do what he could to lighten the sufferings of the population.

In a tired broken voice, he testified how once he had asked Menshagin to secure the release of a certain schoolteacher from a prison camp and to request some improvement of the inhuman German treatment of Soviet war prisoners. Several days later Menshagin had informed him that his requests had been rejected by General von Schwetz, who had further announced that instructions had come through from Berlin to make camp conditions harsher yet.

To Basilyevsky's incredulous query as to how conditions could possibly be made harsher, Menshagin answered that whereas Russian prisoners merely perished from "natural causes"—from hunger and cold—orders had come for the liquidation of the Polish war prisoners "in the literal sense of the word." On another occasion Basilyevsky said he had encountered Sonderführer Hirschfeldt, chief of the local Gestapo branch, in Menshagin's office and had heard him declare that the Poles deserved extermination as an inferior race.

We heard Basilyevsky testify in front of the Soviet Commission for the Investigation of German Atrocities, which for some time now had been operating in the Smolensk area, gathering evidence of various war crimes, including the massacre of the Poles in the Katyn Forest. The Committee members were seated at a long table at one end of a room in one of the few surviving buildings.

Seated in the middle was the distinguished-looking chairman, Alexander Potyomkin, scion of a famous Russian family. Potyomkin, who at present holds the post of Commissar for Public Education for the R.S.F.S.R. (Russia proper), has had a brilliant diplomatic career. He served as ambassador first to Italy and then to France. In 1938 he was called home from Paris to become First Vice-Commissar for Foreign Affairs under Litvinov. As I watched the agile professor-like bobbing of his neat white goatee and pince-nez, I recalled an old Moscow story to the effect that during his Rome assignment he had played chess with the Duce regularly once a week and had always beaten him.

Flanking Potyomkin were my old friend Alexei Tolstoi, who during part of the proceedings peeled and munched a tangerine, and Orthodox Metropolitan Nikolai of Kiev and Galicia, a clear-eyed, delicate-skinned old man with a fragile almost saintlike beauty of feature and expression. His face was framed by long, well-groomed strands of thin, silvery hair and beard. When he spoke, which he did several times in the course of the interrogation, he had a voice that matched his appearance. Looking and listening to this gentle old man, one wondered how he had fared through all those hard years. Today Nikolai has succeeded the late Sergius as Metropolitan of Moscow and Patriarch of all the Russians.

The Commission read us their findings, based on the testimony of members of the local population, on how the Germans had converted Katyn Forest, once a favorite picnic ground for excursions from the city, into a shambles for the systematic execution of Polish war prisoners. These prisoners, who included both officers and privates, were described as the inmates of Soviet war prisoner camps for Poles, three of which were located within a thirty-mile radius of Smolensk. Owing to the suddenness of the German break-through, there had been no time to evacuate them and they had fallen into German hands.

It was all very secret.

The German unit assigned to the task of exterminating the Poles had been given the misleading designation of "537th Construction Battalion." It had established its headquarters in a spacious rest house previously used by the Soviet NKVD (Internal Security) on the high banks of the Dnieper only about a hundred yards from the scene of the slaughter. The surrounding woods had been fenced off with barbed wire, and sentries were posted to keep out casual visitors.

Two girls from a near-by village were employed by the Germans in the rest house as domestics. One of them, Anna Alexeyeva, testified in our presence that she had constantly heard trucks drive into the woods from the neighboring highway, and that soon after she invariably heard shots. Her employers, she said, took many precautions to prevent her from finding out what was happening. But once, as she was walking homeward along the main highway, she saw truckloads of Polish prisoners coming from the direction of Vitebsk and turning into the woods. Shortly after, she heard the familiar shots.

Threading its way through the endless flow of military traffic, a motor cavalcade whisked us up the broad, straight Vitebsk highway to the scene of the tragedy. A chill breeze was blowing from a leaden sky, and the air was wet and soggy like the slush-carpeted earth underfoot—one of those miserable January-thaw days when you wish the mercury would drop below freezing so that at least your feet would be dry. When we reached Katyn Forest, we had double reason to wish for cold weather, for the stench from the open grave pits was overpowering. In some, the bodies were piled in neat, parallel tiers, like carefully packed sardines; but in other pits they had simply been dumped pell-mell in obviously careless haste. Some were fairly well desiccated, like pemican, some partially mummified; others were fleshless skeletons, clothed in nothing but rags. This difference in the state of preservation, we were told, was explained by the varying degrees of temperature and humidity at different levels and in different pits. This and other fine points of the investigation were explained to us on the spot by the members of the Special Commission—all of whom wore white smocks and rubber gloves as though they had just come from the surgical operating table.

Chief of the Commission was Nikolai Burdenko, Surgeon General of the Red Army and one of the world's most distinguished brain surgeons, but rather severely handicapped by deafness. Under the Commission's direction, Red Army labor battalions were still engaged in disentangling bodies and laying them out on stretchers outside the tents where the autopsies were conducted. Masses of tattered clothing, unmistakably Polish, were hung on racks. There were also neat rows of skulls, invariably with one bullet hole at the base and another through the forehead. The hands of the corpses were still tied behind their backs, and the theory was that the Poles had been forced to a kneeling position and then shot with revolvers that were pressed against the backs of their heads. This provided a striking parallel with the method used by the Germans in similar mass executions elsewhere.

If the stench had been overpowering even in the open air, inside the tents where the autopsies were being performed it was beyond description. For there in the heat of woodburning campstoves the corpses had had a chance to thaw out thoroughly. One woman, a Russian interpreter with our party, fainted after the first whiff and had to be carried out. But not Kathy. She got herself a front row position alongside one of the dissecting tables where a rubber-gloved Commission member with a scalpel was slicing the corpse as zestfully as though he were carving a Thanksgiving turkey. He held up chunks of the putrified flesh for our inspection triumphantly exclaiming how "fresh" the tissue was, thus proving that the body couldn't possibly have been there nearly four years as the Germans had asserted, but dated from 1941 at the earliest. Holding our noses, we politely assented—though not being medical experts ourselves we had to take his word for it—and rushed out into the comparative freshness of the open air. But Kathy, apparently conscientiously determined to make a full report back to the Ambassador—on this occasion she was her father's nose as well as his eyes and ears—lingered on until the last. Even the Russians marveled.

That night we had another dose of it. After a concluding session with the Atrocities Commission, we were taken to a room in the same building where material evidence—odd objects extracted from the pockets of the Poles—was exhibited. There were old newspapers, personal letters, postage stamps, paper money, and coins—

mostly Polish *zloty*. But there was also American currency—some bills, including a fifty-dollar one, and several twenty-dollar gold pieces. One of the most pathetic exhibits was a letter, unmailed, written by a Stanislaw Nemczinski to his wife in Warsaw.

After the tragic desolation of ruined Smolensk and the gruesome sights and smells of Katyn Forest, it was good to get back to the comparative comfort and cleanliness of our sleeping cars and polished-walnut, plush-carpeted diner. Still, we had the feeling that the stench had saturated our clothing and that we were somehow contaminated.

This feeling was heightened by the lurid stories Tolstoi, Kudrievtsev, and others told us of the many fatalities caused by "corpse poison." But nobody on our trip suffered any ill effects except Kathy, who broke out with what looked exactly like bedbug bites. If so, they were very discriminating bedbugs, for none of the rest of us were attacked. As soon as I got back to Moscow, I took several hot baths and sent everything I had worn on the trip to be laundered or dry-cleaned.

SOVIET PARLIAMENT

✩ ✩ ✩ ✩ ✩ ✩ ✩ ✩ ✩ ✩ ✩ ✩ ✩

THERE are many things that can be kept a secret in Moscow, but a session of the Supreme Soviet is not one of them. For one thing, the deputies from the sundry Central Asiatic republics swarm all over town in their vividly picturesque national costumes.

In mid-January, 1944, the entire city was a-buzz with rumors of a forthcoming session of the Supreme Soviet. Though as yet there had been no official announcement to that effect, every incoming train discharged delegates from the far corners of the country. All the hotels were filled to overflowing, and regular residents were requested to double up. Theater tickets, always hard to get, became practically unobtainable.

In the absence of any information, people in Moscow speculated about the subject of the coming session.

"Peace with Germany," some stated flatly. "Remember that Cairo rumor story about a separate peace? Well, this is it."

According to one school of thought it was the Soviet Union that had signed a separate peace; according to another, the Western Allies. All of this was because the Cairo rumor story had made such a deep impression and was still so fresh in everyone's minds that they felt bound to connect it somehow with the forthcoming session. Some voices were raised in behalf of a declaration of war on Japan, or at least an ultimatum to Tokyo, warning the Mikado either to lay down his arms or else Russia would join the war against him. But however wide the range of guesses, one thing everyone agreed. Only some matter of major moment could explain the calling of a session of the Supreme Soviet at this juncture.

When early one February morning Muscovites read in their papers the announcement that a session of the Supreme Soviet had been called to approve the budget and transfer the conduct of foreign and military affairs from the jurisdiction of the Central Government to the separate republics, there was complete bewilderment.

"Gee whillikers," exclaimed one American diplomat, "sixteen *Narkomindels* (Soviet Foreign Commissariats) just think of it!"

"That's not the half of it, brother. Just imagine sixteen different *Burobins* to deal with instead of one," replied a colleague. *Burobin* —the Russian abbreviation for Bureau for the Service of Foreigners —was the agency that the embassies, diplomats, and newspapermen had to apply to for everything from foodcards and firewood to airplane tickets to Teheran. Grishin, manager of *Burobin,* was thus supreme ruler and arbiter over the weal and woe of the entire foreign colony. If Grishin smiled upon you, life was a bowl of cherries. Conversely anyone who incurred his displeasure might just as well pack up and go home. No wonder ambassadors vied with each other to woo his favor. Actually those foreigners who grumbled about *Burobin* underestimated the difficulties that organization was up against in trying to perform its duties. Compared to Russians, the foreigners were treated like pampered darlings. Still, the thought of sixteen *Burobins* and sixteen Grishins was a bit appalling.

The box reserved for the foreign press at sessions of the Supreme Soviet in the Great Hall of the Kremlin was so far back that it took sharp eyes to sort out and catalogue the people seated on the dais at the far end of the hall, back of the speakers' stand. The size of the figures was further diminished by a giant, full-length statue of Lenin against the center of the far wall. Stalin, of course, was unmistakable, looking very fit and spruce in his Marshal's uniform; so was Mikhail Ivanovich Kalinin, with his familiar goatee, iron gray when I first saw him, now snowy white.

Kalinin holds a special place in Russian hearts. He is an institution, a living link with Lenin and the era of revolutionary struggle. No great intellect, he, but an honest, straightforward, goodhearted Russian workingman, whom the afteryears of success and elevation have neither spoiled nor robbed of his natural, homespun simplicity. From one end of Russia to the other he is "Mikhail

Ivanich" to plain folk who consider him one of themselves. And to this day he reads and answers a voluminous correspondence from those who solicit help on some personal problem.

There were the faces, almost as familiar, of the other members of the all-powerful Political Bureau of the Communist Party: jovial, robust Jewish Lazar Kaganovich, who deserves the lion's share of the credit for the amazing wartime performance of Russia's railways; Alexander Scherbakov, overweight and no wonder, since as head of the Soviet Information Bureau and the Party Press Committee, he was the Soviet Elmer Davis, Byron Price, Steve Early, and a good many other people rolled into one; swarthy, sharp-featured, snap-eyed Armenian Anastas Mikoyan, the Soviets' keenest businessman, admirer and close student of everything American; pince-nezed, taciturn Lavrenti Berya, an old Georgian pal of Stalin's, now serving as Commissar for State Security; Andrei Andreyev, long-standing, colorless gray eminence of the Party organization, said to be close to Stalin; Klimenti Voroshilov, Donbas coal miner's son who rose to be head of Russia's Armed Forces, a little old and obsolete now, but honored and esteemed; and Molotov, his hair noticeably whitened but his face still young, sitting next to Stalin and much of the time engrossed in *tête à tête* conversation with him.

Our press box, to the right of the main balcony, was a good three stories above the vast floor of the hall. We could gaze down directly on the heads of the deputies seated at their little desks with neatly stacked sheafs of papers before them. It was a joint session of the two houses, and the Council of the Union and the Council of Nationalities sat on opposite sides of the central aisle, grouped according to districts. A good portion were in uniform and there was a sprinkling of vacancies, since many of those deputies who were in the Army were absent.

I recalled earlier prewar sessions of the Supreme Soviet I had attended, when every seat was filled. The deputies, too, must have been reminded of the prewar sessions, for they had also been there. No new elections had been held since 1937, when the Supreme Soviet was first convened under the terms of the new Stalin Constitution of 1936. How the people had rejoiced in that new charter of democracy! It symbolized the triumph crowning the long, lean years of struggle and privation. With the foundations of the new socialist order firmly laid, the Russians could at length relax a little and, for the first time in their national history, breathe the air of freedom. The slogan launched by Stalin, "Life has become better, life has become happier," was on everyone's lips in those days. Food was abundant and cheap as never before; consumers' goods were becoming available in ever-increasing quantities. Even the lowest unskilled worker drew a living wage, enjoyed a seven-hour day, and was entitled to a yearly vacation. The road to future abundance seemed to lie straight ahead—broad, smooth, and unobstructed. No wonder the Party leaders thought that now at last the severity of the dictatorship could be modified and the gradual transition to a more democratic form of government begun. Such was the reasoning and purpose behind the Constitution, with its universal suffrage for all citizens who had attained the age of eighteen, with secret ballot, freedom of speech, freedom of the press, freedom of conscience, and other features which caused it to be hailed both at home and abroad as "the most democratic constitution in the world."

But no sooner had the Constitution been adopted than menacing war clouds began to darken the European horizon. The civil war in Spain, dress rehearsal for the wrath to come, broke out. Hitler began his ascent to madness. Almost simultaneously the Kremlin leaders discovered that unbeknownst they had been harboring a nest of vipers. Came the treason trials and the drastic purge years of 1937-38.

Against this background of political *Sturm und Drang,* of increased danger of war from without and of struggle with treason and counter-revolution within, the Stalin Constitution, conceived in happier days, was delivered on the Kremlin's doorstep, a premature child. Obviously under the new conditions it was impossible to go through with the planned relaxations of control and the liberalization. But the Kremlin was already committed by the previous adoption of the Constitution, and it was therefore necessary to observe its form. Its spirit must wait till later.

Yet the flame of hope kindled by the Stalin Constitution has never been extinguished. Today it burns with a passionate conviction in the hearts of millions of Russians and other Soviet nationalities—the promise of a better world to come. And through the years, the Supreme Soviet, even though it has chiefly gone through motions, has remained the prototype of the democratic parliament of the future.

Foreigners are often amused when they read in the Soviet press about "Soviet democracy," or when the Russians claim to be a democratic country. Indeed, Soviet Russia as constituted today seems to have little in common with Western democracy. Yet despite the rigid measures of control and the present absence of democratic liberties, there exists in Russia a form of democracy, elementary if you will, but more genuine and pure within its limited scope than any American institution except the town meeting, to which in many ways it closely corresponds. Thus in every collective farm village throughout the land it is the meeting of the members that elects all the collective farm officers, that within the framework of the general plan determines the crop plans, and, once the harvest is in, apportions the value, in kind or money or both, of each work day. In the factories, shop meetings, departmental meetings, and general factory meetings discuss the production program; send in their own proposals, suggestions, and criticisms; and take the management to task. To be sure, urgent war needs and lack of time have curtailed the scope of these factory meetings, but there is every reason to believe that, once the emergency passes, they will be restored to their former place. Where in America— or for that matter in any capitalist country—is there anything comparable? The Communist Party, too, has preserved a large degree of inner-Party democracy. And in every organization, from the Government to retail trade, any Party member, regardless of his rank or importance, may be called on at a Party meeting to account for his actions or answer criticisms.

It is on this firm foundation of elementary local democracy that the Soviet leaders expect to build the future edifice of Soviet democracy around the frame of the Stalin Constitution. And, regardless of how skeptical of these intentions some of the outside world may be, the Communist leadership has the confidence and endorsement of the Soviet peoples. And this is, after all, the prime consideration.

It took several days for the session of the Supreme Soviet to get over the first and somewhat tedious hurdle of the budget. The figures, mostly in billions of rubles, were impressive, but frankly somewhat mystifying in view of the uncertain value of the ruble, which varied according to who was buying what and where.

The only correspondents who held on grimly through all the long procedure—the original report was followed by "discussion" in the two houses meeting separately—were the three Japs. For the sessions the Press Department had not deemed it necessary to segregate the American and British correspondents from our Far-Eastern enemies, and it was a curious and unpleasant experience to brush against them in the entrance to the press box or in the narrow pews. The awkwardness of the situation was augmented by the fact that in pre-Pearl Harbor days, one of the Jap correspondents, Hatanaka of the Domei News Agency, had been rather popular with his Anglo-American colleagues. He spoke excellent English (to this day all the Jap correspondents in Moscow file their cables in English because no Soviet censor reads Japanese) and was generally acknowledged to be a well-informed and extremely competent newspaperman, presumably not at all in sympathy with General Tojo and the militarists. Be that as it may, his erstwhile friends were now careful to cut him dead. Although the Jap correspondents were accredited to the Press Department of the Soviet Foreign Commissariat and carried press cards identical with our own—formally there was no distinction in our status—they were not, of course, included on any front trips or other junkets, and their contacts with Soviet life were far more restricted than ours. They were clearly not representatives of an Allied or friendly power. At the Metropole they lived cloistered lives—ate in segregation and had their own parties. Somehow they had found girl friends (goodness knows where!) whom they took to the commercial restaurants where they imbibed quantities of champagne and invariably got uproarious. These failings were shared by the members of the Japanese embassy—but more of that later.

The budget was finally approved with minor amendments and the way cleared for the *pièce de résistance*—the transformation of the Soviet Foreign and Defense Commissariats. All the apathy and boredom of the last few days evaporated as Foreign Commissar Molotov leisurely climbed to the speaker's stand. In that vast hall you could hear a pin drop as the familiar halting voice boomed from the public address system.

For full forty-five minutes Molotov told his audience and the world how the direction of foreign and military affairs was to be taken out of the hands of the Central Government and placed under the jurisdiction of the sixteen separate union republics.

Imagine, for purposes of comparison, that Secretary of State Edward Stettinius got up before a joint session of both houses of Congress and out of a clear sky announced that the State and War Departments were to be disbanded and that control over foreign and military affairs was to be returned to the separate states, each of which would henceforth have its own diplomatic service and its own army. Imagine what an uproar such an announcement would cause among the members of Congress—not to mention the press gallery. On the face of it, the new Soviet changes were equally as startling. There had been no build-up, no prior explanations. Yet if the Supreme Soviet delegates and the Russians in the spectators' gallery were startled, they certainly did not show it. They received Molotov's announcement in completely unruffled calm, broken only by bursts of applause at the proper pauses in the punctuation. And then, instead of debating it for several days at separate sessions of the two houses, they proceeded with the "discussion" then and there after only five minutes' intermission.

Representatives of the republics along the western border and of Adzerbaidjan (which borders on Iran) got up and voiced their support. I remember particularly that Paleskis, the Lithuanian spokesman, mentioned Lithuania's special relations with America by virtue of the fact that in the United States there were some 600,000 Lithuanians who had always kept in close touch with the old country and who, he might have added, ever since Lithuania's establishment at the close of the last war, had balanced the national budget by their remittances. There was a speech by a Ukrainian representative named Grechukha, who, referring to the Soviet Government's offer to arbitrate the Polish-Soviet frontier dispute on the basis of the Curzon Line, declared that Ukrainians were not in full accord with this plan—that they would press demands for the inclusion of several overwhelmingly Ukrainian districts west of this line.

Late that same evening the discussion was wound up and the measure adopted by unanimous vote. And when it was all over, the correspondents at any rate were as puzzled and baffled over the purposes behind the new move as they were at the outset. This lack of clarity has persisted down to the present, chiefly because there have been no new developments. Having adopted the measures, the Soviet Government apparently decided to shelve them for the duration at any rate. The only sequel, and that seemed to make no more sense than the rest of the riddle, was the appointment of Alexander Korneichuk as Foreign Commissar for the Ukraine. Korneichuk, popular, convivial Ukrainian playwright, amid the snows of the Stalingrad campaign had fallen in love with and married Wanda Wasilewska, the formidable chairman of the Moscow-sponsored Union of Polish Patriots. Korneichuk's new appointment and marriage provoked endless quips, including a remark in *Time* that the Russians "had tried wedlock to solve the Polish deadlock." One could imagine Korneichuk and his bride discussing the boundary situation far into the night. Dick Lauterbach of *Time* and *Life* suggested that Korneichuk's theme song should be entitled: "I can give you anything but Lwow (pronounced 'Lvove'), Baby." If the Polish-Ukrainian boundary situation was to be left to settlement between those two, it was easy to see who would get the last word in.

While we in Moscow were searching for the answer to this latest Soviet move, in America and Britain, as usual, there were plenty of people ready with alarmist interpretations. The purpose, they declared, was obvious. It was to simplify the incorporation of additional countries into the Soviet Union when the time came.

The first on the list, they asserted, would be Poland; and from that they jumped to the conclusion that the entire Soviet policy toward Poland was directed to such an eventual incorporation.

A far simpler and more rational explanation seemed to be that the Soviet Government was looking for ways of decentralizing Government functions. It was in fact fully in line with the spirit of the Stalin Constitution, Article XVII of which states: "Every Union Republic retains the right of free secession from the USSR."

Basically, like the new tolerance toward religion, the present measures reflected the growing confidence of the Communist leadership in the inner strength and stability of the Soviet system, and expressed their ultimate aim of inaugurating a greater degree of freedom and democracy, as embodied in the Constitution.

This decentralization of the powers of the Foreign Affairs and Defense Commissariats would not weaken the system, because, regardless of the state structure, supreme control remained firmly in the hands of the Communist Party. Indeed, the new decree greatly strengthened the role of the Party as the one interlocking All-Union organization. At the same time, it gave the local republican governments greater leeway and flexibility in negotiating with their immediate neighbors. Though the application of the new measure seems likely to be postponed for the duration of the war, even now it provides evidence that the democratic plans that found formulation in the Stalin Constitution of 1936 have by no means been discarded, and await only the proper time to find their full expression.

In Russia, as in other countries, the war has set in motion social and political processes whose outcome cannot yet be foreseen. Millions of Soviet citizens who have defended their country with such sacrifice and heroism, both at the front and in the battle of production, feel a bigger stake and pride of ownership in their country than ever before. They are likely to demand a commensurate voice in its affairs. The Government, too, after the record of the war, is doubtless convinced that the people can be trusted with a full measure of political responsibility.

LENINGRAD

☆ ☆ ☆ ☆ ☆ ☆ ☆ ☆ ☆ ☆ ☆ ☆ ☆ ☆

E VER since the offensive that broke the German siege ring had opened on the Leningrad front, the correspondents had pleaded with the Press Department to permit them to visit Russia's second capital. It was therefore with much rejoicing that we received the news, one day toward the middle of February, that we would be going to Leningrad. As usual, we left on short notice— a few hours, in fact. Our train pulled out at five in the afternoon, and for the next thirty-six hours we chugged through the snow-bound vastness of northeastern Russia. For though the German siege ring had been broken, the train still adhered to the circuitous route established the previous year when the first narrow overland corridor was opened, following the capture of Schlüsselburg. We were a party of twenty-odd—some very odd—correspondents, including several women. Their getups were extraordinary as only the getups of foreign correspondents in Moscow can be.

We arrived in Leningrad early one misty, wintry morning and were whisked from the railway station to the famous Hotel Astoria. Despite the lack of running water, except at odd hours, the correspondents agreed it was a vast improvement on the Metropole.

Two of our precious days in Leningrad were spent touring the recent battlefields. At Finskoye Koirovo west of the city, we saw the strongly fortified ridge from which the Germans had surveyed the city for two and one-half years. From their observation posts we could see with the naked eye all of Leningrad's main landmarks—the slender spire of the Admiralty, the dome of St. Isaac's Cathedral, the overhead cranes in the dock area, the big modern blocks of apartments, and the Workers' Club in the Kirov district. With a pair of field glasses and a *Baedecker,* any German could do the sights of Leningrad. During a lull they could even hear the city sounds—the clanging of the trolley cars, the honking of automobile horns. It must have infuriated the Germans to have this rich prize dangling before their nose—so near, yet as inaccessible as the moon.

Here it was that the Russians had launched a frontal attack. There was no way of flanking the position. The infantry assault had been preceded by a two-hour artillery workout, and literally every square foot of the ridge was churned up by shells. Yet many of the underground German bunkers, with concrete walls three and four feet thick, were still undamaged. The Russians admitted that their casualties in this assault had been heavy, though they declined to give any figures.

We drove along the shore of the Gulf of Finland to the palace of Peterhof. What had once been the fashionable suburbs of St. Petersburg were now desolate stretches of burnt-out destruction, where even the forests had been reduced to melancholy vistas of charred stumps. Only a few ruined walls and vast shapeless rubble mounds remained of the fabled Russian Versailles. The Germans, we were told, had carted away its priceless museum furnishings and taken up its parquet floors, blasting whatever remained. The statues had been removed from the line of fountains that extends toward the shore.

A few miles beyond Peterhof we came to Oranienbaum. There, through all the darkest days of the siege, under the protective shadow of the heavy guns of the Russian naval base on the island of Kronstadt offshore, the Russians had managed to retain a bridgehead. Oranienbaum was the Tobruk of the Leningrad front—a thorn planted firmly in the German flank. Through the long months it had effectively weakened their striking power against Leningrad itself.

And when the time came for the general offensive that was to destroy the German "steel ring" and complete Leningrad's deliverance, the first heavy blows were struck from Oranienbaum, whence the Germans least of all expected them. At the appointed hour on the morning of January 4, 1944, the guns of Kronstadt, supported by those of battleships of the Baltic Fleet, started shelling objectives deep inside the German defenses. Simultaneously the hard-hitting, low-flying *Stormoviks* and the field artillery on the Oranienbaum bridgehead opened up against the enemy front-line positions. This double barrage was no blind, hit-or-miss proposition. All targets were carefully mapped and the ranges computed. Enemy return fire, fairly heavy at first, gradually slackened as battery after battery was knocked out. And one hour and forty minutes after the barrage began, the Russian infantry went over the top.

Dislodging the Germans from their dug-in positions around Leningrad was as baffling and difficult an undertaking as any army has yet attempted in this or any other war. The German defenses extended in depth for many miles. As soon as the infantry had succeeded in wedging into the defenses, the artillery moved up and again swung into action. When it had softened up enemy resistance, the infantry once more waded in, deepening the wedge. After four days of this closely synchronized use of artillery, air, and infantry, the Soviet Command was able to announce a break through the German defenses south of Oranienbaum.

Even though our trip to the battlefield was in the nature of a post-mortem, we were able to trace the course of the battle play by play, right to the point near the town of Ropsha where the forces from the Oranienbaum bridgehead and those advancing westward from Leningrad itself had made contact. This junction had cut off the remnants of the German garrisons at Ligovo and Strelnya. Even now, two weeks after the battle, Germans were still being dragged out of dugouts and cellars of ruined buildings. Too frightened to give themselves up voluntarily, they had sought shelter in these holes when they were caught in the break-through.

From Peterhof we drove southwest toward Gatchina. By now we were out of the zone of the heavy fighting, and many of the villages we passed through were virtually intact. But the thing that immediately struck us was the fact that they were utterly deserted. The little log peasant cottages that straggled along either side of the road still had a lived-in look. There were curtains in the windows, farm implements in the yards, and well-trodden paths through the surrounding snow. Many of the doors were open and at any moment we expected a child or a peasant woman to appear in the doorway and stare at us. But the only sign of life was an occasional abandoned dog wandering about the yard bewildered, disconsolate, and hungry, waiting for its master's return. Major Lozak of the Leningrad garrison, our conducting officer, explained that the retreating Germans had rounded up the local population of these districts and driven them off into bondage. When the Red Army took Gatchina, after first cutting the railways beyond the town, they were in time to free many thousands of these civilians.

Gatchina itself was not entirely destroyed and there seemed to be a good many civilians around. But the vast Gatchina Palace, favorite residence of Nicholas II, last of the Tsars, was a still-smoking ruin. The Germans had set fire to it at the last moment. A similar fate had overtaken the Catherine Palace at Tsarskoye Selo, save that there the Russians had managed to extinguish the flames before they enveloped the entire building. But the furnishings had either been removed to Germany or destroyed.

The importance of the Nazi defeat before Leningrad was measured by the scale of their repeated attempts to capture the city. In October, 1941, an assembled force of forty-four divisions had attempted to storm the city. Success was taken for granted. In fact, each German soldier was provided with a pocket guide of Leningrad and units had been assigned their billets. The German military governor had his organization ready to take over, and a special corps of military police whose members were all over six feet tall—paragons of the "master race"—was waiting to move in. Typical of Leningrad's indomitable spirit was the fact that on October 28, the day when the Germans staged their most determined assault on the city, the Symphony Orchestra of the Leningrad Radio Committee broadcast Tchaikovsky's Fifth Symphony on a program for relay to British home listeners. Shortly before broadcasting time, while the orchestra was rehearsing, a bomb explosion blew all the studio windows in and wounded two of the musicians. But even the wounded men took part in the performance.

After sacrificing half a million men in unsuccessful attempts to take Leningrad by storm, the Germans settled down to the slower business of trying to reduce the city by blockade and starvation.

Then it was that they started bragging of their "steel ring" around the city. In November, 1941, Hitler boasted to the world: "Leningrad of its own accord will put up its hands in token of surrender. It will fall inevitably, sooner or later."

That marked the beginning of one of the most tragic and heroic episodes of the war—the siege of Leningrad. With the capture in mid-November, 1941, of the fortress town of Schlüsselburg, at the point where Lake Ladoga empties into the Neva River, the Germans severed all overland connection between Leningrad and the rest of the Soviet Union. The great northern Russian metropolis was for a time completely cut off from the rest of the country. Its days seemed numbered. Then it was that the bread ration shrank to 125 grams daily. Eyewitnesses who had lived through the siege told me how gold, jewelry, fine clothes, and priceless art treasures were bartered for a crust of bread. In addition, the starving inhabitants had neither firewood nor water nor electricity, while the cold of one of the bitterest winters on record blew into the unheated rooms through windows whose glass had been shattered by bomb blasts.

People perished by the hundreds of thousands from starvation and exposure. But the fact that Hitler's boast failed and the city held out was a tremendous tribute to the heroic fortitude of the ordinary civilian population—a population consisting largely of old people and children, since all able-bodied men who could be spared had joined the defense garrison.

Practically all of Leningrad's factories continued to operate, including the vast Kirov (formerly Putilov) Engineering Works on the western outskirts of the city—within three miles of the German front lines.

Although on clear days through field glasses the Germans could observe practically every move in the factory yard, some five thousand workers, 60 per cent of them women, mostly young girls between the ages of fifteen and twenty-two, worked ten-hour shifts all through the siege, making artillery shells and repairing tank motors. Many of these girls were from families whose menfolk had been employed in the plant. At the time of our visit to the plant, husky girls, fully recovered from the effects of famine, were pounding red-hot shell cases into shape. I spoke with one girl, Anna, aged seventeen, who was already an old hand. For two years, she had been working on Diesel motors here under the Germans' very noses. Before the war, her two brothers and her father had worked in the plant and had walked to work each morning from their home. When the Germans advanced to the edge of town, Anna and her family were forced to abandon their house in a suburb that was captured by the Germans. Her father and one brother were killed in the early days of the siege, and Anna and her mother were given a room in an apartment in town. One day Anna came home from work to find that a shell had struck in a neighboring apartment and that flying glass from a blast-shattered window had blinded her mother. But she didn't quit her job on that account.

The electric power plants stopped operating for lack of fuel. The street cars stopped running and people, weak from famine, had to walk to work long, weary miles. Many perished on their way to and from the factories. Just as in some medieval city swept by the plague, the death carts daily made their rounds, gathering up the victims. Then, when the limit of human endurance appeared to have been reached and Leningrad seemed doomed, new hope was born. Braving the German aircraft that then ruled the skies, thousands of Leningrad's inhabitants, weakened by hunger and privation, found strength to build docks and railway sidings at Osinovets, northeast of Leningrad, on the shores of Lake Ladoga. This point became the terminus of a supply line that ran across the southern end of the lake to Kabon on the eastern shore, whence a railway spur was built to the main line. Meanwhile, the all-important railway junction of Tikhvin, south of the lake, had been recaptured, thwarting German plans to complete the encirclement of Leningrad on a wide arc by linking up with the Finns on the Svir River.

Thus, early in January, 1942, when the Leningrad famine had reached its most terrible proportions and the daily ration was cut to 125 grams of black bread made largely from substitutes, trucks loaded with flour and ammunition began plying across the ice of Lake Ladoga, almost within sight of the German lines. In the spring when the ice broke, the trucks were replaced by long lines of barges. On the return run from the Leningrad side, they brought back evacuees, mostly children and old folk whose presence in the city was a burden to the defense.

Several times the Germans sought to cut this slender life artery. In October, 1942, they attempted landings on the small island of Sukho athwart the supply line, using invasion barges based on the Finnish-held shore line of the lake. But the Soviet Fleet defeated them, sinking more than half the barges. That was the last serious German offensive effort on the Leningrad front. In the spring of the same year the Germans had again tried storming tactics, bringing up special assault divisions from the Crimea under Field Marshal von Mannstein. This time, instead of trying to thrust from the west, they attacked from the south, across the marshes towards Kolpino, with heavy dive-bomber support. But again they failed. Hundreds of Germans were either mowed down or else perished in the treacherous peat bogs that fringe the southern approach to the city.

In January, 1943, the Leningrad garrison under the command of General Leonid Govorov, an old artilleryman, and the Russian forces on the Volkhov River front under General Kyril Meretskov, started a double play designed to squeeze the Germans out of Schlüsselburg, their anchor on Lake Ladoga, and thereby restore the land connection with Leningrad. In the course of ten days of some of the heaviest fighting of the war, the Germans were thrown back and a narrow corridor was opened along the shore of the lake.

Under long-range German artillery fire, a bridge was thrown across the Neva River at Schlüsselburg and a railway line built into Leningrad along the lake shore. Thereafter regular train service to and from Leningrad was established.

But though the supply situation eased, the city's suffering was not over. To the west and south the Nazis were still on the city's outskirts; while on the north the Finns were within easy artillery range. For the next year, until the final Leningrad offensive that was to complete the city's liberation from blockade, the Germans and their Finnish allies daily pumped shells into Leningrad from a ring of heavy siege guns. There was not a single building in the whole vast city that had not been hit at least once.

Several shells had landed on the immense Winter Palace and the adjoining Hermitage, from which the collection of paintings and other art treasures had been previously removed and evacuated for safekeeping. The fact that the place was bare, however, did not prevent our hosts from touring us through the empty chambers. A guide gave us her stock Intourist patter, recalling from memory what picture had hung where. A one-ton bomb had been dropped in the square just in front of the Palace and had shattered every window in the façade.

The denizens of the Leningrad zoo had somehow survived the siege, though here, too, the bombs and shells took toll. One of the air raid victims was Betty, a gentle, elderly elephant and a great favorite with Leningrad children, who were sometimes permitted to ride on her back. In the same raid the zoo's sable had managed to slip out of its cage and was later found hiding in the cellar of the Philharmonic Hall.

The Kirov plant, being on the western edge of the city, nearest the German lines, was one of the favorite targets for the German artillery—the enemy was aware of the factory's importance to the Leningrad war effort. The foreman of the foundry declared that his workers, girls included, had become so accustomed to the shelling that whenever it started up he had trouble persuading them to suspend work and go to the shelter. Once a shell ripped off most of the foundry roof and caused casualties among the workers, but within twelve hours production was again in full swing.

Not all the shells that struck Leningrad had been fired from the German positions. In the northern part of the city, around the Finland Station, it seemed apparent from the angle of the shell holes that the missiles had come from the north—from the Finnish lines fifteen miles north of the city on the Karelian Isthmus.

Despite the terrific pounding to which the city had been subjected, the damage was not particularly noticeable, save in particular sections—mainly in the western outskirts. This was largely because much repair work had been done in the course of the siege itself, and even in places where the damage was too great for such current patching, the ruins had often been covered with canvas, painted in the semblance of a façade. This was done partly for psychological purposes and partly to occupy the architects and draftsmen of the City Planning Commission, who right through the thick of the siege worked on projects for the city's postwar improvement and beautification.

The most striking feature of beleaguered Leningrad was not the extent of bomb and shell damage, but the fact that this city, for two and a half years on the front line of some of the heaviest fighting of the present war, had stood up as well as it had. It was hard to believe that the Germans, close as they were, could not have reduced the great city to rubble and ashes. The most probable explanation appears to be that until a fairly late date the Nazis still clung to the illusion that presently the city would fall into their lap like a plum, and they wanted to save the prize for themselves. This assumption seems borne out by the fact that the heavy, systematic shelling of the city did not begin until the autumn of 1943. From then until January, 1944, the Germans, having abandoned hope of ever reaching the city, did their level best to pound it to pieces; but their sands were running out and the time left them proved too short to accomplish the job. Meanwhile, the *Luftwaffe,* in view of its depleted resources and the effectiveness of Leningrad anti-aircraft defenses, could no longer stage a costly, heavy air blitz.

Even so, the damage was tremendous when expressed statistically in terms of casualties and buildings destroyed. Clearly it would require years and tremendous effort to heal the wounds, many of them deep-hidden beneath the surface.

Driving about the city, we saw how preparations had been made, in case of a German break-through, to defend the city block by block, house by house. The entire city was covered with a network of defense lines. Thick earthen ramparts and barricades had been thrown up, anti-tank ditches had been dug, barbed wire entanglements strung. And at every street corner the windows on the ground floors had been bricked in and heavily cemented, leaving only a narrow slit opening. There were pillboxes from which machine guns and anti-tank guns could be operated. At the time of our visit, they were just beginning to remove the road blocks from the main avenues.

The city's over-all appearance of shabbiness was greatly accented by the fact that even where bomb and shell damage was slight, windowpanes were shattered and, because of the glass shortage, had generally been replaced with beaverboard. This gave building after building a blind, expressionless look. According to Popkov, Chairman of the Leningrad Soviet, it would take some thirteen million square meters of glass to replace all the city's windows. Popkov, together with Andrei Zhdanov, Secretary of the Leningrad Party Organization, had directed the life of the city all through the siege. He was a capable, level-headed citizen, with the unassuming directness and earthiness that characterizes so many of Russia's present-day leaders. In appearance and mannerisms he was extremely like a capable, self-made American executive.

A kindred type to Popkov was Nikolai Puzyryov, manager of the Kirov Works. During our interview he answered squarely every question that was put to him: How many of the plant's workers had been evacuated? Thirty-two thousand. How many were now employed: Five thousand. What were they producing? Artillery shells and parts for Diesel tank motors which were brought into the shop for complete overhauling.

No, the workers evacuated would not be returning, even after the war. They would stay on at the new plant which had been built beyond the Urals and which now employed a total of sixty thousand workers. That plant was run by the former manager of the Kirov Works, Puzyryov's predecessor. Yes, much of the machinery had been moved. Evacuation had started shortly after the German attack on Russia. Yes, it was planned to restore the Kirov Works to its prewar production level, but with new workers and machinery, not by bringing back either men or equipment from the new plant which would stay where it was.

Later, in a tour through the empty shops whence the machinery had been moved, Puzyryov remarked, "I don't know what my Government will decide, but personally I've put in a request for the purchase of the latest American machines and equipment. I hope your country will have nothing against letting us buy them.

I'll take American machines, any time, in preference to German or British."

Puzyryov had a way of prefacing many remarks with: "I don't know what my Government will think." He was anything but a rubber stamp or a "yes man."

Not even in the darkest days of the blockade, when there was no electricity, had the daily newspaper *Leningradskaya Pravda* suspended publication. Later, when light and power had been restored, a score of printing plants and publishing houses were kept busy turning out a half-dozen daily papers as well as weekly and monthly magazines on a wide variety of subjects. They also printed books extensively—new editions of Russian and foreign classics, as well as much prose and poetry written during the siege by Leningrad authors.

It was significant that even in its depleted and battle-scarred condition, the former Tsarist capital, the noble city of Peter the Great, immortalized in the works of Pushkin, Gogol, and Dostoyevsky, retained much of its cultural and intellectual leadership, even though the political and economic center of the country had long shifted to Moscow.

Its broad streets, its buildings and palaces with their harmonious classic lines, the manner and speech of its inhabitants—all were imbued with a European urbanity and civilized graciousness that could not be manufactured to order, but came of generations of taste and culture. By comparison, Moscow, for all its post-Revolutionary growth and importance, still retained a trace of that semi-Asiatic provincialism that once earned it the title of "Big Village" from European travelers.

To be sure, this definition dated from the old days when Moscow life and customs were largely dictated by an ultra-conservative, stodgy, and provincial merchant class. But even today the city has grown so fast (more than doubled in size in the past two decades) that its inhabitants have not been duly processed. In a previous chapter I described the experience of riding in a Moscow subway. In Leningrad, even on the most crowded trolley car, there was none of the shoving, cursing, and shrill quarrelsomeness that characterized all Moscow public conveyances. The average citizen had good manners.

More than any other Russian city, Leningrad had preserved the continuity with the past—its old dreams and memories, its ghosts. At a reception held for our benefit at the House of Scientists, we were ushered into a plush and walnut atmosphere of distinguished white-haired old men in celluloid collars and a few gray-haired ladies with lace about their throats—for all the world like a setting from Chekhov.

This genteel, old-fashioned setting ill-became our outlandish party of correspondents. Sartorially we were a queer collection of fish, with costumes ranging all the way from ski suits to one woman's flannel slacks. But our hosts were naturally too well bred to make any disparaging remarks.

Though their appearance and memories linked these learned people of Leningrad with the past, they were also very much part of the living present. They had applied their knowledge and skill to the practical problems of the city's defense and survival. At the peak of the famine one chemist had found a satisfactory way to use linseed cake as a substitute for wheat and had also perfected a process for the synthetic production of proteins. There was a former "pure" physicist who had improved the local production of explosives. An engineer had devised improvements for machine guns and anti-tank rifles. A famous brain surgeon had given his time to treating wounded soldiers and civilians. A noted psychologist and student of Pavlov had devoted his attentions to problems of civilian morale and shell-shock.

But though most of Leningrad's surviving population, even those of pre-Revolutionary vintage, had thus kept abreast of the times and accepted the new order of things, there was about the city a certain aristocratic pride and aloofness. It was the buildings rather than the people. Not the outskirts, which, with their huge blocks of modern apartments, look very much like any other Soviet city; but in the old city. There were little narrow embankments along the Fontanka or the Moika which still looked just as they did a century ago in Gogol's time. At any moment you half expected the door of some stately town house to open and emit the gay chatter of voices, the tinkle of glasses, and the strains of a cotillion.

People might change in conformity with the times, but these old mansions and palaces belonged inseparably and immutably to the vanished past. Designed for a different mode of life, no amount of adaptation or remodeling could reconcile them to the alien present. No wonder prewar Leningrad had more museums to the square block than any other city in the world.

Yet besides this older city, the ghost of old St. Petersburg—city of the aristocracy that even in death remained uncompromising—there was the Red Petrograd of the Revolutionaries, the cradle and setting of the October Revolution. The tradition of the Petrograd proletariat survived in the modern Leningrad working class. Talking to the workers at the Kirov Works, many of whom belonged to families which had worked for generations in the plant when it was called the Putilov Works after its former owners, I was struck with their keen grasp of the issues of the war and their strongly international outlook. They deluged me with questions about America, and while they brought up the inevitable questions about the Second Front, they spoke appreciatively of the American and British air raids on Germany. Somehow one felt that mentally as well as geographically Leningrad was far closer to the West than to Moscow. As in the time of its founder, Tsar Peter the Great, it was still Russia's "Window on Europe."

The heroic tragic months of the siege had served to strengthen Leningrad's sense of its own tradition and local patriotism. The people had been completely cut off from the outside world for so long that they had developed a strong sense of independence and self-reliance. And the portrait of the Leningrad Party Secretary, Andrei Zhdanov, who was also head of the Leningrad Defense Council, was almost as conspicuously displayed as that of Marshal Stalin.

One manifestation of this strong local spirit was the fact that in the heat of the siege many of the new names bestowed on streets and localities in the city had been erased and, by spontaneous popular agreement, the old historic names restored. Thus the famous Nevsky Prospect, officially renamed "Prospect of the

Twenty-fifth of October" after the Revolution, was now again officially the Nevsky Prospect. Another famous street, the Liteiny or "Street of the Moulders," which had been renamed "Volodarsky" after the Revolution, was now once again the Liteiny. There were many such instances of reversion.

All of this proved that despite the frightful ordeal of two and a half years on the front line, despite the hundreds of thousands who perished of hunger or were killed by shells and bombs, despite the thousands of evacuees who, like the thirty thousand workers from the Kirov Works, will remain in their new homes beyond the Urals, Leningrad has emerged from the war with renewed vitality. The city which the more rabid wing of the Finnish press once boasted would be returned to swamp will yet play a leading part in Russia's political and economic life.

There is a strong contemporary ring to the immortal lines of Pushkin's "Bronze Horseman."

> Shine brightly, Peter's Town, and stand
> Like Russia, stalwart firm and free.
> And may the vanquished elements
> Be reconciled at last to thee.
>
> Well may the Finnish waves forget
> Their ancient bonds and anger deep,
> Nor in their futile rage attempt
> To trouble Peter's endless sleep.

MOLOTOV THROWS A PARTY

☆ ☆ ☆ ☆ ☆ ☆ ☆ ☆ ☆ ☆ ☆ ☆ ☆

HIGHSPOTS of the Moscow foreign colony social season were the receptions tendered by Premier Molotov on November 7, anniversary of the Revolution, and February 23, anniversary of the founding of the Red Army.

Then it was that those envoys and military attachés who had dress uniforms tucked away could shake out the mothballs and deck themselves in full regalia. These receptions provided almost the sole opportunities for foreigners to rub elbows with those Russians who were sufficiently important—but not too important—to be on Molotov's guest list. The foreign correspondents were usually dealt in on the invitation cards.

The Twenty-seventh anniversary of the founding of the Red Army was the occasion for a remarkably fine turnout. Seldom before had so many Soviet celebrities, including high Government officials, graced one of Molotov's diplomatic parties. This was doubtless in token of the improved relations with Britain and the United States. But the representatives of two Axis countries that still maintained relations with the Soviet Union, Japan and Bulgaria, were also present.

The party was held at the mansion on Spiridonovka Street which the Foreign Office invariably used for entertainment. It was built in a sort of Gothic style with big churchlike windows, high vaulted ceilings, and row upon row of interconnecting salons.

As the guests arrived between the hours of eight-thirty and nine-thirty, an efficient plainclothesman, versed in the looks of the foreign colony, gave them the swift once-over to see whether they "belonged." Meanwhile, relieved of their wraps, they climbed the broad stairs of the hall, ideally suited for "making an entrance," to where Premier Molotov, princely in his Foreign Office dress uniform, and Mme. Molotov, gorgeously gowned in white satin, stood at the head of the receiving line.

Early arrivals were the Japs, who, doubtless figuring that there was safety in numbers, came in a body. A military attaché and two naval attachés in dress uniforms towered above the bandy-legged ambassador and three Jap correspondents, all of whom wore tails. Repairing to the music room where the concert, invariably first item on the agenda would presently start, they could find no better place to ensconce themselves than along the wall directly beneath a huge life-size canvas of the signing of the Soviet-British treaty of alliance in London by Premier Molotov, Ambassador Ivan Maisky, Churchill, and Eden, with Big Ben showing through a window in the background. So close were the sons of the Rising Sun to the receiving line that several Allied diplomats, after howdydos with the Molotovs, narrowly averted shaking hands with the Japs, who doubtless would have welcomed an opportunity to talk to someone besides themselves.

When the time arrived for the concert to begin, British Ambassador Sir Archibald Clark-Kerr, Averell Harriman, and Kathy were seated in the front row in the places of honor, flanked by the Molotovs, the Litvinovs, and the Maiskys. Elsewhere it was first come, first served. But the wiser portion of the company preferred to preserve their freedom of movement by standing at the back of the hall or circulating in the adjoining rooms where they could greet their old friends. There was an amazing turnout of marshals, generals, admirals, and people's commissars, as well as the cream of the literary and theatrical worlds. But through it all, a certain clannishness prevailed. The marshals seemed to consort mostly with marshals, the commissars with commissars, the literati with the literati, and so on. There was no effort made to introduce people to each other. Consequently the foreign correspondents, as happened all too often, spoke chiefly with the foreign correspondents or with the waiters, most of whom had been brought over from the Metropole for the occasion.

The concert, given by the country's finest talent, nevertheless began to pall eventually, and people cast impatient glances toward the rooms on the opposite side of the entrance hall where the sumptuous refreshments were waiting.

In a corner of the hall I saw Alex Werth, Russian-born correspondent of the London *Sunday Times,* discoursing with Wanda Wasilewska and her husband, Alexander Korneichuk. In a long, white silk gown and a modish fur jacket and towering a head above her husband, Wasilewska looked more statuesque than ever. Alex introduced me. Korneichuk, just appointed to the newly established post of Ukranian Foreign Commissar, was saying that he had just been down to Kiev to take inventory of the various buildings there that had once housed foreign consulates and to see about getting them in readiness to accommodate the foreign missions which would, he was sure, be sent to Kiev before long by various powers.

"We shall also have our own press department," he added smilingly, "and I trust you will come and visit us. The air is warmer in Kiev."

"Will we need special visas in our passports, Mr. Commissar?" asked Alex jokingly.

"The general public, yes," answered Korneichuk, "but for you gentlemen of the press we shall make a special exception."

The music in the background ceased and there was a rising hubbub of voices and shifting of chairs as the people poured out of the concert room. Not waiting for any formal invitation, they all made a bee line across the hall and through the double doors that had just been thrown open to reveal long, tempting vistas of tables piled with everything from heaping plates of glistening black caviar to huge roast turkeys, planted amid forests of glasses and wine bottles.

Again the people seemed to sort themselves out by profession. As though by prearranged signal, the writers and artists headed for one room, the generals for another, while the lesser fry, too, were drawn together by the common tie of obscurity.

The supper was a stand-up affair—all except for the last hall, where the marshals, Government members, and top diplomats congregated. Here again Molotov sat down between Sir Archie and Kathy, with Harriman next to Kathy

Sir Archie was sartorially impeccable in his tails and his sash of a Privy Councilor. Kathy was chic and attractive in blue. Only Averell, in a double-breasted business suit and soft collar, seemed strangely out of keeping with the brilliant, lavish gathering. But still a business suit was better than a siren suit. The Russians obviously didn't mind.

At every Molotov party, it had apparently become the custom to "gang up" on one of the leading foreign representatives and deluge him with hospitality. The foreign colony still reverberated with the tales of the November 7 party, when the Russians had concentrated on Sir Archie, who, according to eye witnesses, had eventually subsided below tabletop level. But the target for tonight was Harriman. Commissar after commissar was brought up and introduced to the U. S. Ambassador by Molotov and Mikoyan. First came the commissars of the various branches of the defense industry, all split up now into separate commissariats: tank production, aircraft production, arms production. These were followed by the commissars of machine tool production, iron and steel, non-ferrous metals, and so on through the list. Each one insisted on a toast to Soviet-American friendship. The gist of each toast was how much the particular commissar admired America, liked Harriman personally, and how sure they were that after the war the USSR and the USA would be friends and do business. Then came the turn of Kaganovich, the bluff, hearty Commissar of Railways. He was in high spirits and when he shook hands with the Ambassador, a fellow railroad man, insisted on a special grip which he said demonstrated the principle of the new automatic safety coupling which he had designed and with which he was equipping his railway cars. This new coupling, he added, was symbolic of the fast friendship and alliance between the United States and the Soviet Union, on whose firmness the welfare of the world depended.

"What about Britain," asked Harriman, "why not include them?"

"Don't worry about Britain," laughed Kaganovich. "If America and the Soviet Union are joined together, Britain will couple on automatically. That's where the automatic feature of my coupling comes in handy. Here's to American-Soviet friendship!"

Wines and liqueurs—anything that would fill a glass, in fact— followed each other in riotous, dizzy, digestion-defying sequence.

And each new commissar saw to it that Harriman drank the toast with him. The Ambassador bore up nobly until an American rescue squad, organized in response to furtive pleading glances, managed to create a diversion and slip him out of the room. By that time he had run the gauntlet of all the main defense commissariats and was toasting through the consumer industries.

In the meantime, Molotov was walking through the rooms, glass in hand, clinking with acquaintances. At one point he was almost ambushed by the Jap ambassador, who advanced toward him with his own glass upheld, smiling as only a Jap can smile. But Molotov, instead of clinking with him, gave him the iciest possible nod and passed on.

About this time, I noticed Wanda Wasilewska sitting in a quiet corner and I headed in her direction. I told her of seeing General Wladyslaw Anders in Cairo and of meeting other Poles in Teheran.

"Anders," she commented slowly, in measured, matter-of-fact tones, "made the mistake of his life when he took his army out of here and moved to the Middle East. I told him so at the time. 'You will never get to Warsaw, that way,' I warned. 'What will you bet,' I added, 'that I get there long before you do by staying on here in the Soviet Union?'

"He laughed at me. So did the others. I would like to see their faces now. I am here because I am a Pole."

As she spoke, a sudden flame flickered in the icy depths of her eyes and a flush tinged the waxen whiteness of her cheeks for an instant only, and then her face resumed its statuesque mask. There was something formidable and impressive about this woman. You sensed behind her carefully controlled exterior tremendous reserves of willpower, cold passion, and determination. You began to comprehend why she was rumored to carry such weight with Stalin. She possessed to a remarkable degree some of his outstanding qualities. Clearly she was not a person to cross. One wondered how popular, easygoing Alexander Korneichuk was enjoying married life.

In a neighboring room at the center of an admiring throng, Andrei Vyshinsky, another Soviet leader of Polish origin, was delivering a patriotic peroration in his best prosecutor's style. Across the way, in another room, the writers, artists, and musicians were having what amounted to their own private party, blissfully oblivious of the rest of guests. Two little Japs, feeling lost and out of place in all the rooms, had finally wandered in there and established themselves in a corner. The writers, artists, and musicians—all except Shostakovich who, obviously bored by it all, had left early, and Alexei Tolstoi, who had been dragged off by his wife with gentle but firm reminders that he had a chapter to work on tomorrow—had applied themselves seriously to the refreshments and had done them ample justice. After all, not often did intellectuals, even the top-notchers have a crack at a spread like that in wartime Moscow.

Elsewhere a band was playing dance music and numerous couples, all Russian with the exception of Kathy and some U. S. naval officer, were navigating around the floor.

In the next room there were soft lights, comparative quiet, and a number of easy chairs. In one of these I notice Harriman seated by Marshal Budyonny, the mustachioed and leathery old legendary hero of the Red Cavalry. Budyonny beckoned for me to come over.

"I would like you to translate to Mr. Ambassador how much I hope some day to go America and visit your horse factories and see your races. Is it true that the Ambassador is interested in horses himself?"

But by this time the Ambassador was interested in one thing and one thing only—getting home.

"Please find Kathy and Admiral Olsen," he told me, "and tell them I'm ready to leave—before this old boy proposes a toast. I don't think I could take another."

The Ambassador's departure was the signal for a fairly general exodus of the more important foreign and Soviet guests. For there was still a war on, and most of them had an early working day to face. Many of the lesser lights lingered on until the early morning hours, though by that time the Metropole waiters had cleared the tables of whatever food and drink remained.

The party had been a decided success from the standpoint of Allied friendship. There was the minor episode, which few people had noticed, of the Belgian military attaché, who, slightly limbered up by the liquor, had got friendly with his colleague the Bulgarian military attaché, forgetting for the nonce that this was fraternizing with the enemy. The Belgian minister, a nervous irascible type, had dragged him away and given him a public dressing down. There was also a major of the U.S. Marines, recently come from the South Pacific, who had to be talked out of going over and knocking the block off one of those dirty Japs. . . .

Suppose he had?

THE FINNS MISS THE BUS

✩ ✩ ✩ ✩ ✩ ✩ ✩ ✩ ✩ ✩ ✩ ✩ ✩

FAILURE of the peace negotiations with Finland, which dragged through the late winter and early spring only to be broken off, was a disappointment but not a surprise. On previous occasions—notably in October, 1939—the Russians had found the Finns difficult to deal with, even though the Russians, anxious at that time to secure the northern approach to Leningrad, had offered them a good slice of Karelia in return for a strip of the Karelian Isthmus.

Proof that experience teaches the Finns nothing was provided by the fact that they had entered the war on Germany's side. After the Soviet victory on the Leningrad front, by all the rules of the game they should have quit the war.

About the time that the German military governor for Leningrad—who had been cooling his heels in Helsinki for over two years waiting to ride down the Nevsky Prospect on a white horse —packed up and returned to Berlin, Juho Paasikivi, thick-featured, fuzzy-tongued, veteran Finnish negotiator with the Russians, called on Mme. Kolontai, the Soviet Minister in Stockholm, to ask for terms. The terms were sent. Whereafter, through March, the Finnish press inveighed against their "harshness." The terms called for internment of German troops, withdrawal to the 1940 boundary, cession of the Petsamo area, and an indemnity of around 600,000,000 dollars. To those of us who had been in Leningrad, these demands seemed comparatively mild. Then, despite the continued hostility of the Finnish press comment, toward the end of March the news was noised about that Paasikivi and Enkel were in town.

The Swedish Legation was in charge of Finnish interests. For once the Hagloffs, the young Swedish Chargé and his charming wife, were in the very center of things, instead of being far out on the ragged edge, as rather suspect neutrals. The Finnish delegation was staying at the Foreign Office guest house—it was Paasikivi's third sojourn there. They had come by Swedish plane with a Swedish crew, which had brought the Hagloffs—wonder of wonders—letters and newspapers from home dated the same day, and a crate of oranges. In peacetime this would have been quite commonplace, for Soviet and Swedish planes plied between Moscow and Stockholm on alternate days. But to the Hagloffs it was a veritable miracle. They had come to Moscow the previous summer after six weeks of traveling—first across Germany, then down through the Balkans, through Turkey, and into the Soviet Union through Batum. When they got to Moscow, home had seemed a long, long way off.

From March 23 to 29, the Finns were locked in daily and nightly conference with Molotov, Vice Commissar Dekanozov, and other members of the Soviet Foreign Office. Stalin attended only by proxy. It was all very hush-hush, and we correspondents were not supposed to know they were there. Needless to say, there were no press conferences. The rumor was that things were going well—that agreement had been reached on all points save the indemnity and that the Finns were returning to Helsinki with the drafted terms of the agreement ready for the signature of President Risto Ryti.

When the delegation finally took off for Stockholm, Paasikivi asked Fru Hagloff if there was any shopping he could do for her in the Swedish capital, saying that he would be glad to bring whatever she wanted back with him on his next trip, which would doubtless be within a fortnight.

Apparently the understanding which Enkel and Paasikivi had reached in Moscow was afterwards repudiated by the Helsinki Government with the support of Parliament. The Russian reading of events was that the strongly pro-German Ryti-Tanner Government had never seriously intended to make peace. It had simply gone through the motions of negotiating in response to popular pressure, and in order to make its own people believe the Russians were "unreasonable." For this purpose they had simply exploited the liberal and anti-German Enkel and Paasikivi, who themselves had been acting in good faith.

The fact was that the Finns in Helsinki did not yet realize the full hopelessness of Germany's plight. They were too isolated and local-minded. Their own troops were still deep in Soviet territory. Though the Germans had been flung far from Leningrad, the Finns were still sitting unmolested in the positions north of the city. Save for the far northern sector, which was garrisoned by Germans, the entire Finnish-Russian front was in a semi-dormant state, with nothing more exciting than a bit of sniping and some patrol clashes in the Karelian forests. All this had lulled the Finns into an illusion of false security and an exaggerated sense of their own strength. Thus, while the negotiations were still in progress, the influential Government paper *Uusi Suomi* declared it was wrong for the Russians to treat the Finns as losers because "everybody knows that Finland is now very strong and our possibilities for defense are very great."

Nor did Helsinki itself feel the war too keenly. There had been a few air raids, but nothing like a systematic pounding. And since the beginning of the negotiations, raids had ceased altogether.

In the Winter War of 1939-40, it had taken the piercing of the Mannerheim Line and a Russian thrust across the Gulf of Viborg on the main road to Helsinki to induce the Finns to make peace. This time it was to require the piercing of all the Karelian Isthmus defenses (more formidable now than they had been in the earlier campaign), the capture of Viborg, and the expulsion of the Germans from the Baltic states, finally to induce the Finns to accept the Russian terms. In the very midst of it came the extraordinary and nonsensical Ribbentrop mission to Helsinki and the dispatch of German troops to the Isthmus front.

Another reason for Finnish stubbornness in the present war, as in the previous, was expectation of sympathy and assistance from the Western Powers—this time America.

Back in October, 1939, American good intentions had helped pave the way for the Soviet-Finnish war. Ambassador Steinhardt, on instructions from Washington, had expressed to the Soviet

Government America's solicitude for the welfare of Finland; and while this note had failed to alter Soviet resolve to secure the approaches to Leningrad, it did stiffen Finnish opposition to the Soviet demands. Later, it had been the praises and promises of aid lavished on "the gallant little Finns" by the Western Powers that had prolonged Finnish resistance beyond the natural limit.

Hagloff confirmed to me that Daladier had personally asked King Gustaf to permit the passage across Sweden of Allied troops to aid the Finns. In Britain, Prime Minister Neville Chamberlain told Parliament that an expeditionary corps of 100,000 was in Scotland ready to sail for Finland. Hagloff claims that it was his Government's refusal of this request for transit that had averted war between Russia and the Western Powers—a conflict that would undoubtedly have been a victory for the Nazis.

Today, when the Soviet Union and the Western democracies are fighting the Nazis side by side, people have almost forgotten how close they came to clashing over Finland. In the light of subsequent events, the public has come to realize that even then Russian policy was primarily aimed against Hitler Germany. For the Russians remembered and knew what the rest of the world did not—that in 1918 Finland had been Germany's ally, that German officers and military missions had continued to play a considerable part in the schooling and organization of the Finnish Army, that many of the Finnish officers were graduates of German military schools, that powerful interests were operating to align Finland with Germany for the eventual assault on the Soviet Union. The Russians acted on this knowledge, and today it is obvious that the extra margin won on the Finnish border in 1939-40 spelled the difference between defeat and victory in the long battle for Leningrad.

While sympathy in the West for the Finns had now cooled to the freezing point, the Finns were not fully aware of the change. The fact that America kept a diplomatic link with Helsinki, even though Britain had declared war, was construed to mean that America might be willing to mediate with the Russians on Finland's behalf. Had America taken timely steps to dispel these hopes, it might have saved both Finnish and Russian lives. But not till June, 1944, when the Russian frontal assault on the Karelian Isthmus front was fully underway, did the United States request the recall of Finnish Minister to Washington Hjalmar Procope, and not till the signing of the Ribbentrop-Ryti agreement in Helsinki some weeks later did the United States actually sever diplomatic relations.

The Russians, for their part, are convinced that without outside interference they and the Finns can reach a working agreement. For besides the anti-Russian Germanophiles, such as Ryti and Tanner, responsible for leading Finland to disaster, there are other strongly influential elements who, regardless of their political complexion, have long realized that Finland as a small nation on Russia's perimeter cannot afford an anti-Russian policy. Recognized leader of this group is Juho Paasikivi, who through the turmoils of the past years has managed to retain the respect of the Kremlin. During the abortive Soviet-Finnish conversations in the autumn of 1939, Stalin himself was reported favorably impressed by this old banker. Without forfeiting the confidence of his own people, in and out of season, Paasikivi has always advocated friendship with the Soviet. His recent elevation to Premiership appears to be a step in the right direction.

Another realist among Finnish leaders is no less a person than Marshal Baron Carl Gustav von Mannerheim. For all his long record of fighting the Soviets, this aging warrior was never basically anti-Russian. His younger years had been spent in St. Petersburg court circles. After graduating from the Cadet Corps, the St. Petersburg military academy, he had served in one of the crack regiments of the Tsar's guard, and in the World War had served as a General in the Russian Army. After the October Revolution he returned to Finland, the country of his origin, to fight with the "Whites" against the "Reds." But despite his old unsavory record as the sponsor of the "White terror," he had, during the fateful negotiations of October-November, 1939, strongly urged acceptance of the Russian demands on the grounds that war with the Soviets would be sheer madness which could end only in disaster. It is significant that when peace with the Soviet Union could no longer be postponed, the Finns turned out President Ryti and replaced him by Mannerheim, the former Russian Tsarist general.

To those who contend that Russia is determined to destroy Finnish independence, the most conclusive answer is supplied by the fact that this time the Russians were under no political, military, or moral obligation to negotiate with the Finns. After the previous rejection of the Russian terms by the Helsinki Government and the Ribbentrop trip to Finland, the Russians had every right to demand full capitulation and military occupation of the country. Their moderation should go far toward laying the foundation for future Soviet-Finnish friendship.

Actually, despite all the propaganda about three and a half million Finns threatened with extinction by the crushing weight of a hundred and eighty million Russians, historically Russia has never been a serious threat to Finland. When Tsar Alexander I took over Finland from the Swedes in 1808, the young Tsar was then under the influence of liberal French political thought. As an autonomous Grand Duchy, Finland became his experiment in progressive government, enjoying a degree of freedom and self-rule beyond that of any other part of the Tsarist domain. And though Alexander III tried briefly and unsuccessfully to restrict Finnish liberties, right up until 1917 Finland enjoyed cultural autonomy and a high degree of economic prosperity. Even during the first World War, Finns were exempted from military service. And the so-called Finnish War of Liberation of 1918 was in reality a civil war between leftist Finns with Soviet Russian backing and rightist "White" Finns with German support under General von der Goltz. The representation of Finland as the outpost of Western European civilization was distinctly an afterthought. Actually, the Finns are in many ways more Oriental and non-European than the Russians, despite a veneer of Scandinavian civilization.

During the weeks and months of the Russo-Finnish War, which I covered from the Finnish side, I was impressed by the deep Oriental strain in Finland. The strange, agglutinative Finnish language is unrelated to any European tongue save Hungarian, which, like Finnish, is of Mongolian origin. The same strain is evident in Finnish features and in the Finnish character, with its fatalistic and brave obstinacy and its streak of cruelty.

But in some ways the Finns and the Russians are curiously alike. There is the same physical toughness and stamina, the same attachment to their native soil, the same fanatical courage and self-sacrifice in defense of their convictions, the same deep melancholy strain, which in the Finns is unleavened by Slavic humor and lightheartedness—the Finns are as dour and gloomy as their northern skies. All of which recalls that there is a strong Finnish strain in northern and central Russia. These regions were once sparsely inhabited by Finnish tribes who intermarried with the Slavic Russians that pushed up from the south. To this day, many place names, including Moscow, are of Finnish origin, and Finnish words survive in the Russian language. In a historic sense the Finns bore the same relation to the early Russians that the Kelts did to Anglo-Saxons.

THE WHITE EAGLE FLIES AGAIN

☆ ☆ ☆ ☆ ☆ ☆ ☆ ☆ ☆ ☆ ☆ ☆ ☆ ☆

THE SOVIETS were still at outs with the London Polish Government, but the White Eagle of Poland had reappeared on Soviet soil. It was an eagle of a slightly different feather from that of the London Poles—not the crowned spread-eagle with distended talons, but a stockier, less predatory-looking bird, with its wings half-folded and its feet apparently on the ground. The difference was not merely ornithological. Like most things in Eastern Europe, it had a political content. The London Government's eagle was the Eagle of Jagiello, adopted in the fourteenth century when Poland swallowed Lithuania and adjoining territory to form Greater Poland, which at its peak included all the Ukraine and much of Russia proper. The more modest bird was the symbol of an earlier period when Poland was a smaller but homogeneous state. Hence its selection by the Moscow-sponsored Union of Polish Patriots, headed by Wanda Wasilewska. And now this Eagle flapped on the battle flags of a new Polish Army, formed under the auspices of the Union of Polish Patriots and led by General Zygmunt Berling.

A career officer of the Polish Army, General Berling had previously served as General Wladyslaw Anders' chief of staff. In this capacity he had been in charge of the evacuation of the Polish troops under Anders from the Soviet Union via the Caspian port of Kislovodsk, where they had embarked for Iran. Under orders from his chief, Berling had performed his duty conscientiously. But when the operation was completed, instead of leaving on the last ship, Berling suddenly announced his decision to remain in the Soviet Union and enlist in the Red Army.

To those who accused him of betrayal Berling retorted that the best way to further Poland's cause was to fight the Germans, and that Poland's liberation could be accomplished only from Soviet soil. Not even the threat of court martial proceedings (the move was quashed by Premier Sikorski) could alter his resolve. He was joined by a score of other Polish officers, whom he had quietly helped to remain in the Soviet Union. For the next year Berling and his comrades fought anonymously in the ranks of the Red Army.

It was not until the summer of 1942, some months after the Soviet rupture with the London Polish Government over the Katyn incident, that the plan for a Polish Army to fight alongside the Russian forces saw the light. As first conceived, it was to consist of but one division—more than anything else a token force that would serve to implement the claims of the Union of Polish Patriots to a voice in the future fate of Poland. The soldiers of this Kosciuszko Division (named after the famous Polish patriot) were recruited from among the Poles who had remained behind in the Soviet Union at the time of the Anders evacuation. Polish refugees, scattered far and wide over Russia and Siberia, responded readily to the new call to arms. It also was discovered that many Poles, much earlier in the war, had found their way into the ranks of the Red Army. Some from the eastern provinces had been drafted; others had volunteered. These were sorted out and transferred to the new Polish division. Berling's hour had now come to emerge from anonymity and don a Polish uniform. Together with his little band of followers, he assumed command of the new Polish force. But the gray eminence of the undertaking, the organizing genius behind the scenes, was a remarkable and little-known man—State Security Commissar Zhukov (not to be confused with his namesake, the Marshal). Zhukov knew the ins and outs of Eastern European politics better than most nationals of the states concerned, and he spoke a variety of languages. Besides his political acumen, he possessed qualities that would, under different circumstances, have made him a topflight Hollywood director. On short notice he could produce quantities of uniforms for any required nationality, flags of any or all United Nations, army chaplains of any denomination, including the Mohammedan, together with all paraphernalia necessary for the discharge of their duties. The Polish division was only one of his charges. He also ministered to the

Czech brigade, the Yugoslav unit, and the French *Normandie* fighter squadron.

Both the Czech brigade and the Yugoslav unit were composed largely of deserters from the German Army or from the satellite Slovak and Croat Armies. Sometimes whole regiments came over in a body under the leadership of their officers. They were, for the most part, men of exceptional courage, eager for a crack at the Germans—even though they knew that if they were captured, they would face a firing squad or worse. The use of these Allied units in battle was complicated by the fact that as soon as the Germans located their positions, they immediately "gave them the works." The Czechs had fought valiantly at Voronezh and in the liberation of Kiev, but they had sustained heavy casualties. Likewise, when the First Polish Division went into action at Lenino in the Ukraine early in January, it immediately became the object of the special attention of the *Luftwaffe* and the German artillery. The Poles bore up bravely, and while the German claims to have destroyed the division were an impudent fabrication, their losses were fairly heavy.

Thereafter the Red Army Command wisely decided to save the Czech, Polish, and Yugoslav units for the time when they would be most useful—for operations on their home soil. The Russians felt sure that all these groups would then serve as nuclei for recruiting from the local population. They would thereby expand into larger fighting forces and at the same time retain the tradition of close collaboration with the Red Army—a political as well as a military factor of the first magnitude.

Before the First Polish Division went into action, the formation of a Second Polish Division, the Dombrowski Division, was announced. It was also recruited chiefly from refugee Poles and from former Polish prisoners of war. Then in March came the news that a Third Polish Division had been formed and that the three divisions would now constitute a self-contained Polish Army under the command of Berling, who was promoted to the rank of Lieutenant General. The Third Polish Division was something of a surprise, for it was generally assumed that with the Second Division the available supply of Poles had been completely exhausted. We learned the answer when a group of correspondents was invited to attend the swearing-in of the new Division in a village some hundred miles southeast of Moscow.

The new recruits, we discovered, consisted largely of Poles from the recaptured former provinces of Eastern Poland—from Sarny, Lutsk, and Rovno—together with a considerable number that had managed to slip through the German lines from Lwow. There were also some Poles from Silesia and Posen, who had been drafted into the German Army and had deserted. All these men were highly regarded because they were closely in touch with the Polish Underground. In addition, any Soviet citizen with a Polish name or of Polish extraction, who in the normal course of events was called up for military service, was given the option of declaring himself (or herself) a Pole and of joining the Polish Army. The most serious handicap was the shortage of Polish officers. It was solved by transferring a few officers out of the First Division and by borrowing officers and instructors from the Red Army.

The Third Polish Division, like its two predecessors, was named after a Polish patriot, this time Romuald Traugut, one of the leaders of the Polish uprising against the Tsar in 1863. Despite handicaps and mixed composition, the Third Division put on an impressive show. Decked out in new khaki uniforms (procured through the efforts of Commissar Zhukov) closely cut to traditional Polish patterns, and equipped with the latest and best output of Soviet war industry—including tommyguns, long-barreled anti-tank rifles, medium and heavy artillery—the Division presented arms in the slush and mud of the village square. Then at a shouted command the band struck up the Polish national anthem while the infantry did a Polish version of the goose-step past the reviewing stand.

General Berling, a towering figure in a huge fur cap, inspected the ranks on foot, pausing here and there for a word with an old friend whom he recognized.

On the reviewing stand, bedecked with American, British, French, Soviet, Yugoslav, Czech, and Polish flags, stood Andrei Witos, Vice-Chairman of the Union of Polish Patriots and brother of the former Polish Premier who was ousted by Pilsudski. Next to him was the Roman Catholic chaplain of the Division, a surplice over his uniform; while lined up behind them were Brigadier General William Crist of the United States Military Mission, General Petit, head of the French Military Mission, and Czech and Yugoslav military representatives. Among the latter was Colonel Lozic, the Yugoslav military attaché who the previous day had decleared for Marshal Tito, and to designate his new allegiance had sewed a Red Star to his blue, British-issue RAF cap. The British, though invited to send a representative, had declined to do so, presumably because they officially recognized the Polish Government in London. Motivating the American acceptance of the invitation, Ambassador Harriman later explained that the United States welcomes and approves of all forces fighting against the common enemy.

A few days later the Third Polish Division entrained to join the other two divisions in the Ukraine. But the Russians were determined to have no repetition of Lenino. Accordingly, the Polish Army was held in reserve until the time should come for it to play a direct part in the liberation of Poland.

It was in their Ukrainian habitat that I had an opportunity to spend a week end with the Polish troops in the early part of May. I was one of five correspondents invited by the Press Department to go on a trip arranged for the benefit of Professor Oscar Lange of Chicago University. Like the Reverend Stanislaw Orlemanski, Professor Lange had come to the Soviet Union by special invitation.

Unlike the rawboned priest from Springfield, who was destined to cause such a world furor, Lange was a mild-mannered, little man—an extremely shrewd observer. An authority in his field, the application of statistics to political economy, he was a man of the world, a typical Middle European liberal intellectual of the pre-Hitler period, who would have doubtless been as much at home in Vienna, Prague, or Berlin in those far-off days as in Cracow, where he had taught at the famous University. Lange was a Pole by nationality, but he had moved his family to America in 1937, and he was now a U.S. citizen. Hence, whenever Lange saw a Polish refugee or read of some atrocity committed by the Nazis in Poland, his normal reaction was "There but for the grace of God and my own foresight go I."

Father Orlemanski, a second-generation Polish-American lacked this European background and personal intimacy with the issues. An obscure parish priest, this was his first trip abroad. Never before had the world at large been aware of his existence. And then overnight he was catapulted to the pinnacle of fame. His was the distinction of being the first Roman Catholic prelate ever to be received by Stalin. Though Father Orlemanski had come to Russia purely as a private citizen to visit the Poles, and though he had no authorization whatever to speak for his Church, Stalin, when he saw the priest's black coat and rounded collar, decided to kill two birds with one stone.

The Kremlin realized that the time was ripe for at least some partial reconciliation with Catholicism. It wasn't simply that this was a necessary step in the solution of the Polish deadlock, although that, too, figured in the computation. But the Soviet Union in its new role as one of the influential members of the family of nations was anxious that no world force should be aligned against it. The Russians recognized the tremendous influence of the Catholic Church over millions of consciences on both sides of the Atlantic—an influence which had hitherto almost uniformly been exerted against the interests of the Soviet Union, and with untold detriment to those interests. If the Catholic Church could now be won over to at least a position of neutrality toward the Soviet Union, it would greatly ease the suspicion and prejudice against her in scores of countries—including the United States. The task of international co-operation would be that much simplified. Stalin thought he could make the Springfield priest the apostle of this reconciliation, and he therefore told him at the end of his first interview that he would have a message of the utmost importance for him before he left the country. The following morning the citizens of Moscow, who had lived through so much in recent years, were destined for another surprise. There on the front page of all the papers were pictures of Father Orlemanski and Uncle Joe beaming at each other. It was the first inkling they had of the priest's existence or of his presence in Moscow. Interviewed the following morning, Father Orlemanski simply said the results of the interview had been excellent.

One week later, when he returned from a visit to the Polish troops at Sumy in the Ukraine, Father Orlemanski saw Stalin a second time. It was after this second interview that he delivered his sensational statement: "Unquestionably Marshal Stalin is a friend of the Polish people. I will also make this historic statement that future events will prove that he is very friendly disposed toward the Roman Catholic Church."

Father Orlemanski, for all his naïveté, had a streak of peasant cunning that prompted him to ask Stalin for something in writing to supplement his orally expressed sentiments of benevolence toward the Catholic Church. Thus Stalin's letter on the subject of the Catholic Church, which Orlemanski released upon landing in America, was written in response to a request by Orlemanski, who rightly sensed that without some such tangible proof his own statements on the subject would be discounted. So ended one of the most extraordinary and fantastic episodes of our time. The parish priest who went to Russia to see some Poles, saw Stalin and became the bearer of a message from the Kremlin to his Church.

Why he chose this peculiar means of transmission is Stalin's secret. A more official and direct approach would have been through Father Leopold Braun, the American Jesuit rector of the Roman Catholic Church of St. Louis des Francais, who had been in Moscow continuously for the past fifteen years. Father Braun, however, has never seen Stalin nor indeed received any form of official recognition, though he carries in his pocket the credentials of Apostolic Delegate.

Perhaps it was because the Soviet authorities had little reason to trust Father Braun. Yet the fact remains that he was apparently greatly pleased with Orlemanski's interview. The two priests spent several hours together behind locked doors before Orlemanski's departure, and Father Braun even came to see him off at the airport at five in the morning. Yet when Orlemanski first arrived, Father Braun expressed little interest in his visit and made no effort to see him. In fact, the first meeting was arranged by Jim Flemming, the Columbia Broadcasting representative.

In selecting such an obscure figure as Father Orlemanski to convey his message, Stalin may have been appealing for the sympathies of the Catholic rank and file and the lower clergy. Perhaps the theory was that an appeal over the heads of the hierarchy—however the Princes of the Church might react to it—would have a favorable effect on millions of Catholics, whereas any message conveyed to the Vatican through official channels would simply be ignored.

It is significant that public opinion forced Orlemanski's reactionary superiors to rescind disciplinary action against him. And though up to now there are no new developments to report, who can say that the seed Stalin planted in the Vatican's ear may not someday germinate? Vatican policy, like Kremlin policy, has always been distinguished by its "realism." Basically, neither has anything to gain from continued mutual hostility.

Lange and Orlemanski shared the Hotel National's Royal Suite, with its ponderously gorgeous sitting room full of gilded, brocaded furniture and flute-legged, marble-topped tables—a relic of Tsardom. When a colleague and I first called on them, the marble-top table was supporting a huge basket of fruit—big, juicy apples and tawny-golden oranges. After a winter in Moscow, you forget what oranges look like. And there the "distinguished visitors" sat, absent-mindedly peeling and munching those Olympian delicacies under our noses—and never once offering us so much as a bite.

While we talked, there was a constant coming and going of Polish uniforms and Russian correspondents. A fixture in the place was a personable young Polish woman who was eating a meal when we arrived. It developed that she was a long-lost niece of Lange's, who had come to Moscow as a refugee and was now teaching English in a school for Polish children at Zagorsk, sixty miles north of Moscow. Until two days previously, uncle and niece had had no knowledge of each other's whereabouts; they did not even know whether the other was still alive. Then the niece had read in the paper of the Professor's arrival and had hastened to see him.

It was evident from the conversation that the Professor was particularly concerned over the possible effects of the anti-Soviet propaganda being spread in the United States by the official Poles anent the forthcoming Presidential election. The Polish question, he told us, was fast becoming a political football in the Presidential campaign. Various Polish pressure groups were disseminating propaganda accusing the President of selling out Poland to appease Russia. The New York Polish-language paper *Nowy Swiat*, mouthpiece of the arch-nationalist, anti-Soviet Matuszewski, had already declared itself against Roosevelt's re-election. If something were not done to counteract this influence, others might follow suit. It was not only the election campaign that was affected, but also the whole structure of Soviet-American relations.

Hence the importance of providing the President's supporters with ammunition on the Polish issue. That was why the professor and the priest had come to the Soviet Union. They were to see for themselves how the Poles were faring in the Soviet Union and to find out whether the army under General Berling was indeed a bona fide Polish Army. They would conduct their investigations separately and later compare notes.

I next saw Professor Lange early one morning at the Moscow airport. We were on our way to the Ukraine. A few days previously Father Orlemanski had been to the Kremlin for his first interview with Stalin. It had come suddenly and without any advance warning. He and Lange had been at the Opera when in the midst of an act the door of their box had opened and a silhouetted figure had tapped Father Orlemanski on the shoulder with the words: "Come with me, please."

Lange had been left behind to see the rest of the show. However, he had been assured that before he left the country he too would be granted an interview. The promise was later fulfilled.

We flew to Kiev in a Lend-Lease C-47 equipped with bucket seats. At the airport we were joined by Wanda Wasilewska, smart in her silver fox furs, but looking pale and tired after a long illness. So it was illness that had kept her out of circulation for the past two months. This spiked the rumors which had inevitably cropped up following her failure to attend the Kremlin banquet given by Stalin for General Berling and other senior Polish officers on the occasion of the formation of the Polish Army Corps and Berling's elevation to the rank of full General.

At the Kiev airport we were met by our old friend Korzh, former chief censor in the Foreign Office Press Department. A native of Kiev, he had been transferred to his home town to serve as head of the Press Department of the Ukrainian Foreign Commissariat under Korneichuk. Korzh's physical presence in Kiev was our first evidence of the application of the new law dividing up the Foreign Office.

Driving through the town, we were amazed to see what progress had been made during the winter in restoring life to normal. The Kreschatik, Kiev's main street, was still a mass of ruins and rubble. But already the street itself had been cleared for traffic and a temporary streetcar track had been laid along one side. Mixed crews of men and women were shoveling seemingly inexhaustible mountains of debris onto little trays which they carried like stretchers, coolie-fashion, and dumped into flatcars standing on the track.

Up the hill from the Kreschatik, with the exception of a burnt-out building here and there, the city was fairly well intact. Compared to Smolensk or even Kharkov, the ancient city of Kiev had been fortunate. The hotel where we were quartered had previously served as a German officers' billet. Besides painting and furnishing the place, the Germans had installed their own plumbing fixtures. The faucets in the washbowls in each room bore the legends *Kalt* and *Warme*—which were purely ornamental, since the water supply in that part of town was still out of operation.

But we were not destined to tarry in Kiev. After one of the extravagant meals which characterized all our trips, we were hustled out to a waiting cavalcade of jeeps, plus a ZIS limouzine for Lange. Lange, in an expansive mood after the dinner and toasts, confided to Eddy Gilmore and myself that a crate of oranges had been slipped into his luggage for the trip and that he simply didn't know what to do with them. We generously expressed our willingness to help him solve the problem, but unfor-

tunately he never again referred to them during the rest of the trip.
No doubt he found others who were equally willing to help.

With a crisp wind lashing our faces, we bounced in our jeeps
down the main highway which runs west from Kiev straight as
a tightrope. Doubtless at one time it had also been smooth, but
now the wheels and treads of countless cars, trucks, and tanks—
Russian and German—plus bomb and shell craters, had chewed
up its asphalt surface beyond all driving comfort. We were but a
small part of a flow of military traffic that coursed endlessly toward
the front, building up the reserves of men and supplies for the
next great push.

On either side of us stretched the lush Ukrainian landscape, now
green in the full tide of spring. Every few miles thick promon-
tories of heavy forest intruded into the open farmland. The Germans had done their best to push the forest back from the road,
clearing large tracts, erecting high barbed wire fences along the
edges of the clearing, and building log blockhouses reminiscent of
old American frontier posts. For the Germans these forests had
been enemy territory, whence any time of day or night Partisans
might raid their convoys on the road. From what we saw, it was
easy to reconstruct their terror of the threatening forest—the tense,
uneasy situation along the German supply lines far to the rear of
their front.

The highway also chronicled the stages of the expulsion of the
Germans from the Ukraine. We saw the blasted, charred evidence
of the tank battles around the village of Korostyshev, where the
German counter-offensive of December had been fought to a
blood-drenched standstill. Beyond, more open country, and finally
the town of Zhitomir, which was considerably the worse for having
changed hands four times. What struck us most on the brief
ride through Zhitomir was that every single building that still had
a roof over it had been turned into a hospital brimful of wounded.

Not far beyond Zhitomir, we left the main highway for a side-
road, and presently the landscape was almost blotted out in the
swirling dust cloud kicked up by our vehicles. Obviously we were
now in the zone of the Polish Army. Every vehicle that passed us
had white and red Polish pennants fluttering from the fenders,

while the M.P.'s directing traffic at crossroads and manning the various military check posts wore Polish uniforms.

Though somewhat nearer the front, we were away from the main battle areas, which usually centered around the larger towns, the railway and highway junctions. Also, much of the evidence of fighting had already been hidden by the fresh, green carpet of new wheat and rye. Only here and there had the plowman been forced to detour the giant, rusted ruin of a Tiger tank. But the little whitewashed Ukrainian villages looked as neat and trim and peaceful as they had in happier days. Even a fair portion of the pigs and poultry appeared to have survived the depredations of the Nazi commissary, and in the village pastures sleek herds of cattle chewed their cuds reflectively.

The Germans, we learned, had been forced to retreat from the region in such haste that they had not had time to apply their usual scorched-earth tactics. The peasants had saved much of their livestock by hiding it in the woods. They had also managed to salvage vast stores of grain, partly by concealment and partly because of German haste and oversight. Our chief escort, Commissar of State Security Kostelanets, declared this had proved a tremendous windfall. The Soviet Government had fully expected to find devastation in the Western Ukraine equal to that in other liberated areas. They had, in fact, made plans to rush in food supplies to feed the destitute population. Instead, a preliminary inventory had revealed that the region not only had sufficient food to care for its own population, but could also contribute to the maintenance of the Army. This had simplified the Soviet High Command's supply problem and had cut two whole months from its operations schedule.

But though this part of the country had escaped devastation, the German invasion had left deep wounds beneath the surface. Thus in the Village of Troyanovo, where the Polish Command was quartered and where we were billeted in peasant cottages, most of the able-bodied men and some of the women had been shipped off to forced labor in Germany. And in more than one house, towheaded offspring of German soldiers had been added to the legitimate brood. Hundreds of ordinary peasant folk had been maimed physically and spiritually. And though they were glad to be rid of the Germans at long last, there was some uneasiness lest the returning Soviets prove overly severe with those who had dealt with the enemy. So far, however, the authorities had been more than lenient.

The Polish troops quartered in the village were ordered to help the families on whom they were quartered with the care of their individual garden plots and domestic animals, and they had aided the collective farm through the heaviest period of the spring sowing. Also, there had been a considerable amount of social life and entertainment. The Poles had organized their own orchestras, folk dance groups, and amateur theatricals, and had invited the villagers to the shows. In addition, traveling Red Army professional shows had put on performances from time to time. All this provided a welcome variation of the endless routine of peasant life.

With Troyanovo as our headquarters, for the next six days we traipsed around with Lange and General Berling, visiting units of the First and Second Polish divisions—the Third Division was in a different locality.

Invariably the visits followed a certain routine. First, there was a short parade while a band struck up the national anthem "Poland Has Not Yet Perished." Then at the blow of a whistle the troops, usually one company at a time, would form a vast huddle with Lange, the General, and other members of our party in the center. That was the beginning of a question and answer period, with the Professor acting as chairman and translator. A former member of the educational committee of the Polish Socialist Party, Lange had a knack for talking to the men and winning their confidence, and once the initial reserve had been broken down—General Berling usually put in a word urging them to speak their minds freely and without restraint—their opinions usually gushed forth.

Their indignation waxed high as they accused the London Polish Government of following a reactionary policy. They were particularly incensed over reports that men and officers of General Anders' army had been arrested for expressions of sympathy with the Polish Army in Russia, and they wanted to know why Britain and America did not force their release. But there was no animus against the Poles serving in the Anders army and other units owing their allegiance to the London Polish Government. As one soldier expressed it, "They are our brothers and we should like to be united in the common struggle."

They also felt that while some elements of the Polish Government in Exile were totally unacceptable and should be barred from postwar Poland, others, including Premier Mikolaiczyk, would be welcome.

When they were asked what sort of economic and political system they wanted in postwar Poland, they gave stereotyped answers that reflected the views expressed in *Wolna Polska,* the organ of the Union of Polish Patriots. Thus the formula of a strong, democratic, and independent Poland—which originated with Stalin—was on the tip of every tongue. But for the most part, they were rather vague as to the kind of democratic system—beyond that it should provide freedom of speech, press, and religion, and that no fascist parties should be tolerated. Several were in favor of patterning the new Polish state after America.

They were unanimously and very positively in favor of a sweeping agrarian reform that would break up the huge estates and distribute the land to the peasants. But at the same time, they were unanimous in rejecting any form of "collectivization." There was general agreement that while big monopolies and perhaps the banks should be nationalized, small industry and business should be left in private hands.

Though the Polish soldiers expressed their thanks to the Soviet Union for helping them to arm and organize, they insisted that the USSR must not interfere in Polish internal affairs, and that the future of Soviet-Polish relations would depend on the fulfillment of Soviet promises in this connection.

We encountered the widest variety of opinion on the Polish boundary issue. The men were generally agreed that Poland should be permitted to expand westward and northward—that she should get most of East Prussia and Pomerania, with their extended coast lines on the Baltic, and the whole of Silesia. But on the question of the boundary with Soviet Russia, several declared themselves in favor of restoration of the prewar frontier while others said the

Curzon Line was acceptable as a basis, provided certain adjustments were made. In this connection the overwhelming majority wished to see Lwow restored to Poland. They expressed general endorsement of the principle of population transfers and invariably announced their intention to move to Poland, even if their old homes happened to be in districts annexed by Russia.

More than once these men voiced solicitude for the welfare of their families, which were still in some remote part of Asiatic Russia. Such expressions prompted assurances from General Berling that the Union of Polish Patriots was arranging to have all Polish refugees brought to assembly points in the Ukraine, preparatory for their repatriation when the time came, and that special issues of food and clothing were meanwhile being distributed.

The soldiers in their turn asked Lange and us a lot of questions, usually about the American war effort and invariably leading up to "What about the Second Front?" Lange wound up each session by asking for a show of hands of those who had relatives in America. Invariably a forest of hands was raised. Whereupon he told them that if they knew their relatives' addresses and wanted to write them letters, he would be glad to play postman.

An extremely sore subject with all these Poles was the Ukrainian Nationalists' persecution of Polish populations in areas still behind the German lines. Every day, recent arrivals from the other side brought lurid stories of whole villages massacred by these Ukrainian fanatics who were aided and subsidized by the Germans. According to one spokesman, more than forty thousand Poles had been killed in the Luck district alone.

In some of the areas thus threatened, Polish Partisans had evacuated the population to the comparative safety of the swamps and forests. Thereafter, wherever the Partisans moved, they were encumbered by carts and wagons loaded down with families and their possessions until such time as they contacted the advancing Red Army.

Many former Partisan units had joined Berling's regulars. New of the formation of the Polish Army, when it filtered through t lines, had had a powerful, magnetic influence on people in German-occupied regions, swelling the influx of volunteers

managed to make their way through the lines. With the sufferings of the homeland fresh in their minds, these newcomers constituted a direct link between the Berling Army and the Polish civilian population. More than anything else, their presence proved that the oppressed Poles were ready to welcome the Red Army with open arms if only because its advent would spell the end of Nazi rule. General Berling and his staff, encouraged by the volume of new recruits, were predicting that their Army would soon pass the 100,000 mark.

As I noted earlier, the equipment of this Polish Army was the best available. Their motor transport was mostly of American make. Besides American jeeps and six-wheeled trucks, they had American half-tracks with anti-tank guns mounted on them. I also saw some Canadian tractors hitched to their heavy artillery field pieces. But the bulk of their armament was of Soviet make—from heavy KV tanks to tommy guns. Among other features, the Polish Army boasted several battalions of husky girl tommy gunners.

Much of the food we saw and sampled was of American origin, including butter from Minneapolis and quantities of the inevitable Spam.

Yet though this Army's equipment was either Soviet or American, and though it had been formed on Soviet soil with the assistance of the Russians, in heart and spirit it was thoroughly and intensely Polish. At our innumerable confabs the proceedings invariably wound up with cheers—cheers for Professor Lange, cheers for Marshal Stalin, cheers for Britain and America. But invariably their loudest, most spontaneous cheer was reserved for "Our Leader," General Berling. Whereupon that giant warrior would grin boyishly from ear to ear, obviously embarrassed at being the object of such popularity, but at the same time enjoying it hugely.

We wound up our six-day tour and headed back toward Kiev, convinced that these men and their leaders believed they had as much right as anyone to speak for Poland.

ROMANIAN PREVIEW

☆ ☆ ☆ ☆ ☆ ☆ ☆ ☆ ☆ ☆ ☆ ☆ ☆ ☆

WHILE attempts to get Finland out of the war and re-establish relations with the London Polish Government were encountering snags, new diplomatic progress was being registered in the southwest. Ever since Stalingrad, the war-weary Romanians had been secretly looking for a way to pull out of the Axis partnership. The inhabitants of Odessa recounted how, after Stalingrad, the local Romanian occupation authorities had lost their cockiness and had gone to almost incredible extremes in their efforts to curry favor. By distributing a few judicious bribes, a local poet had managed to publish and circulate a book of pro-Soviet patriotic verse. A Soviet flier who crashed near the town in August, 1943, was given an elaborate funeral with military honors—senior Romanian officers acting as pall-bearers while one of their number walked behind the coffin bareheaded, carrying the flier's decorations on a red velvet cushion.

The Red Army, when it retook the town in April, 1944, and a group of foreign correspondents who arrived a few days later, were surprised to find most of the local girls walking around in silk stockings and other bits of finery. Market prices on foodstuffs and a variety of luxury items were ridiculously low compared to Moscow market prices. For one hundred rubles a Soviet correspondent whom I knew bought himself a whole pig—about 4000 rubles' worth by Moscow prices. It almost broke his heart that he couldn't fly the whole animal back, but instead had to have it slaughtered so that he could at least take the choicest cuts home with him. Even so, it was a bargain.

While they had the chance, the Romanians did a fair job of looting that portion of the Ukraine which was assigned to them. But as soon as they saw how things were stacking up, those Ro-

225

manian carpetbaggers who had feathered their nests made haste to
get home as inconspicuously as possible and with as much of their
loot as they could carry. The real stampede began after the Italian
surrender. The Romanians, who pride themselves on their Latin
origin and kinship with the Italians, would have broken with the
Axis then and there, had it not been for the German stranglehold
on their country. For weeks thereafter, even the Antonescu Government, which goodness knows had sold itself to the Nazis
body and soul, was reluctant to sever relations with the Badoglio
Government. At last Berlin forced it to break. Even then, the
Romanian authorities agreed to provide a ship for the evacuation
of Italian Minister Pellegrino Ghigi and his staff to Turkey. At
the last minute, when the Italians were already on ship board, the
Germans intervened. But the Italian diplomats, instead of being
interned, were taken back to their legation where they continued
to live under fairly lax surveillance. Later, when a representative
of Mussolini's new "Republican Government" arrived in Bucharest
and sought to present his credentials to King Mihai, he was put
off indefinitely by a long and lingering "diplomatic illness." Meanwhile, with the King's consent, Romanian Elder Statesman Prince
Barbu Stirbey, one-time favorite of Queen Marie, was sent to the
Middle East to contact the Allies.

Red Army Intelligence had duly read the falling barometer of
morale and the rising anti-German mood among the Romanian
war prisoners captured at various stages of the fighting in the
South. The Soviets also kept track of events in Bucharest through
their Balkan listening post—the Soviet Legation at Sofia, Bulgaria.
Their information added up to the conclusion that Romania was
the weakest link in the Axis chain, and that it could in due course
be broken by diplomatic rather than military pressure. The first
move was to let it be known that the Soviet Union, while intent
on recovering Bessarabia and Northern Bukovina (no news to the
Romanians), would see to it that Hitler's Vienna dictate awarding
Northern Transylvania to Hungary was annulled, and that the Red
Army was ready to assist the Romanian Army recover the province
from the Hungarians and Nazis. This was shrewdly calculated
to win the ear and support of Romanians regardless of their

politics, and to build a fire under any remaining sympathy for the Axis. The result, in the early spring of 1944, was a tremendous increase in Romanian desertions to the Soviet side. They now came over in whole regiments. The Germans, hard-pressed in the southwestern Ukraine, had to take over the entire front. They could no longer rely on their "Allies."

At the end of March, troops of Marshal Malinovsky's Second Ukrainian Army, having thrust across northern Bessarabia, reached and crossed the Prut River. Romania thus became the first Axis partner and first foreign state to be invaded by the Red Army.

Naturally, the hopes and fears of much of the world were centered on that Soviet-occupied, remote corner of Romania as a test of how Russian troops would behave on foreign soil.

Much of the distrust of the Soviet Union in Western countries could be traced to the fear that when the Red Army advanced beyond the borders of the Soviet Union it would seek to overthrow the existing social order and set up a Soviet system. There was a time—not so long ago—when forecasts as to Russian intentions could be divided into two schools of thought. According to one school, once the Russians completed the liberation of their own territory, they would call a halt and negotiate a separate peace with Germany, leaving the rest of us either to follow suit or else to bear the burden of the war alone. The other school of thought contended that instead of halting at their frontiers, the Russians would keep right on going until they had overrun and communized the rest of Europe. Both schools agreed that whatever the Russians did, there was cause for alarm.

The first school had been disposed of by the course of events. But the adherents of the second school continued to frighten solid citizens with the specter of a Europe communized in the wake of the victorious Red Armies.

It was doubtless partly to answer these misgivings that Foreign Commissar Molotov, one evening at the end of March, called in the correspondents and read a written statement to the effect that the Red Army, in the course of military operations, had crossed the Prut River and entered Romanian territory. It went on to say that Russian troops had set foot on Romanian soil solely in the interests of the war, and that they would in no way interfere with the existing social relationships in Romania.

The outside world seemed much relieved by this declaration, but at the end of June the Soviet Government decided to back up its assurances with more tangible evidence. Accordingly, representatives of the Allied press were loaded into two planes for a seven-hour flight to the Bessarabian town of Balti, whence we were to proceed overland another 120 miles to the Romanian town of Botosani. The length of the journey served to measure how far the war had moved away from Moscow since the days when a front trip involved only a few hours' ride by car from the capital.

Cut off by the front from the rest of Romania, and isolated from any contact with the Soviet Union save through the military, the town of Botosani and the surrounding district provided excellent laboratory conditions for testing and demonstrating Soviet policy in occupied territory.

Botosani was a pleasant provincial town with a residential section of shaded streets lined by neat, modern, stucco villas, each set in a flower garden. There was little industry in the town—three or four flour mills, a leather goods factory, and a sugar refinery. Most of the well-to-do citizens were "engaged in commerce"—generally a polite Romanian name for speculation. Their object in life was to buy cheap and sell dear, and though they competed among themselves, they all combined against the peasants to keep the prices of food and other agricultural produce ridiculously low and the prices of manufactured goods absurdly high. Even before the retreating Germans had cleaned out the shops, a pair of shoes cost 25,000 lei, which meant that in order to buy one pair of shoes, a peasant had to sell six sheep. It was no wonder that practically all the peasants we saw were barefoot.

At the time of our visit, commerce was severely hampered by the fact that Botosani was cut off from its normal supply centers in Bucharest and Constanta, still in Axis hands. The Russians had other things to think about besides bringing goods from the Soviet Union to make up for this shortage, even though the local merchants besieged the Red Army Commandant with their voluble complaints. Another source of grievance on their part was the fact that the Red Army Commissary bought what it needed direct from the peasants, shortcircuiting the town middlemen.

With no goods available, the merchants and speculators turned to the black market in currency as the sole outlet for their initiative and enterprise. Here, at least, they had a wide opportunity. For there were three different kinds of paper money in circulation— regular Romanian leis, Red Army occupation leis, and Soviet rubles. The Russians had set an official exchange rate of ten Romanian leis to the occupation lei and ten occupation leis to the ruble. But the only time they attempted to enforce it was in paying for their purchases of foodstuffs for the Red Army. In practice, every shop-keeper set his own rate. There were no banks open; all the Romanian banks, together with their employees' and depositors' funds, had been evacuated. Hence currency transactions were carried on in the innumerable cafes on the town's main business street.

The method was for a certain group of operators to form a pool and then circulate rumors, for example, that the Russians had suffered a serious defeat near Lwow. As a result, the price of the ruble on the black market would come tumbling down; when it got low enough, the pool would promptly buy up rubles. Then they would launch another rumor to the effect that the Germans had sustained serious reverses near the East Prussian border, which would cause the price of the ruble to skyrocket. By such means, those in the know managed to amass paper fortunes in the course of a few weeks.

Though the inhabitants of Botosani speculated in lei and rubles for lack of more substantial values, they had a truly reverential attitude toward the American dollar. On the local black market, dollars were being quoted as high as four thousand lei and five hundred rubles each. On one occasion I went into a shop to buy a sheepskin cap I had seen in the window. When I asked the price, the shopkeeper went into a huddle with several of his friends. After several minutes' discussion in rapid Romanian, he emerged to ask me in what currency I wanted to pay for my purchase. When I explained I had nothing but rubles, his face fell perceptibly; he returned to the huddle, which this time retired to a back

room for major consultation. After five minutes the shopkeeper
came out to announce the cap would cost 350 rubles. This, I objected, was exorbitant—even at the diplomatic rate of exchange this
came to almost thirty dollars.

"Haven't you some dollars?" the shopkeeper asked pleadingly.

I shook my head.

"If you had dollars," he said mournfully, "I would let you have
it for sixty cents."

In normal times, Botosani had had a population of thirty thousand. But the Romanian authorities had done their best to persuade people that if they remained behind when the Romanian
and German troops retired, they would be butchered by the
Bolsheviks. Hence about eight thousand had been either forcibly
or voluntarily evacuated, including the entire local government
and most of the wealthier Romanians. But the town's sixteen thousand Jews had stayed behind in a body, preferring to take their
chances with the Bolsheviks. And during the ten days' interregnum,
between the departure of the last Axis troops and the arrival of
the first Red Army units, the Jewish community organization took
charge of the maintenance of law and order, forming for this purpose a Jewish police force to prevent looting of shops and houses
by deserters and stragglers from the army. But though the police
were predominantly Jewish, at least one of them was a former
member of the anti-Semitic Iron Guard. He told me he had become
disillusioned with Hitler and Antonescu after his two brothers
had been killed fighting for the Germans on the River Don.

On April 7, 1944, the day the Red Army entered the town, a
coalition of civic groups in which the Jewish community had the
decisive voice appointed a mayor to replace the incumbent who had
fled with the the other authorities. The honor fell to a local German or *Volksdeutcher*—a good Aryan by the name of Altberger.
He was eminently qualified for the job, his Jewish sponsors explained, because he had never been mixed up in politics in the past
and was well-known and liked by everybody. "He is a good boy,
they concluded—almost like a Jew." The truth of the matter was
that nobody was at all cetrain that the Germans had left for good
and that the Russians had come to stay. In picking a mayor, the

civic groups had consequently looked for someone who, in the event the Germans returned, would not be objectionable to them, thus lessening the danger of reprisals.

Altberger clearly filled the bill, not only because of his "pure Aryan" antecedents, but also because he had served for two years in the army, rising to the rank of sergeant driver in the Motor Transport Service. He had been mustered out in 1943 when the Romanian Government decided to demobilize a portion of those units which had seen two or more years of active fighting.

It was evident that the Soviet military authorities had no high opinion of "Hizzonner," nor did our interview with him convey the impression of great force or executive ability. But if the Jews of Botosani wanted a German mayor, so far as the Russians were concerned, they were welcome to him. They—the Russians—were sticking to the letter of Molotov's statement that the Red Army would keep hands off in Romanian affairs.

So punctilious were the Russians about not interfering in Romanian internal matters that they had refused to repeal the anti-Jewish laws on the grounds that only the Romanian Government in Bucharest had the authority to do this. Actually, of course, they were no longer observed. The Jews had re-entered their confiscated houses, and had taken possession of their business and other property. But a section of Jewish opinion was nevertheless indignant that their ownership could not yet be legally confirmed. One of the main topics of contention in this connection was the fate of landed estates that had been confiscated from Jews under the anti-Semitic laws. The Jewish community, in which the wealthier Jews had the leading voice, clamored for the return of these estates to the former Jewish owners, now that the Romanian incumbents had fled. But in the face of peasant opposition to such a restitution, the Soviet authorities had refused to support the claim. And the former Jewish estates, together with other estates which had been abandoned by their Romanian owners—in the Botosani district only two out of 152 big landowners had stayed behind—were being worked and managed by the peasants. This was the sole indication of economic change. And the Soviets declared that it had been necessitated by the flight of the landowners.

Sharp cleavages on economic lines were apparent inside the Jewish community, between the wealthy Jews and the Jewish poor. The wealthy Jews, intent on safeguarding their riches, lived in mortal fear of some move toward confiscation and sovietization. But they were careful to avoid all criticism of the Soviet military authorities in this connection. Instead, they accused the poorer Jews of being communistically inclined and of plotting to take advantage of the present situation in order to set up a soviet regime. The poor Jews, for their part, accused the wealthy Jews of duplicity, and denounced them for their previous collaboration with the pro-Axis Antonescu Government. Both factions seized every opportunity to buttonhole us and pour their grievances into our ears.

Actually, so far as we could discover, the local Communists appeared to be on their good behavior. And though the trade unions, abolished by Antonescu, had now come out from underground, their leaders, with whom we talked, insisted they were strictly economic and non-political in character.

The charge that leading members of the Jewish Community had collaborated with the Antonescu regime was true—it was the price of their survival. The Jewish Community had made a voluntary contribution of four million lei to Antonescu's war chest; they had also resorted, in typical Romanian fashion, to large-scale bribery of Romanian officials to lighten the burden of the anti-Semitic laws. The Romanian Jews had been far better off than their coreligionists in other Axis-dominated countries. For it was discovered early in the application of the anti-Semitic laws that to eliminate the Jews altogether from Romania's economic life was to invite chaos— there were simply not enough qualified non-Jews to replace them. This discovery had been the main reason for curbing the extremist Iron Guard, which in the fall of 1940 had precipitated an economic crisis by its terrorism against the Jews. Paradoxically it was the Germans, bent upon extracting Romania's full potential for their war needs, who demanded that the Iron Guard be checked. In the Nazi classification, Romanian Jewry was listed in the category of "useful Jews."

Thus it was that while the Jews of Poland, Lithuania, White Russia, and Bessarabia were being mercilessly and systematically slaughtered, their kinsmen in Romania enjoyed comparative immunity from the extreme forms of anti-Semitism.

Even those provisions of the anti-Jewish laws which prohibited a Jew from owning land or factories were circumvented in many instances by the simple expedient of taking a gentile into partnership and transferring the business to his name. The gentile served as a "front" while the Jew continued to run the business as before. Such had been the arrangement in the Botosani flour mills and other enterprises. Then when the German and Romanian armies retreated, the Romanian "owners" left with them and the Jews stayed on and continued business as usual.

The activities of the Jewish Community organization of Botosani were co-ordinated with those of all Romanian Jewry through the resident delegate of the Bucharest Jewish Community, which, as the leading Jewish body of the country, sent its representatives to all the provincial towns. Behind its official policy of collaboration with Antonescu, the Bucharest Community from time to time managed to do a little something to lighten the sufferings of Jews in other countries. Thus it obtained the repatriation of Romanian Jews deported to "Transnistria"—the name invented for that section of the Ukraine which Antonescu, with Hitler's consent, had annexed. It also managed to save from extermination several thousand Jewish orphans in the Ukraine, who were brought to Romania and farmed out in small batches to various local Jewish Communities for care. The Bucharest Jews also sent clothing to some of the concentration camps in Transnistria. All this was no more than a drop in the ocean of suffering, but it helped to save a few individual lives—and salve more consciences.

Such humanitarian gestures were far easier to make after the Stalingrad debacle, which had taken much of the starch out of Antonescu's self-assurance and made his underlings more receptive to bribery.

As the Germans were forced to yield in the Ukraine, and the front rolled ever closer, the Jews of Botosani lived in constant trepidation lest the Hitler hordes, reeling backward through Romania, vent their chagrin in savage pogroms. That they had reason to fear is shown by what happened in other communities of north-

ern Romania. Thus in Radauti the retreating Germans went
through the town like a swarm of locusts, plundering both the Romanian civilian and military stores, and setting fire to what they
couldn't carry away. In Radauti the Red Army had been welcomed
as deliverers.

In keeping with their professed intention of interfering as little
as possible in the conduct of local affairs, the Soviet Military Administration in the occupied areas of Romania was a model of
simplicity. The military commandants in the various cities we
visited were regular Army officers without any special training comparable to that received by the members of the AMG.

A rather harassed young man was Major Vladimir Chernyayev,
aged twenty-five. On him had fallen the distinction of serving as
commandant of Botosani, first sizable town on foreign soil to be
occupied by the Red Army. Prior to his entry into the Army in
1939, Chernyayev had driven a tractor on a collective farm near
his native town of Nikolayev in the Ukraine. Since then, he had
completed the rush, wartime course of the Frunze Military Academy (the Soviet West Point), and had served with frontline troops
up until his present appointment.

Chernyayev's chief complaint was that the local population
wouldn't leave him alone. He was constantly besieged by citizens'
committees with various grievances or proposals—right up to and
including helpful suggestions as to how the Red Army should
conduct its military operations for the capture of Jassy or some
other point. There was also a constant stream of callers anxious
to profess their loyalty and enthusiasm for the Allied cause and
to offer their services in some capacity.

Thus the Romanian recruiting officer who had previously been
in charge of recruiting soldiers for Antonescu's army to fight the
Russians was now eager to recruit Romanians for the Red Army.
He had been deeply hurt and disappointed when Chernyayev declined his services on the grounds that non-Soviet citizens were
not accepted in the Red Army.

Then there had been a deputation from a local colony of Russian
Old Believers, whose ancestors had immigrated to Romania at the
end of the seventeenth century to escape religious persecution.

They arrived in Chernyayev's office like an old painting come to life, with flowing beards and robes, speaking courtly and quaintly archaic Russian. The purpose of their visit was to assure the Soviet Commandant of their full support and loyalty as true Russians and to warn him against overmuch trust in the Jews or the Romanians, who, they said, were all tricky and double-faced.

Chernyayev's chief source of concern was the black market—not so much currency speculation, but speculation in commodities, which, if unchecked, might interfere with the job of obtaining food supplies for the Red Army. Accordingly he was trying to get the local administration to adopt some form of price control. But so far, all his suggestions and efforts in that direction had been politely but consistently sabotaged. He welcomed our presence, he said, because since our arrival people had been so intent on following us around that the black market had virtually suspended operations.

And indeed whenever we appeared on the streets, we were in imminent danger of being mobbed, not through hostility, but quite the reverse. For some time, it appeared, there had been rumors that an Allied military commission would visit Botosani, and to the local inhabitants we were that commission. It seemed that practically every Jew in Botosani either had relatives in the United States with whom he wished to communicate or else had himself planned to emigrate to America and had accordingly applied for a visa. A goodly number had, in fact, been to America at one time in their lives, and it was surprising how many people in this remote, provincial Romanian town had a smattering of English. Hence they were constantly trying to get a word with us, or slip us a letter or an address on a scrap of paper. One question they all asked: Would an American consular representative come to Botosani?

Perhaps the most extraordinary character among the people that buttonholed us was an old Irishwoman from County Cork. She had lived in Botosani these thairty years, she had. But from her brogue she might have left the "owd sod" yesterday. When I eventually succeeded in getting her story unsnarled from her loquacity, it appeared that she had worked all this time as housekeeper for a wealthy Romanian family. Before the Russians came, her employers had fled to Bucharest; but they had left her behind purposely to look after their property on the theory that as a British subject she would be in a good position to do so. Just at present she was convinced that all the Jews in Botosani and all the Russians were conspiring to rob her of the family furniture. While her eyes snapped from side to side like the crack of a whip and three long hairy moles on her chin danced to the tune of her speech, she told us with a straight face that the Germans had halted the Russian advance at the Seret River by the simple expedient of rolling out large barrels of wine and leaving them along the roadside. The Russians had stopped to drink up the wine and had become so drunk that they were in no condition to continue the offensive.

"Don't believe anything anybody else tells you," she added, "all the Jews are Bolsheviks at heart."

We asked her if during the German occupation she had ever been molested as a British subject. No, she replied, she had never actually been bothered, except that they had forbidden to permit her to nurse the wounded when she volunteered, even though she was a trained nurse.

"They refused," she added, "not because of my British passport, but because they discovered I was an Irish Jew." After that I gave her up.

Though the gentile Romanians were far less conspicuous in town than the Jews, those of them who had stayed behind seemed eager to be friendly and co-operative. It was astonishing how readily Romanian string orchestras—which not so long previously had been ready to fiddle the *Horst Wessel Lied* or some other Nazi gem at the drop of a hat—had mastered an extensive repertory of the latest Soviet songs. Wherever we went during our stay in Romania, we were overwhelmed with banquets, always accompanied by music. The orchestra would play "God Save the King" for the benefit of our British colleagues, and for us, "Yankee Doodle," which the Romanians believed was the American national anthem.

The one Romanian we met who did not fall all over himself in an attempt to demonstrate his friendliness was Vasile Lovinescu, mayor of the town of Dorohoi. A nationally known member of the Romanian bar, Lovinescu made a ponderous speech in which he stated that Romanians, though opposed to the English in the present war, had reason to respect them because Britain had first helped to free Romania from the Turks in 1829. Furthermore, their beloved Queen Marie had been of English blood, though, in the Mayor's words, her soul was Romanian. Beyond that, it was all too evident that beneath his suave exterior "Domnul Vasile" loathed the Russians and us, cursed with all his soul the vagrant destiny that had landed him in his present job, and wished he were in Bucharest in his comfortable town house. It was all, he intimated, the result of his wife's illness, which had prevented his departure in good time.

The other Romanians didn't behave in the least like citizens of an occupied enemy country. Nor did they exhibit the slightest remorse or embarrassment over the fact that their country had aligned itself with Hitler and furthered his war plans. They seemed to absolve themselves from all complicity on the grounds that it was a case of *force majeur*. And you wondered, looking into their smiling faces, which of them had previously taken enthusiastic part in the spoliation of the Ukraine. Even though at that time the rest of Romania was still on the Axis side, the conduct of these Soviet-occupied Romanians clearly foreshadowed the future political pole-vaulting which less than two months later would transform Romania overnight from foe to ally. The Russians, who until so lately had looked upon Romanians as only a shade different from Germans, were distinctly embarrassed by all this show of friendliness. But they, like the Red Army men who subsequently took Bucharest, had their political instructions. Only once did I find evidence that they had not forgotten the Romanian contribution to the sufferings of their own country. Neatly inlaid in white stones on the roadside by the Russian checkpost at the entrance to Botosani was the old slogan "Death to the Romanian Invader!"

RUSSIA WANTS GOOD NEIGHBORS

☆ ☆ ☆ ☆ ☆ ☆ ☆ ☆ ☆ ☆ ☆ ☆ ☆

THE FUTURE security of the Soviet Union's western frontiers has been the prime consideration of that country's policy toward her immediate European neighbors in the current war period. From the Soviet standpoint, the prerequisites of this security are: first, that these frontiers themselves shall meet strategic defense requirements; and second, that the neighboring country shall not become a center of anti-Soviet political intrigue and hence a springboard for a future attack on the Soviet Union.

To the achievement of their ends the Russians have used their military, diplomatic, and political means in close co-ordination. Thus when peace negotiations with the Finns had definitely broken down, the Red Army on the Karelian front, after a long lull, mounted an offensive that broke the main Finnish defense lines. This, by all logic, should have settled matters. But instead, the Finns signed a new pact with Ribbentrop and it was nearly two more months before they finally hearkened to the voice of reason. Yet when the time came, the Russians did not penalize the Finns heavily for the additional losses and inconvenience caused. The final terms were virtually the same as those proposed all the way back in February. This in itself was a powerful answer to those who had claimed that Finland was threatened with national extinction.

In the case of Poland, the Russians presented the terms upon which they would recognize the Polish Government-in-Exile, and clung to them. However, as the London Polish Government, against even the advice of Churchill, continued to stall, the Soviet Government, without closing the door to further negotiations with the London Poles, went ahead with alternative plans. The Union of Polish Patriots, formed in Moscow, merged with a section of the Polish Underground to form the Lublin Polish Committee, now functioning on Polish soil. This Committee supplied the foundation on which to build Polish political home support for the common struggle against the Germans, just as the Polish Army under General Berling supplied the nucleus for rallying military support. Both the composition and program of the Polish Committee, as well as the spirit and outlook of the Berling Army, were a cogent refutation of alleged Soviet plans to Bolshevize Poland— to make that country a "Seventeenth Soviet Republic," as the London Poles had darkly imputed.

The Russians were determined to retain the ethnic frontiers of which they had been deprived in 1920, solely because they were then too weak to defend them. Even back in September, 1939, when the Russians moved into Eastern Poland, the British Government, which then had no reason to feel kindly disposed toward Moscow, admitted that the Russians had simply moved up to the line which in 1920 had been offered them in the name of the League of Nations by Lord Curzon, the British Foreign Secretary. But while the Russians proposed the Curzon Line to the Polish Government-in-Exile as a basis for negotiating the boundary, they made it clear that they would be willing to make concessions.

Actually, the underlying reason for the failure of the London Poles and the Russians to reach an understanding has not been the boundary dispute; that is only the pretext. There is deep-rooted reciprocal suspicion. The London Polish Government was still dominated by elements fundamentally hostile to the Russians—including people who not so long ago dreamed of extending Poland's frontiers to the Dnieper. They continued to see their country's sole salvation in a conflict between the Western Powers and the Soviet Union, and they did their best to promote discord between the two groups.

Soviet opposition to the exiled London Polish Government is based precisely on the knowledge of the anti-Soviet complexion of many of its components, proof of which is not lacking.

The installation of an anti-Soviet government in Poland would be as fatal to the Soviet Union's future peace and security as the existence of an anti-American Government in either Mexico or Canada would be to the welfare of the United States. Suppose the Government in Mexico City were constantly agitating for the return of Texas and California to Mexico, on the grounds that they had formerly belonged to that country? A basic error we sometimes make is to use one set of standards in judging the policies of others, and then to employ an entirely new set in considering our own. Yet in the given instance the case for Russia is even more cogent. Time and time again through history, Russia has been devastated, her cities and fields laid waste, her people slaughtered, by invaders who always approached from the same direction—from the west, across the Polish plain. Beyond Poland lies Germany, and in the postwar years the major task in keeping the peace in Europe will be to prevent German rearmament. This Russia cannot do if an anti-Soviet Poland, who conceives of her foreign policy in terms of balancing between a hostile Russia and a hostile Germany, stands in the way. The Russians cannot forget that one of the chief stumbling-blocks in the unsuccessful Anglo-French-Soviet negotiations of 1939 was Poland's refusal to accept Soviet military aid in the event of a German attack.

The guiding principle of Russian diplomacy, now and in the postwar world, is security, freedom from the danger of again being attacked by Germany or some combination of powers. Therefore, while the Russians are determined to eliminate German militarism, they are equally opposed to any bloc or alliance of the small nations of Europe, including the Scandinavian and the Balkan, which might serve as a future source of anti-Soviet intrigue. The old fear of "capitalist encirclement" is still a powerful influence on Soviet foreign policy. The Russians well remember that in pre-Hitler Europe, France and its small Eastern allies—the countries of the *Cordon Sanitaire*—constituted the main threat to the Soviet Union. Hence the misgivings caused in Moscow by recent rumors, emanating from London, of a Western European Bloc.

In their quest for security, the Russians may be expected to participate in any world peace organization of the type contemplated at the Dumbarton Oaks Conference. But they have not forgotten the lessons of the League of Nations. They are somewhat distrustful of British Continental aims and uncertain of what America will do. Some Soviet observers are frankly uneasy lest America become the new focal point of an anti-Soviet world coalition, which the architects of Soviet foreign policy still consider a very real threat. They further realize that no American administration can commit its successors, and that regardless of the present trend in America toward international co-operation, American isolationism is by no means dead.

The Russians can never delude themselves into thinking they can escape from Europe and retire behind an ocean. What happens in the rest of that Continent, and particularly in the countries adjoining their frontiers, is of deep and immediate concern to them. The lives of their people and the safety of their cities are at stake.

Hence the Soviet Government, while welcoming and supporting plans for international peace machinery, may be expected to rely for security first and foremost on its own efforts. It feels that its size, geographical position, and vital interests entitle it to a voice in European affairs roughly commensurate with the role exercised by the United States in the New World.

The Russian version of a Good Neighbor Policy in Eastern Europe is exemplified by the relations that have existed for some time between the Soviets and Czechoslovakia. Never has the progressive and democratic Government of Dr. Eduard Benes regarded Soviet Russia as a "menace." On grounds of mutual interest it has worked consistently for cordial understanding with the mightiest power of Eastern Europe. Russia has fully reciprocated this friendliness and good faith. Up to the tragic day of Munich, the Soviet Union was fully prepared to carry out in concert with France its treaty obligations under the Soviet-Czech Mutual-Assistance Pact, negotiated when Dr. Benes came to Moscow in 1935. In December, 1943, Benes again visited the Soviet capital to conclude a revived and strengthened Soviet-Czech Treaty of Mutual Assistance and Friendship. This time the pact was sealed by the comradeship in arms of the Czechoslovakian Brigade and the Red Army.

The Russians would like nothing better than to conclude similar pacts with their other neighbors. Indeed, the Czech pact makes specific provision for Poland to join it on a tripartite basis, if she so desires. The Russians hope that their present alliance with Czechoslovakia will provide the nucleus for a comprehensive alliance of the states of Eastern and Southeastern Europe with each other and with the Soviet Union.

Such a close-knit defensive alliance would constitute the Soviet Union's diplomatic main line of defense. The Soviet concept differs fundamentally from the concept of the Baltic-Black Sea Bloc, to which exiled Polish diplomats still cling. Inasmuch as such a bloc would be completely detached from and opposed to Russia—a revival, in effect, of the old *Cordon Sanitaire* that followed the last war—the Soviets look upon it as a "natural" for any future anti-Soviet combination.

Soviet plans for Eastern Europe's future diplomatic organization are aided by the tradition of Russia as "Big Brother Ivan" among the South Slavs. Russian encouragement and support of Marshal Tito and the Partisans in Yugoslavia, and the Red Army's direct part in the liberation of Yugoslav territory, including Belgrade, provide a firm foundation for future diplomatic collaboration with the peoples of Yugoslavia—another instance of how Soviet military strategy and diplomacy go hand-in-hand.

In Bulgaria the deep-rooted pro-Russian feeling was strong enough even in the peak period of German ascendancy, to deter a pro-German Government from taking the final step of severing relations and declaring war on the Soviet Union. And now the Bulgarians are indebted to the Russians for helping them to break out of the Axis partnership and swing over to the Allied side with a minimum of humiliation and punishment.

Bulgaria, which was not at war with Russia, had sent a delegation to Cairo to negotiate armistice terms with the British and Americans. These negotiations dragged through the lattter part of the summer without getting anywhere. Then, early in September, the Red Army appeared on the Bulgarian border, having pushed through Roumania. Russia declared war on Bulgaria; the venue of the armistice negotiations abruptly shifted to Moscow, and within ninety-seven hours the armistice had been signed and Bulgaria had meanwhile declared war on Germany. Once again, the Russians had used warfare and diplomacy in skillful combination.

While in all the countries which the Red Armies have entered the Russians have been uncompromising toward pro-Axis elements, they have not shown any particular favor toward the local Communists. Rather, they have everywhere urged the broadest unity of all anti-fascist elements, including the monarchists. Thus in Romania, with their troops everywhere, the Russians have been quite content to leave the conduct of civil affairs to governments serving under young King Mihai.

Of all the Balkan states, the Russians love Hungary the least. They regard that country, with its feudal agrarian economy, as the main bastion of political and economic reaction in Southeastern Europe. The Hungarians lent both their moral and physical support to the Nazi attack on Russia; and, according to the Commission to Investigate Nazi Atrocities, on several occasions the Hungarian troops excelled the Germans in perpetrating crimes against civilian populations. Also, Hungary was the last to break with Hitler. Hence the readiness with which the Russians agreed to restore Transylvania to the Romanians.

Though Soviet foreign policy looks on Eastern Europe as its special sphere, the Russians watch events in every European country, with unrelaxed vigilance, for signs of any survival or revival of fascism. They are on the alert lest, defeated on the battlefield, the fascists live to fight another day under some protective coloring. Before Teheran they were constantly suspecting Britain and America of planning to compromise with pro-fascist elements in various countries. Such was the interpretation placed by them upon the dealings with Admiral Darlan and Marcel Peyrouton in the initial stages of the North African campaign. Later they were on the lookout for similar tendencies in Italy. The frank talks at Teheran did much to clear the atmosphere of suspicion, though the Cairo rumor story, previously discussed, was proof that uneasiness persisted.

Today the Russians feel largely reassured about the political situation in most countries. In the Balkans they have clearly carried the day against all plans for rightist restorations. Even Churchill, with his tenderness for kings, has been forced to abandon whatever plans he might have had for foisting King George of the Helles onto an unwilling people. The fate of King Peter of Yugoslavia is likewise in doubt. In Bulgaria the regent and the Child-King Semyon fled the country. In Italy, France, and Belgium the trend is strongly toward democracy. In Spain, however, the Fascist puppet Franco, apparently having patrons in high Allied circles, is making frantic efforts to maintain himself in power.

In the interests of Allied amity, the Russians expurgated from their lengthy published résumés of Churchill speeches passages that were likely to jar the ears of Soviet readers. This was notably the case with the Prime Minister's friendly references to the Caudillo. But the passages in question were doubtless read with care—and possibly raised eyebrows—by Kremlin leaders.

Russia and France, the two countries most directly menaced by German militarism, are inevitably drawn together for mutual protection. The Russians cannot forget that if French demands had not been overruled at the close of the last war, the present war might have been prevented. The French see in Russia's land might the one force capable of holding Germany in check.

Hence the same logic of necessity which brought about the Franco-Russian entente before the first World War, and the Franco-Soviet Pact of 1935 when the German threat again became acute as a result of Nazism, is operating today. In retrospect many Frenchmen ascribe the fact that France was overrun to failure to make the alliance with Russia an effective instrument. Had Russia come in on France's side in 1939, they argue, France would never have fallen. But after Munich and the disappearance of Czechoslovakia, the Franco-Soviet Pact lapsed. And many Frenchmen place the blame squarely on their own politicians and diplomats, whom they accuse of subordinating French interests and policy to Whitehall. That was why, when reports of a Western European Bloc, apparently encouraged from London, caused uneasiness in Moscow, the French Foreign Minister publicly declared that France was unalterably opposed to any alliance that did not include Eastern Europe. His terminology suggests that he had Czechoslovakia in mind as well as the Soviet Union, in which case Czechoslovakia is again destined to play the role of bridge between her Western and Eastern Allies. But with no more Munichs.

NAZISM DELENDA EST

☆ ☆ ☆ ☆ ☆ ☆ ☆ ☆ ☆ ☆ ☆ ☆ ☆

ALTHOUGH in November, 1941, the Germans advanced within sight of Moscow, most of the city's civilian population had never seen a German soldier. Hence one morning in mid-July, 1944, there was considerable excitement when the word spread that sixty thousand German war prisoners, a brace of Generals in the lead, would be marched around the outer boulevard ring. Hours ahead of time, throngs congregated along the line of march—even in a war-busy city like Moscow, it was amazing how many people could find the spare time. By the noon hour, when all approaches to the boulevard had been cordoned off to traffic, the sidewalks on either side of the broad smooth asphalt were packed with eager humanity, shoving and pushing as only a Moscow crowd can. Then down the center came the long, gray column, with some twenty nattily-uniformed Nazi Generals in the lead. It was a strange, grotesque parody of that victory march through Moscow which Hitler had promised and which didn't quite come off. Down either side rode Soviet guards, keeping the prisoners in line.

The people watched in stony silence—not a hiss, not a boo, not a single outburst of emotion. I too watched, and I wondered how an American crowd, a British or a French crowd, would have behaved under similar circumstances. The sole expression of feeling which I saw was from a little old woman. Too small and frail to elbow through the tight-packed throng to where she might glimpse the Germans, she appealed to a policeman for help.

"*Tovarisch* militiaman," she said timidly, "I've had three sons killed by the Germans. I'd like to see what a German soldier looks like."

With the policeman gallantly acting as interference, the old lady got into a frontline position. For a couple of minutes she

watched the gray serpent crawl past; then spitting emphatically—
a typical Russian peasant gesture of disgust—she exclaimed:
"*Tepiehr mnieh hvahteet* (I've had enough)," and made her
way out of the line.

Close on the heels of the last Nazi column came the City Street-
cleaning Department in full force. Sprinkler trucks wetted down
the pavement and then the huge rotary brushes scrubbed it. Suddenly the tense silence broke. A great wave of laughter surged over
the massed thousands.

A Russian friend with whom I compared notes told me he had
seen several women weep. They had felt sorry for those poor Germans! One of the most common observations among the Muscovites who had witnessed the parade was: "How young and husky
the Germans looked!" They inferred that maybe the enemy, even
after his tremendous losses, wasn't so short of men as they had
believed.

But the remarkable thing about all the comment and reaction
was the lack of personal animosity against the Germans. There
are reports that during the severe period of the famine in Leningrad it was dangerous to lead prisoners through that city, but that
was only when people had been driven to extremes of desperation.
Though much bitterness and hatred had been engendered by the
war, it was directed primarily against Hitler and the Nazis—not
the German rank-and-file. Doubtless the crowd that had watched
the sixty thousand prisoners so impassively would have been ready
to tear the Feuhrer limb from limb had he been led in chains
through Moscow. But in the eyes of many Russians the individual
German soldier was still an object of pity.

When with a group of correspondents I visited Minsk three days
after the Germans had been driven out, I observed much the same
attitude toward the German prisoners on the part of the Russian
soldiers. Several German divisions had been cut off in the woods
south of the town, and though the front had advanced many miles
westward, the Russians were locally engaged in mopping-up operations. Thousands of Germans were either surrendering or being
captured and routed through the town and back along the broad,
straight Minsk-Moscow highway. They would march many miles

before they reached a railhead, where they would be loaded into boxcars for shipment to prison camps. Some of the prisoners had made abortive attempts to disguise themselves as civilians, so their attire was often a strange conglomeration of odd bits of military and civilian clothing. As usual, our group of correspondents was an outlandish sartorial mixture of military and civilian items. Therefore it was no wonder that one morning, while we were waiting on a street corner to be taken somewhere, a Red Army cavalryman cantering past mistook us for a batch of German prisoners.

"Why didn't you give yourselves up long ago?" he yelled at us. "Don't you realize Hitler's *kaputt?*"

But the remark was made good-naturedly, without venom— merely as a friendly remonstrance or piece of advice.

Later we had our own turn at capturing German prisoners. Under protest, our conducting officer had finally agreed to take some of us down to the area where the German remnants were being liquidated. We were duly warned to be ready to take cover in the ditch if we ran into any sniping.

Riding in jeeps, we turned south from the town onto another broad highway, littered with the fresh evidence of fighting. (Early that same morning a desperate group of Nazis had reached the outskirts of Minsk under the mistaken impression that the town was still in German hands, and now they lay just where a machine gun and mortars had mown them down—on the approaches to the Jewish Cemetery.) Presently, we turned off the highway toward a forest from which the booming of artillery alternated with the chatter of machine guns. The way was strewn with German corpses. Sometimes the boots were missing, while near-by a pair of tattered Russian shoes told an eloquent story. Once our jeeps were forced off the road by a huge overturned German wagon and the bodies of its two giant dray horses. Sprawled in the dust were two German soldiers. Another lay just off the road, at the edge of a field. It was evident that he had been clipped in the act of running away; even in death his whole posture expressed swift movement.

Less than a hundred yards farther on, we came to the first house of a small village, built flush with the road in typical White

Russian fashion. A young girl watched us through the window and two small children played on the front stoop while an ancient shawled crone puttered in the little vegetable garden. They seemed oblivious of the slaughter under their very eyes. Thus had these ordinary peasant folk become inured to war.

Meanwhile, the shooting in front of us seemed to have receded, so we headed into the deserted, spooky silence of the woods. Suddenly, through the trees ahead of us we glimpsed three Germans. They were waving white handkerchiefs and apparently were anxious to surrender. Speeding up, we proceeded to capture them, somewhat to the surprise of a near-by Red Army patrol which had also seen them.

We soon discovered that only one of our three prisoners was a bona fide German. One was a Czech, the other an Alsatian. They told us that two days previously their battalion had been ordered to split up into small groups and to try and make their way as best they could through the Russian lines to Minsk, which was still believed to be in German hands. After getting lost in the woods, they had run out of water and food and had been searching frantically for someone to surrender to. They were delighted to meet us.

We handed over our catch to the colonel of the Red Army patrol that had been sent to clean out this section of the woods. He told us the command estimated that some two thousand Germans were still hiding in the area. In fact, they had come near mistaking us for Germans—which would have made the second time in one day. He then proceeded through an interpreter to direct our prisoners where to go and report. They were given water and some biscuit and were told to proceed toward the rear unescorted. Later we passed many such groups of prisoners traveling on their own. Some of them were even mounted on horseback, for the woods were also full of German horses. We passed one Red Army mobile kitchen whose driver was cursing a stolid, husky-looking mare, hitched to the traces.

"I can't make her understand what I want," he explained to us with a grin. "I can't speak German and she doesn't know Russian."

Many of the German prisoners had not yet recovered from their tremendous astonishment at still being alive. Their own propaganda had given them scant expectation of surviving capture. Even now they half-expected that presently they would be led off somewhere and lined up against a stone wall.

Actually, though the Soviet Union is not a signatory to the Geneva Convention on war prisoners, it abides by its rules. Captive Germans have been getting the same rations as Red Army men of equivalent rank. This is in marked contrast to the lot of Russian prisoners in German hands.

While the Russians treat their prisoners humanely, as long ago as the victory at Stalingrad—which gave them their first big haul of a quarter of a million captured Germans—the Soviet authorities decided that since prisoners had to be fed, they might as well be usefully employed. Then and there they were put to work clearing the rubble of towns and cities they had destroyed. It is part of the Russian plan for Germany that after the peace, Germans, besides paying reparations, shall help to rebuild what Nazi fury destroyed in Russia, Poland, Britain, and practically every European country that suffered in the war.

But labor is only one part of the Russian program for their German prisoners. This great, gray mass, whose numbers now exceed the million mark, provides the backdrop for the activities of the Moscow-sponsored Free-German Committee and the Union of German Officers.

In the Soviet Union there is no ban on the circulation of anti-Nazi literature and propaganda among German prisoners. All such activity is under the auspices of the Free-German Committee, which directs its efforts toward weaning the rank-and-file Germans away from Nazism and its inhuman creeds. Thus the work of re-educating the German people, which the post-war planners talk about, is already under way in Soviet Russia.

Actually, the Free-German Committee embraces Germans of widely differing ideologies, ranging from Communists to generals who revere the traditions of Bismarck.

There are in the Soviet Union today several thousand German political refugees of the left who fled the Reich in the years between 1933 and Hitler's attack. Some, but not all, are Communists. They include men of achievement and prominence, such as the author Friedrich Wolff and the former Reichstag deputy Wilhelm Pieck. During the purge years of 1937-38, it was discovered that the Nazi Government had been sending spies and diversionists into Russia in the guise of political refugees. Accordingly, at that time there was a careful sifting; but many of those who were arrested have been exonerated since the war. It is a tribute to the Russians' sense of balance that little of the anti-German animus aroused by the war and the Nazi atrocities has been directed against these refugees. They have been accorded throughout the consideration to which they are entitled under Article 129 of the Soviet Constitution which says: "The USSR affords the right of asylum to foreign citizens persecuted for defending the interests of the working people or for their scientific activity or for their struggle for national liberation." Today they continue to live in Moscow unmolested.

In the black days of October, 1941, many of them were evacuated to the East along with the Russian population, but practically all have since returned. They preserve their old political affiliations, including membership in the German Communist Party. In the formation of the Free German Committee they have been joined by a sizable contingent of captured German officers, headed by General Walter von Seydlitz, former Chief of Staff of the Sixth German Army, who surrendered together with Marshal von Paulus at Stalingrad. These German officers, who maintain their own separate organization, the Union of German Officers, are in general strongly nationalistic but anti-Hitler. They take their text from Bismarck's insistence, ignored by his successors, that Germany and Russia were natural Allies.

The publications of the Free-Germany Committee—the weekly *Freies Deutschland* and a constant stream of pamphlets on a variety of military and political subjects—emphasize opposition to Nazism and advocate German-Russian friendship—the two main points on which all the members of the Free-Germany Committee can agree. But the colors on the *Frei Deutschland* masthead are the old Imperial, red, white, and black.

While it is not yet clear what part will be assigned to the Free-Germany Committee after Hitler's defeat, already it has become an important factor in shaping the future. The caliber, background, and connections of many of its members vouchsafe them an audience and a following inside the Reich. The eventual release and repatriation of half a million German war prisoners, who for long months have been exposed to a steady barrage of anti-Nazi and pro-Russian propaganda, should also have some results.

In this connection it is worth recalling that right up until Hitler's seizure of power in 1933, the German Communist and Social-Democratic Parties swung six million and seven million votes respectively. Though in the intervening Nazi years these groups have been submerged, once Hitler has been overthrown, the parties of the left are almost certain to recover some of their old following and influence. No doubt the Russians are weighing these elements in their plans for postwar Germany.

Though the Russians are committed to the transfer of considerable slices of German territory to Poland as compensation for Russia's retention of the lands east of the River Bug, it is unlikely that they would favor any further drastic breakdown of Germany's territorial integrity. While the Russians will seek to educate the German masses rather than wreak vengeance on them, on some points they will brook no leniency or compromise. They will demand the punishment of every last German whose name appears on their extensive lists of war criminals. And in determining just what constitutes a war criminal, they are not likely to err on the side of liberalism. Their list will include all members of the *Wehrmacht* implicated in the commission of atrocities against civilian populations or in the operation of Nazi extermination camps; it will include the entire roster of the Gestapo, the SS, the Nazi Party, and all those who aided and abetted Hitlerism politically and economically—a very sizable slice, indeed. For some of these—including all top Nazi leaders taken alive, beginning with Hitler himself, and all others involved in the planning and perpetration of the Nazis' crimes—the Russians will demand the supreme penalty. The others will most likely be put into the labor gangs.

Nazism, the Russians insist, must thus be destroyed root and branch. Any milder policy would enable the beast to hibernate in some dark Underground. In the advocacy of this program, the

Russians anticipate opposition from the West. Not so much from Britain, where buzz-bombs and rocket bombs have steeled public opinion, but from the United States, where various pacifist groups and even a member of the U.S. Senate have raised their voices on behalf of mildness for defeated Germany. But the Russians are fully confident their program will have the wholehearted endorsement of the nations of liberated Europe who themselves suffered so much and so long under the Nazi jack boot.

THE ITALIANS STAGE A
COMEBACK

☆ ☆ ☆ ☆ ☆ ☆ ☆ ☆ ☆ ☆ ☆ ☆

THE Soviets had numerous irons in Europe's diplomatic fires. One frosty evening back in February I recall having dinner with Arnold and Eve Smith, a refreshing Canadian couple, old friends of mine from Cairo days. After dinner a British Embassy secretary was talking rather aimlessly: "We had a caller the other day, an Italian gentleman by the name of Ercoli, only that isn't his real name. He asked us to help him gets visas and transportation back to Italy. We're waiting now for word from London. . . ."

Thus did I discover that the Italian Communist leader, Secretary General of the Comintern before Dimitrov took over in 1935, was making plans to return to his native land after more than two decades of exile in Russia. When he got home, he dropped his pseudonym of Ercoli and resumed his own name of Palmiro Togliatti, to which he presently added the title of Minister without Portfolio.

Presumably Ercoli-Togliatti, like other former Comintern officials, had been out of a job ever since June, 1943, when he among others had affixed his signature to the document dissolving that organization. Certainly a return to political life even in war-lacerated Italy was more pleasant than rusting in Moscow.

Ercoli's departure for Italy was no isolated phenomenon. The Russians were beginning to evince a lively interest in Italian political developments. Ever eagle-eyed for indications of compromise with fascism, they did not consider the Allies were pressing sufficiently for the unification of the democratic and anti-fascist forces within the country. Vice-Commissar Andrei Vyshinsky, who had toured Italy as Soviet member of the Allied Mediterranean board, had come home with misgivings. Editorial comment to this effect was followed by the announcement that Moscow had established relations with the Badoglio Government. Meanwhile Ercoli, by now definitely Togliatti, was doing his best for unification.

The news that the Soviet Union had recognized the Badoglio Government brought forth the comment from the new Ethiopian Minister that his Government still considered Badoglio—who had directed Italian operations in the war of conquest of Ethiopia when the Fascists used bombs and poison gas on defenseless native villages—war criminal Number One.

The excitement over Soviet recognition of Badoglio had subsided by May, when one morning the press announced the arrival of the Italian envoy, Signor Pietro Quaroni, and his wife. Eddy Gilmore and I hastened together to call on the couple. We found the Quaronis ensconced in two small connecting rooms of the Hotel National, surrounded by piles of trunks and suitcases and two water spaniels. Signor Quaroni was a debonair diplomat of the pre-Fascist school. He spoke fluent English, learned as a captain in the army at the close of the last World War, when he had served as one of General Pershing's Allied aides. He also spoke presentable Russian, which he had acquired as Italian chargé d'affaires in Moscow during the late twenties. His acquisition of Signora Quaroni dated from the same period. She was a Russian, a large, statuesque woman with the label *buyushee* (literally "has-been," used in modern Russia to designate members of the former wealthy classes) practically emblazoned on her forehead. A native Muscovite, she was quite excited to be back, and she spent the next several weeks airing her dogs and her fox furs up and down the little byways that lead off the widened Gorky Street. She was "quite disappointed," she said, at how run-down everything looked, but nodded her comprehension when I explained that there was a war on.

Nevertheless to the Quaronis Moscow, even in wartime, was still a modern European metropolis. For the past seven years they had been tucked away in Kabul, capital of Afghanistan, where, from 1941, to Italy's surrender, as representatives of an Axis power, they had been completely cut off from the outside world.

Two days after their arrival the Afghan Minister in Moscow was

holding his annual reception in honor of some national holiday or birthday. Since Afghanistan was neutral, the Minister invited the Japs and the Bulgarians as well. But to avoid embarrassment, he ran the party in two shifts. The Japs and the Bulgarians came first and left very early—even before the Norwegian Minister, an inveterate party-goer, turned up.

The Quaronis came with the other Allied diplomats. It was their first appearance at a diplomatic function in some years, and they were enjoying themselves thoroughly. Signora Quaroni, a head taller than her husband, sailed majestically from room to room through buzzing seas of diplomats and Soviet Foreign Office officials, partaking of the lavish refreshments. Since Eddy and I were among the few people who knew the Quaronis, we introduced them right and left and watched the reaction. Signora Quaroni treated every new acquaintance like an old friend. Once I overheard her—the Signora's voice matched her looks—asking a group, "Can any of you tell me something about this man Badoglio we're representing? We've been away from Italy so long. . . ."

The Signora was an instant success with Major General Burrows, head of the British Military Mission, and with several junior British diplomats. But while she was talking to a cluster of these sons of Albion, I noticed Jock Balfour, the British Minister (as distinguished from Sir Archibald Clark-Kerr, the Ambassador), standing cross-legged in a corner and glaring his disapproval. Apparently it wasn't quite protocol to be sociable with the Quaronis when no instructions on the subject had yet come through from Whitehall.

While the Signora was deep in converastion with Alexei Tolstoi one of our lady corerspondents, her lack of sex appeal strikingl set off by a rather vivid tea gown, barged in with a request Tolstoi for material on atrocities for an article she wanted to wri Tolstoi, patient and kind as ever, told her to call up his secret in the morning and that he would himself instruct the secre beforehand. As the female newshound withdrew, Signora Qua turned to me in her booming voice and asked, "Who is atrocity?"

Despite Jock Balfour feeling a bit sticky over protocol, the

diplomats were ready to welcome these new additions to their colony. After all, wasn't Italy a co-belligerent now? Ambassador Harriman invited them to come to the next movie at Spasso House, and the general consensus was that the Quaronis would be a distinct addition to the gaiety of nations. There was one exception. The little Ethiopian Minister darted one fiery look at the couple, then called for his hat and coat. But his defection passed almost unnoticed.

A curious bit of diplomatic contratemps was caused by the fact that when Italy, following Germany's suit, broke off relations and declared war on the Soviet Union in June, 1941, the Japanese took charge of Italian interests in Moscow. Hence when Quaroni arrived, he found the Japanese Embassy had the Italian files and the keys to the Italian Embassy—one of the most palatial in Moscow. The Japs recognized, not the Badoglio Government, but the fascist "Republican Government" which Mussolini had set up in northern Italy in the shadow of the Brenner. Hence they at first refused to hand over anything. Only quiet but effective intervention by the *Narkomindel* broke the deadlock by breaking the lock.

WAR IN EASTERN ASIA?

☆ ☆ ☆ ☆ ☆ ☆ ☆ ☆ ☆ ☆ ☆ ☆

THE Hotel Metropole night was shattered around two o'clock one morning last mid-June by blood-curdling shrieks of "Help! Help! He's murdering me!" The voice was a woman's and the language Russian. Roused by the noise, a motley posse of hotel guests in every conceivable style of negligee attire, from women in paper curls and pajamas to bald men in long-tailed nightshirts, congregated in the hallway outside the locked door whence came the screaming. From time to time the continued shrieks were interrupted by the crash of some heavy object and the tinkle of glass. The room was identified as being that occupied by the Jap chauffeur of the Jap military attaché. Jack Margolis, Soviet-naturalized, Cockney-born hotel manager was on deck, obviously distressed by the scandal.

When Margolis and others pounded on the door, demanding that it be opened, there was no response. By this time the shrieking had subsided to hysterical sobbing and moaning. The apparent impasse was solved when someone remembered that the chauffeur's master lived at the far end of the same hall. In due course a young Jap in a swanky silk kimono swished up to the door and barked something in Japanese which worked like "Open sesame!" The door was flung wide upon a scene of destruction fearful to behold. A big full-length mirror had crashed off the wall in a thousand fragments. Tables, chairs, and a couch were overturned helter-skelter amid a chaos of broken bottles, dishes, and glasses. In a far corner next to the window a woman was huddled; another lay prostrate on the floor amid the litter of broken crockery; while in the middle of the room stood the Jap chauffeur, brandishing a carving knife.

The first of the audience to recover his speech was Jack, but all he could think of to say was *"Eto prawsta nyeh-hawrawshaw,"* the

257

nearest English equivalent of which would be "That just isn't nice"—an example of the British genius for understatement.

Everyone fully expected that following this incident the chauffeur would either commit hara-kiri, or, failing that, be shipped home in disgrace. Apparently, however, his superiors decided he was just having a bit of good, clean Japanese fun, and so forgave him. To the Russians they offered the face-saving explanation that the women had tried to rob the chauffeur, who had acted in self-defense. As nobody had been injured, the incident was considered closed when the Japs agreed to pay fifteen thousand rubles to cover the damage to the furnishings. But the story got around, and it did not improve the general standing of the Japs.

Actually there was scant sympathy wasted on Japs either by Muscovites or anyone else in the Soviet Union. Anti-Japanese sentiment was especially strong in the Red Army, many of whose top leaders—like Marshals Konyev and Zhukov—had won their spurs in border warfare with the Japs. And whenever I had occasion to be with Red Army officers, they invariably referred to the Far Eastern War without any prompting on my part, and expressed their fervent wishes for a Japanese defeat. Some even went so far as to suggest that the Soviet Union would presently also take a hand.

In America probably more explosive and irresponsible nonsense has been talked about Russia's Far Eastern neutrality than about any other phase of Soviet world policy. This talk has ranged up to and included demands that the Soviet Union either enter the war against Japan immediately or else provide the United States with air bases in the Far East—which would amount to the same thing. These demands were voiced long before the Allied invasion of Western Europe, at a time when Russia was still fighting the brunt of the Axis land forces singlehanded. Russian Far Eastern neutrality has been deliberately exploited by anti-Soviet propagandists.

To be fair, any examination of current Soviet-Japanese relations must go back to the summer of 1938. At that time, when the Western Powers were still helping the Japanese build up reserves of gasoline and scrap iron, the Soviet Union was the first country to call the Japs' bluff. In a three-day battle on the Manchurian-Soviet border the Russians administered to the Japanese their first major military setback since the Mukden Incident inaugurated the Tokyo policy of aggression.

Even after this reverse, Japan kept testing Russia's strength, and for the next year there were minor and major frontier incidents almost monthly. All of this prompted seasoned observers of Far Eastern affairs to talk of an undeclared Russo-Japanese war.

Balked on the Soviet-Manchurian border, in the summer of 1939 the Japanese launched a full-scale invasion of the Mongolian Peoples' Republic, which is closely allied with the Soviet Union.

The result was the Halkingol campaign, with tanks, planes, and all the implements of modern war engaged on both sides. Again the Japanese were worsted, but the Russo-Japanese undeclared war continued to provide future commanders of the Red Army with proving grounds well into 1940.

At the time of the Pearl Harbor attack in December, 1941, Japan was deterred from attacking Russia, too, by recollection of its previous embarrassments, plus the knowledge that the Far Eastern Red Army was still on the job. Also, the Japanese were waiting for Moscow to fall, as Hitler had assured them it would.

The continued presence of that Far Eastern Red Army has kept a goodly portion of Japanese land forces riveted to the Manchurian-Soviet frontier ever since, rendering substantial help to the Allies, whose Governments were keenly conscious that Russia was bearing the full brunt of the German Armies in Europe at the time and scarcely could be expected to do more.

Russo-Japanese relations during the past two years may be best described as frigidly correct. While each country has fervently desired the other's defeat, both have also felt they had their hands full already without an additional front. But contact was reduced to a minimum. The Japanese diplomats in Moscow lived completely isolated. The only other members of the diplomatic colony they could talk to were the Swedes, the Turks, and the Bulgars, and now they are left with only the Swedes.

Early last spring the Russians terminated the Japanese oil and coal concessions on Northern Sakhalin twenty-six years ahead of time and compelled the Japanese to clear out at short notice. Likewise, when time came for the renewal of the Japanese fishing concessions, traditionally the subject of long diplomatic haggling, the Russians simply announced their intention of excluding the Japanese from certain areas. And the Japanese, hard pressed in the Marshalls and Solomons, pocketed their loss of face with never a whimper.

The Soviet Union obviously has a stake in Japan's defeat fully as great as, if not greater than, that of Britain and the United States. Now that the continuity of Russian military tradition has been restored, there are the old affronts of the Russo-Japanese War of 1904-5 to be requited. Though the concessions on Northern Sakhalin have been summarily liquidated, the Japanese still hold the southern half of the Kurile Islands which, strung from the northernmost member of the Japanese Archipelago—Hokkaido—to the tip of Kamchatka, effectively seal the Russians off from access to the Pacific Ocean except through Japanese territorial waters. And the Japanese exercise the right of stopping and inspecting Soviet ships passing through these waters.

Then there is northern Manchuria. Russia was squeezed out of that long-standing zone of Russian influence by the Japanese in a series of maneuvers after efforts at a united stand against Japan had been frustrated by the appeasement policy of the British. Haunted by the threat of an anti-Soviet coalition in Western Europe, the Russians could not challenge the Japanese alone, and in 1935 they sold to Japan the Russian-built and Russian-owned Chinese Eastern Railway—the direct link with Vladivostok. Its loss made the strategic position of Vladivostok and the Far Eastern Maritime provinces extremely precarious in the event of war with Japan.

The issue of Russian security in case of a future Japanese attack is increased by Soviet knowledge that in the event of a Japanese victory in the present war, Russia is slated as the next target. Moscow is fully aware that the Tanaka blueprint of Japanese aggression calls for the inclusion of Siberia in the "Greater Asia Co-Prosperity Sphere." Such are the powerful factors favoring Russia's participation in the Far Eastern War against Japan.

But before the die is cast, there are several "if's" to be resolved—

political as well as military. The vast bulk of Japan's still undefeated and undepleted land army is on the Asiatic Continent—the most troublesome and fanatic part of it, the Kwantung Army, is just across the Amur River from Soviet territory, which it has long been training to attack. And while, as is pointed out by those who demand Soviet bases for American bombers, it is much closer from Vladivostok to Tokyo than from any fields from which American planes are now operating, yet from the Manchurian border, where the Japanese Army is massed, to Vladivostok is even shorter.

It is a grave mistake to imagine that recent American victories in the Pacific have in the least impaired the fighting qualities of these Japanese troops. Anyone who so imagines should be disabused by what happened near Kweilin in South China, where the United States Air Force was deprived of several bases.

As distinct from the United States with its ocean-girt remoteness from the battlegrounds, Russia's entry into the Far Eastern War means exposing yet another broad sector of its home territory and additional Soviet cities to devastation. Also, the fighting doubtless would be on a scale quite comparable to operations on the major European fronts, involving new heavy casualties for the Red Army.

Before undertaking such new commitments, Marshal Stalin doubtless would want to make certain that Russia's security requirements in Europe had been met, which means that the question of Russia's participation in the war against Japan is bound to be a strong Russian bargaining point in dealings with the other powers.

Indications that Soviet Far Eastern policy may be approaching a major turning point were contained in Stalin's speech on the anniversary of the Revolution, November 7, 1944, when he directly classified Japan as an aggressor along with Nazi Germany.

This in itself was not new. Signed articles appearing in leading Soviet publications had in the past referred to Japan in almost identical terms. Of course, the names signed to those articles formally absolved the Soviet Government from any official responsibility for the views expressed, even though the world at large, including the Japanese, could draw their own conclusions.

In Soviet policy it isn't always what is said that carries decisive weight, but who says it. When Stalin says something publicly for all the world to hear, he does so in his three-fold capacity of Premier of the Soviet Government, General Secretary of the ruling Communist Party, and Commander-in-Chief of the Red Army. His words are weighted with the concentrated might of the entire Soviet nation. It is not surprising, therefore, that Stalin never ad libs. Deeply conscious of his immense authority and the responsibility that goes with it, he saves his utterances for moments of supreme historic decision, when they are figuratively handed down on tablets of stone. Hence the excitement his references caused in Tokyo. But while this Stalin speech may well prove a turning point, until the die is cast it is impossible to venture any final prediction, or to count one's airbases before they hatch. Meanwhile, though American bases in the Soviet Far East were still in the realm of speculation, American airbases at the other end of Russia became a reality. And this our Air Force Generals considered half the battle. To these air-minded warriors, from Poltava in the Ukraine to Vladivostok is only a day's run in a Super Fortress

AMERICAN AIR BASES

☆ ☆ ☆ ☆ ☆ ☆ ☆ ☆ ☆ ☆ ☆ ☆

THREE days before "D" Day the world was informed that the first flight of American heavy bombers had landed at bases of the Eastern Command of the U.S. Army Air Force "somewhere in the USSR."

The story of these bases went back to October, 1943—to the time of the Moscow Conference between Hull, Eden, and Molotov. It was then that Averell Harriman also arrived in the Soviet capital to assume his ambassadorial duties. In his party was a quiet, pleasant-spoken Army officer—Major General John Russell Deane. Deane was the new head of the United States Military Mission to the Soviet Union, succeeding Brigadier General Philip Faymonville, the War Department's long-standing Number One expert on Russian affairs, who had been recalled under mysterious circumstances. It was no easy assignment for Deane. For everyone, including the Russian military men with whom he came in contact, would be mentally measuring and comparing him with the popular Phil. Also, some of his subordinates in the Mission were hold-overs from the Faymonville regime—men whom Faymonville had raised from N.C.O.'s to the rank of major or better. These officers were naturally devoted to their former chief and were likely to resent his successor as an intruder.

But Deane took everything, including the latent opposition, in his quiet, friendly, unassuming stride. Quite early in the game it became noised about that he and the Ambassador were out for some particularly big game. Harriman himself was forever saying—as a justification for turning down sundry requests for diplomatic intercession—that he couldn't waste his ammunition on secondary targets when he had something really important at stake.

Later in the course of the winter there were constant comings and goings of Liberator-fulls of Air Force personnel—radio detection experts and sundry officers who just didn't seem to fit in with the routine of Lend-Lease to Russia. A few of us made guesses which we kept strictly to ourselves. Later it transpired that Harriman and Deane had brought the project for the bomber bases with them and had first broached the matter to the proper Soviet authorities soon after their arrival. The scheme was said to have been fathered by no less a brain than that of General Hap Arnold. As the first step toward Far-Eastern bases, it was highly significant, even though it was certainly starting at the far end. It would also serve to impress the Russians with the American technique of high-altitude precision bombing, for which they had no equivalent in the Red Air Force.

The initial Soviet reaction to the plan was more favorable than the Americans had dared hope. The Russians promised to take it under consideration and get some broad decision as to policy. At Teheran the matter was again brought up, this time at the top level, where it seemed to meet with favorable response. Finally in January the green light came, and from then on it was a question of working out the details, choosing the sites, deciding on the size of the establishment, and arranging for the shipment of the necessary equipment for the ground staffs.

The project, like other Army projects, was given a code word, and packing boxes labeled "Frantic" began to accumulate in various American Atlantic ports. Some of the supplies were sent in by the northern route to Murmansk; others through the Persian Gulf and across Iran. The Russians did everything they could from their side to expedite supplies for the bases; evidently the scheme had enlisted strong support among the Chiefs of the Red Air Force, who doubtless felt there was much they could learn from working with Americans at close quarters. At Murmansk and Archangel, priority was given to the unloading and trans-shipment by rail of "Frantic" cargo, while efficient and intelligent Major General Alexei Perminov of the Red Air Force, who was placed in command of the Russian part in the project, showed an amazing knack for cutting red tape and getting results. Perminov worked on the friendliest terms with Colonel (now Brigadier General) Alfred Kessler, the American Chief of Staff. Kessler, a rugged West Pointer of forty-five, New Jerseyite by birth, Californian by adoption, soon found that he and his Russian colleague spoke a common airforce language. At the same time a large share of the credit for the smooth functioning of the project, both in its earlier and later stages, should be given to studious, quiet Captain Henry Ware, who acted throughout as official American interpreter. Ware had come over to the Soviet Union in the early thirties as an economics student. He had lived in a Russian household as a member of the family and had acquired an excellent working knowledge of the language and people. Later he had returned to the United States and taken a job in the Department of Commerce in Washington. When the U.S. Military Mission heads, desperately in need of an interpreter, heard about Henry, they had him out of his Washington office, commissioned, in uniform, and on his way to Russia—all within the span of forty-eight hours.

On a chilly day in April the first contingent of American personnel stepped out of the special railway cars that had brought them up from Baku into what looked like the midst of nowhere. On closer inspection, it proved to be a badly mangled airfield outside the shattered city of Poltava. The retreating Germans had demolished all the hangars and most of the buildings that had once accommodated Red Air Force personnel. Only one wing of a big five-story building had somehow escaped the holocaust. There the first American contingent was housed. The entire area, including the building, had been carefully de-mined some months before, when the Russians first retook it from the Germans. But one day a Red Army sentry, on duty outside the American quarters, discovered a suspicious looking wire. Immediately, the Americans were asked to vacate their quarters. Sappers traced the wire to the building's foundations and gingerly removed several tons of carefully concealed high explosives.

The traditionally hospitable Russians did their best to make their American guests comfortable. The plumbing in the building was beyond repair, so Russian workmen proceeded to clothe in lumber the Russian conception of a multiple-seated American privy. In the beginning the Americans and Russians ate together; the latter

ran the mess and supplied the menu. It did not take them long to
discover the American liking for rare juicy steaks, and since some
of the Americans failed to finish off the huge helpings of boiled
cabbage—the only available green vegetable—the Russians decided
that Americans were an exclusively carnivorous nation. So for a
time, with appalling regularity, the Americans were served nothing
but juicy steaks three times daily. Fearing they might offend the
Russians' feelings, the Americans hesitated to say anything until
they were finally driven to it by sheer desperation. The Russians,
far from being offended, asked them why they hadn't spoken up
sooner.

This experience taught the Americans a valuable lesson: the direct approach, rather than the devious, was the best way of getting
along with the Russians. Whenever there was something you
wanted or didn't like, you came right out and said so, without trying to be too subtle or diplomatic.

Quite early in the proceedings the Americans were introduced
to the vodka treatment. Whenever there was a party or a banquet,
which was often, they found that their Russian colleagues expected them to drink toast after toast, bottoms up, to Stalin, Roosevelt, and Soviet-American friendship, tossing down the hatch whole
tumblerfuls of liquid fire. And anyone who didn't hold up his end
lost face. To deaden the effects and to protect the linings of their
stomachs, the Americans tried such time-tested stratagems as swal-
lowing chunks of butter or tablespoonfuls of salad oil before the
ordeal.

Henry Ware, who, as interpreter, had to keep a clear tongue in
his head in spite of hell and high water, had mastered a deft
sleight-of-hand trick of dumping his vodka under the table. Observ-
ing that Colonel Kessler was invariably the main target of the
Russian Air Force, he let him in on his little secret. But the results
were disastrous. The very first time he tried it, the Chief bungled
and was caught red-handed. Thereafter the Russians carefully
watched his every move and never let him get away with anything.

The major obstacle to complete harmony and co-operation between Russians and Americans was the language difficulty. The
Army personnel department had done a bang-up job of easing this

problem by rounding up for the project a fair proportion of men of Russian, Ukrainian, Polish, Czech, or some other Slavic stock, whose knowledge of Russian or a related language would give them a head start in making themselves understood. But even those men who knew not a word of Russian soon became experts in the art of sign language. Of course, they sometimes misfired—as when an American mechanic asked his Russian assistant for his cigarette lighter and the latter brought him a blowtorch.

Misunderstandings also occurred when some quite innocent English word sounded like something quite different in Russian. At one point the Russian General complained to the American Chief of Staff that the waitresses in the mess were on the verge of quitting because, they said, they had been insulted. Everyone had a good laugh when they traced the trouble to innocent requests for a second helping of peaches.

Sometimes practical jokers made the most of the language difficulty. Thus one American mechanic taught his two Russian understudies to yell "Jerk!" when they saluted American officers. There was one word, however, which all the Americans, from the Colonel down, were taught to master right from the very first day. That was *Stoi!*—Halt! The camp was guarded by Red Army sentries, and when any Russian sentry yelled *"Stoi!"* the Americans were told, he meant *"Stoi!"* And if you failed to comply, you ran a pretty good risk of getting shot.

One day in mid-May the Anglo-American press corps was invited to a press conference with General Deane at Spasso House. There it was that we were officially let in on the secret of the bases. The General, disarmingly frank in admitting that he had had little experience with such matters, asked our advice about handling the publicity releases. On the basis of our suggestions an appropriate communiqué was drawn up for release when the first group of bombers would fly in from the west and land at the new bases, thus inaugurating the "shuttle-bombing" operations. The date for this first operation, the General told us, had not yet been set. But he planned to arrange for all of us who wanted to go down to the bases in time to witness the arrival of the planes.

That was how, for the first time since the start of the war,

American and British pressmen in the Soviet Union were able to cover an operational story first-hand, and not by copying their stuff out of the columns of the Soviet newspapers. The Press Department of the Foreign Office arranged transportation, and with a few hours notice, on the morning of June 3 we flew down to the main American bomber base.

The first impression was unforgettable. On the vast, Nazi-devastated Ukrainian steppe was a bit of America, as unmistakable in its identity as a baseball diamond. Everything from the big square khaki tents to seventeen-ton gasoline trucks was strictly G.I. The base personnel, both the officers and men, included representatives of practically every one of the forty-eight states. Russia, they frankly acknowledged, was the last place they had ever expected they'd end up in, and even now, after more than a month, they were still wondering how it had happened. But they gave a collective impression of enjoying the experience thoroughly. Many of them remarked that the surrounding landscape, with its broad fields of grain, rich pastures, and green forests, was more like an American landscape than anything they'd seen since leaving home. This was especially true for those who had been stationed for a considerable period in barren, sun-baked sections of North Africa or Southern Italy. The people, too, they said, looked clean and healthy—quite different from the Arabs or poverty-stricken southern Italians. And from the outset, everyone—from the Russian soldiers to the inhabitants of the neighboring town of Poltava—was hospitable. So it hadn't taken the G.I.'s long to make friends, especially with the girls, whose looks compared favorably with home standards, they said.

To the local Ukrainian inhabitants—some of whom had lived through the German occupation, others of whom had recently returned from the Soviet interior to which they had been evacuated early in the war—these Americans were like men from another planet. They had not, of course, been tipped off beforehand; so that when they saw the first group of American uniforms, a few wondered if they had again been invaded by some other nation. And in some ways it was like an invasion—at any rate when the first combat crews arrived.

At the enlisted men's mess, we found a dozen strapping Russian girls in bulging G.I. coveralls helping out on K.P. They were opening cans of rations, dumping the contents into huge pails, and then dishing out the warmed-up stuff on the chow line. These girls, regular soldiers in the Red Army, were anything but fragile. I noticed one of the girls watching with an amused look while two G.I.'s swayed and staggered with the weight of an enormous soup pail, whose hot contents was sloshing on their feet. Finally, taking pity on them, the Amazon stepped over, motioned to the G.I.'s to set it down, then lifted it and easily carried it away herself, unaided.

The boys in the cookhouse, having given up trying to memorize the girls' Russian names as a hopeless job, had re-christened them with American nicknames. So that now the Russians answered to such descriptive monikers as Fatty, Curly, Blondie, Tubby, Freckles—while one girl was called "New York," for no apparent reason since she hailed from Kharkov. The girls took all this and any amount of kidding with puzzled good nature, setting it all down to the eccentricities of the *Americantsi*.

Besides their wages, the girls got three square meals a day of G.I. food. They looked as though they were thriving on it, although they complained that American food was too sweet and that they missed their sour cabbage soup and black bread. They were amazed at the small amount of bread Americans ate as compared with Russians, and wondered how the Americans survived.

On one particular, back in the days when the project was being blueprinted, the Russians had remained adamant. The total American permanent ground staff for the bases was to be restricted to one thousand, and no amount of argument would budge them. And now the explanation for this stand came to light. The Russian High Command conceived of the American bases as schools where Russian personnel could study and master American methods and American equipment. If American personnel were limited, it would mean that American mechanics would have to work with Russian assistants. And so most of the crews trained to service the bombers consisted of three Russians under the direction of one American. To this work the Russians assigned a picked personnel, and every evening, after working all day on mixed service crews, these Russians would attend classes conducted by their own officers. Requirements were stiff, and anyone who lagged was weeded out. No wonder the Americans were amazed at the apparent ease and swiftness with which their Russian assistants "caught on." The Russians were also under orders to learn English. In fact, Americans and Russians working on the same service crews would often place bets as to who could learn the other's language fastest. In general, the G.I. had to acknowledge that the Russians were winning hands down. All the Russians carried around little notebooks in which they jotted down English words and phrases (spelled phonetically in Russian characters) together with their Russian meanings.

Contact between Americans and Russians was not limited to working hours. Almost every evening some sort of entertainment was put on—either a movie, a concert, or a song and dance and vaudeville program—by some traveling Russian troupe. All these shows were held in the open air, in the ruins of a former theater that had lost roof, walls—everything but the stage. During the intermissions a Russian would come out and translate explanations or announcements into halting English, which always got him a big hand. Sometimes he made brave attempts to translate the jokes, and everybody laughed whether he got the point or not.

The shows would be followed by dances. There were only three American nurses in camp, and no Wacs; so most of the G.I.'s dated Russian girls. The G.I.'s taught the girls to jive and cut a rug, and the girls taught them Ukrainian folk dances. Usually the evening ended up in a round of community singing. All these gatherings were permeated with the warmest spirit of friendship and camaraderie, despite the language barrier.

At one shindig I met a group of five inseparable companions—Joe from New York, Shorty from Pittsburgh, Nikolai from Leningrad, Kostya from Moscow, and Misha from Rostov. For the most part they just sat around and grinned. When I saw them, the two Americans were initiating their Russian side-kicks into the mysteries of chewing gum and trying to get across the point that you weren't supposed to eat or swallow it. Only the restricted supply of gum prevented the habit from taking firm root in Soviet soil.

The real fun at the base began when the first mission flew out of the low western clouds two mornings after our arrival. The planes were from the Fifteenth Air Force in Italy, and its commanding officer, General Ira Eaker, was riding the lead plane. One ship had blown up in the air over the target—not from flak, as far as could be observed, but from some internal trouble. Otherwise there were no casualties.

Despite their long flight, the members of the combat crews were in no mood for rest. They were all keyed up over being in the Soviet Union for the first time in their lives, and they were raring to see the sights. Previously there had been some talk of the town being off limits until after the planes had taken off on their return flight. But in less than no time, most of the combat crews, washed and shaved, were on their way to town. For the next two days American fliers were in evidence everywhere. They conquered the town utterly and completely, and in a brief period got closer to the Russian people than many of the foreigners stationed in Moscow had in a year or more. They liked the people from the outset. Said Major John S. Cunningham of Milton, Massachusetts, "These people go around holding their heads up, and making every effort to look presentable. This is more like the States than anything I've seen since I left home."

The inhabitants of Poltava, as well as the towns near the other bases, gave the fliers a heroes' welcome and threw open the doors of such houses as were still habitable. Though all the boys made out pretty well, the biggest success was probably scored by Lieutenant William Dacko of Roslindale, Massachusetts. The son of Ukrainian parents, he had learned to speak Ukrainian in a school run by an Orthodox priest in Boston. This was his first opportunity to use it on home soil. On his first visit to town, he met a girl named Valya. She took Dacko and his buddy to her house and introduced them to her sister and family and fed them a substantial meal of borsch and potatoes with sour cream. The next day was Sunday, and Valya took Dacko to church. Dacko was enjoying his stay so thoroughly that he was rather downcast at the prospect of an early departure—Valya had promised him her photograph the next time he came to see her. After two days of being grounded by the weather, most of the fliers were eager to get air-borne; but others, like Dacko, had unfinished business in town. So that it was with mixed emotions that they assembled for brief-ing on the evening of the third day. The news that they would be returning to Russian bases and not flying on back to Italy after the next mission was received with widespread satisfaction.

There was one member of the Fifteenth Air Force in Italy who made an unscheduled and unheralded flight to the Soviet Union. He was Lieutenant George Myers, twenty-one, of Flora, Illinois, and Indianapolis. The day before the bombers took off for Russia, with other members of his group, he was sent out in a P-38 on a photographic reconnaissance mission. Somewhere around the crest of the Carpathians he lost track of the others. After cruising about, he spotted some planes in the distance and, thinking they might be his mates, flew toward them to investigate. They turned out to be five German *Focke-Wulf* 190's. They chased him, but he outdis-tanced them.

Since by this time he was running low on gas, he decided to head for the Soviet Union instead of trying to get back to his base in Italy. On the ground below he could see gun flashes, which he took to be the line of the front. Then, seeing a good-sized city with an airport, he headed for it. But just to be on the safe side, he decided to buzz the field before landing. As he raced over the field, ack-ack and small arms fire started coming at him from all directions.

It was distinctly unhealthy; so he gathered altitude and flew on. Checking his map, he discovered that the hot place must be Jassy, and decided rightly that it was still in German hands. Presently he saw water below him, which according to the map looked like the Black Sea. He headed inland, and seeing another city with an air-port, circled and landed. This time he was inside the Soviet lines, all right. The city turned out to be Nikopol on the lower Dnieper. The Russian authorities were distinctly puzzled by the irregularity of it all, for Myers had no papers, or passport, or any means of identification beyond his uniform and dog tag. They were also perplexed because neither pilot nor plane was armed. However, the colonel in charge of the airport took George home with him, introduced him to his wife and daughter, and gave him dinner and lodgings. Next morning he was flown up to Poltava. Having no foreknowledge of the Eastern Command's existence, he was more than mildly astonished to find Flying Fortresses parked all over the airfield. His amazement was complete a few minutes later, when, in the midst of a typical American camp, he ran into the four members of his own group.

Thus was launched a major practical demonstration of the thesis that Americans and Russians can get along and work together. In this respect, the political aspects of the Eastern Command far outweighed its military importance. It was no routine combat assignment that its members were detailed to perform. They were diplomats, laying the groundwork of the future peace. The fact that the Germans were keenly aware of the significance of this development was demonstrated three weeks later, when, following the second shuttle mission, the *Luftwaffe* came in. This time the Eighth Air Force had flown in across the length of the Reich. They had evidently been trailed by German reconnaissance, which must have taken fairly good photographs. For at midnight that very night the *Heinkels* were over. For nearly two hours they pounded the runways in waves, using flares to light the job until fires on the ground made this unnecessary. Though they inflicted severe damage on the planes, for some reason almost no bombs fell in the area of the camp. Hence there were only two casualties among the American personnel. A group of very frightened American correspondents spent a good part of the night in slit-trenches, but damage to them was psychological only. Less fortunate were two of their Soviet colleagues, who picked the wrong moment to leave their slit-trench and dash away from the field. Both were killed. Fatalities were highest among the Soviet sentries standing guard over the planes. Their orders were not to leave their posts whatever happened. Besides high explosives, the *Heinkels* sprinkled the area thoroughly with butterfly bombs, nasty little anti-personnel contraptions that land without exploding but then go off at the slightest disturbance—even if it's only a footstep near-by. These made the task of clearing the damage and the runway especially ticklish.

The raid on the base was all the more surprising in view of the fact that *Luftwaffe* activity in the Ukraine had for some time been on a fairly small scale—never deeper than two hundred miles. Poltava was nearly five hundred miles from the front line. This was a clear indication of how much importance the Germans attached to the American bases. A few nights later they attempted to raid one of the other bases, but all aircraft had been shifted elsewhere.

There was much which the Russian airmen could learn from watching the U.S. Army Air Force operate. For the Russians had no strategic air force comparable to the American or British. They did not receive any American or British heavy bombers under Lend-Lease, nor did they build any of their own. Their Soviet-made bombers were all two-engined mediums that they generally used against enemy supply dumps, railway junctions, and troop concentrations in the forward area. They were strangers to the technique of high-level precision bombing. In fact, American airmen were amazed when they discovered that the Russians had torn the oxygen equipment out of most of the several thousand A-20 Douglas Medium Bombers they had received from the Douglas Aircraft Assembly Plant at Abadan on the Persian Gulf. The explanation was that the Russians did not go in for high-altitude work, and therefore regarded the oxygen pipes and cylinders as so much encumbrance.

The Red Air Force specialized in the close support of ground operations, either offensive or defensive. Its chief attack weapons are the *Ilyushin-2* and its improved version, the *Ilyushin-4*, both popularly called the *Stormovik*—a low-flying, short-ranged monoplane, heavily armored and with a cannon in the nose that fires an armor-piercing shell. The *Ilyushin* is also variously termed the "Flying Tank" and the "Tank Buster." It is used for low-altitude strafing attacks on enemy armor and gun positions in the battle area, or against enemy supply columns close to the front. According to all reports, it is a most effective plane for its purposes.

The *Yak* and *La* fighters, named after their respective designers,

Alexander Yakovlev and S. A. Lavochkin, were speedy, maneuverable planes well suited to the job of providing fighter cover for the *Ilyushins* or for combing the German *Stukas* out of the hair of the Russian ground forces. But they, too, were not adapted to high-altitude work. Nor had the Russians anything comparable to the American and British long-range fighters for general hell-raising behind the enemy lines. When a squadron of American P-58's flew in to provide escort for the bombers on their way to and from the Ukrainian bases, for a while they had a field day shooting up German transport planes and other sitting ducks. These planes had been in the habit of flying right up to the front lines without fighter cover because the Russians never interfered with them.

This partiality to low-level work and heavy fire-power explains the Russians' enthusiasm for the P-38 Bell Airacobra, a plane which few American or British pilots I have talked to ever had much use for, owing to its poor performance above twenty thousand feet. But to the Russians that is a matter of indifference. I remember how once during the offensive on the Karelian Isthmus last June, two German reconnaissance planes—probably Me-210's—came over at something over thirty thousand feet, trailing long plummets of vapor like sky-writing. Down below, *Ilyushins* with their fighter escorts were taking off from a near-by field on routine missions over the battle area, paying not the least attention to the Fritzes way upstairs.

In its specialized field of ground co-operation, the Red Air Force is doubtless unexcelled. Russian pilots are as skilled and brave as any. Among other things, they have developed to a fine art the technique of ramming enemy planes.

Thus there was much that the Russians could learn and were eager to learn by their direct contact with an American operational base. From their standpoint it has been well worth the effort, regardless of how it may influence the over-all strategy of the war.

THE BRITISH SCOOP OWI

☆ ☆ ☆ ☆ ☆ ☆ ☆ ☆ ☆ ☆ ☆ ☆

I WAS still at the bomber base the morning of "D" Day. In the early dawn the boys of the Fifteenth Air Force had taken off on a mission to Romania. Their target was the *Luftwaffe* airfield at Galats, and most of the crews heard General Eisenhower's historic first communiqué over their radios on the return run. We at the base had picked it up on a regular BBC newscast at nine in the morning. From that moment on, we busied ourselves testing Russian reaction by breaking the electric news to any Red Army men or officers whom we chanced to encounter. The first reaction I recall was from a young Air Force lieutenant who was escorting General Perminov's daughter, herself a uniformed member of the Air Force.

"Thank Heaven," were the first words, "three years we've waited for this day." And he and his fair companion ran off to tell others.

That afternoon we flew back to Moscow. The outdoor loudspeakers in the streets and squares, originally installed to announce airraid warnings, were still blaring the announcement at fifteen-minute intervals with potpourris of martial music in between. Earlier in the day, I was told some people had rushed around embracing and kissing perfect strangers in the old Russian Easter tradition. Others had wept happily.

Yet emotional reaction was confined to a minority. Such, in truth, was the magnitude of the event that the average Soviet citizen needed time to grasp and assimilate the full meaning. Perhaps the Russians had waited for a second front so long and endured so many disappointments that the edge of their expectancy had dulled like the appetite of a hungry man who tires of waiting for his dinner. They had in the past developed a certain skepticism on the subject. It is best illustrated by the following anecdote long current in Moscow: A small boy asks his daddy what the Second Front is, and the parent answers, "Maybe when you grow up, you'll be able to find out for yourself."

So, when they first heard the news of the landings in France, some people didn't want to give full rein to their feelings until they were sure this wasn't just another Dieppe Raid.

Yet soon a remarkable change in the atmosphere took place. The spring sun seemed warmer, the air clearer. There was a new spring, too, in the stride of Moscow citizens as they went about their business, and the expression on Moscow's collective face was transformed—the corners of its mouth lifted perceptibly and a new light in its eyes.

Much of this might have escaped the casual observer, who might have concluded from the comparative absence of emotional exhibitionism that the Russians were indifferent and unmoved by the news. Russian feelings run deep and seldom get out of control. In sorrow and joy alike they are an extraordinarily patient and disciplined people. Had the same casual observer been in Moscow on that fateful morning of June 21, 1941, when the same loudspeakers that were now telling of the Allied invasion of France announced that other invasion—the German attack on the Soviet Union, he might have been fooled by the absence of panic and alarm into imagining the Russians were unpatriotic or cared little for their country's welfare.

One outward indication of how Soviet citizens really felt about the opening of the Second Front was the tremendous eagerness with which they bought up the newspapers. So terrific was the crush around the newsstands that the militia had to keep the crowd in line. The first announcement had come too late for the morning papers. As a rule, Moscow's only evening paper, *Vechernaya Moskva,* simply reprints the morning news. But on Tuesday, June 6, 1944, for the first time in its history it scooped *Pravda* and *Izvestiya*—and on the biggest story of the war.

Next morning, also for the first time in history, the Soviet Press published the text of a prayer. It was President Roosevelt's prayer on "D" Day, and it touched the hearts of average Russians as few messages had ever done. Now, at last, the people began to grasp

278 *Russia Is No Riddle*

that they were not alone—that after all the long years of isolation, of "capitalist encirclement," they were part of a great world coalition. And for the Russians, who still had to overcome the remnants of an inferiority complex toward the West—the heritage of past centuries—this was indeed a revelation.

In the days that followed the invasion, for the first time since the war began—in the trolley cars and subways, in the shops and theater lobbies—the people were talking of peace, not as a remote and unattainable desideratum somewhere beyond where the blue begins, but a certainty of the near future, a goal to which the distance could be measured. They began making plans for the time when they would be able to resume their individual lives and their pursuit of happiness where they had been suddenly broken off that other June three years before. A time limit had been set at last to the seemingly endless ordeal of sorrow and suffering. Had not Stalin himself declared that once the offensive against Germany was launched simultaneously from West and East, the days of the Nazis would be numbered?

The evening of "D" Day, most of the Anglo-American colony turned up at the commercial restaurant in the Hotel Moskva, which in the cold grandeur of its marble columns and vaulted ceiling was about as cozy as Grand Central Station.

The atmosphere was not rendered any warmer by the fact that ranged around one of the largest tables in the place, strategically located, was a quorum of the Moscow Japanese colony, including the three correspondents. They, too, were obviously celebrating, though it was hard to say what. They were lavishly swilling Soviet champagne at thirty dollars a bottle, and with every gulp the smirks on their mugs grew more truculent as they leered across the room at us. Some of the British and American officers and embassy secretaries were all for going across and wiping the smirks from those Japanese faces then and there, but the embassy councilors, counseled caution and thereby prevented a possible international incident. Presently the Japs, having reached a stage of glassy-eyed stupor, staggered off. After that, things brightened up considerably. There was widespread fraternization with whatever Russians happened to be patronizing the restaurant that night.

Most of them were senior Red Army officers, who were entitled to a discount of up to 40 per cent on the exorbitant commercial prices. The other patrons were factory directors and top-flight technicians from out of town—the Soviet equivalent of the clientele of Billy Rose's Diamond Horseshoe. No Muscovite in his proper senses would pay those prices even if he could afford them, which was highly unlikely to begin with. Just to give you an idea: once when Eddy Gilmore and I invited Signor Quaroni and his wife to dinner at the Moskva, our check for an extremely modest meal for five people, plus the tip, came to about 4000 rubles or, at the Embassy exchange rate, around 330 dollars.

For the British and American diplomats, who seldom if ever associated with Russians socially, that evening's fraternization marked the dawn of a new post-"D" Day era of rapprochement with the Russians. Though it was impossible to change the ingrained habits and policies of a quarter-century overnight, American and British stock went up by leaps and bounds. Henceforth when a uniformed member of the American or British Military Missions appeared in public, he was no longer the butt of bitter and pointed jibes, but the object of admiration. Not only the people, but also the Soviet Government became more benevolent.

The British were far more ready to exploit the opportunities of the new situation ushered in by "D" Day than were the Americans, even though intrinsically the Russians are more interested in America than they are in Britain.

Back in August, 1942, about the time of the first Churchill visit to Moscow, the British Ministry of Information had begun publication in Moscow of a weekly Russian-language newspaper under the title *Britansky Soyuznik—British Ally*. From the outset the new publication enjoyed instantaneous success with the Russian reading public. In was the first time since the Revolution that anything published by a non-Soviet source had been made available, and it was as welcome as a breath of fresh air or a change of diet. Whenever it was time for a new issue to appear on sale, the crowds queued up for it at the newsstands; and though it sold for one ruble per copy, after the newsstand supply was exhausted, which didn't take long, a copy would bring as much as sixty rubles on the open market.

Although only 25,000 copies of each issue were printed, every copy was read by from twenty to a hundred people. And its circulation was not limited to Moscow. Small quotas were sent to other towns, including Leningrad throughout the blockade, and to the front lines, where it was read as eagerly as in the rear areas.

Not that the *Britansky Soyuznik* was brilliantly written or edited, but it was new and it had the field to itself. The contents steered well away from controversial political issues. It carried folksy informative articles about British everyday life, told about the British home war effort, about the British forces overseas—the desert war, the RAF, the submarine war, the British merchant marine. It gave graphic descriptions of the Blitz. It was packed with an immense amount of other everyday information that revealed Britain to the Russians in an entirely new light, establishing closer bonds of sympathy and understanding.

In the spring of 1944, Moscow received a visit from Mr. Peter Smollet, head of the Russian Section of the British Ministry of Information. Mr. Smollet was a man of parts and dynamic energy, though to look at him casually one would never have suspected it. Father of many brain children, at thirty-three he was already beginning to look like a family portrait, with a trend toward obesity. His King's English was of a flawless diction seldom encountered outside the description of an international spy in an E. Phillips Oppenheim novel—far too perfect for a native Englishman. Smollet, in fact, was an Anglicized Czech, born to the name of Smolka. Perhaps his Czech origin made him doubly *persona grata* in Moscow. At any rate, a few weeks after his arrival he completed plans for the publication and distribution of books in Russian, including an edition of thirty thousand copies of translated selections from Churchill speeches, a book on the Eighth Army, and sundry British fiction and war books—all with the full co-operation of the Russians. But Smollet's crowning achievement in the publication field was to arrange for increasing the size of the weekly *Britansky Soyuznik* from eight to twelve pages and the printing from twenty-five thousand to fifty thousand copies. The increase would be made with the issue of June 4, 1944, which suggests in retrospect that Mr. Smollet had a pretty clear notion of when "D"-Day was due. The British were so thoroughly on their toes that the day after the invasion they put out a special "D"-Day issue of the *Soyuznik*.

At the same time, the Ministry of Information was shipping English books to Russia in increasing quantities, and was placing them on the shelves of Soviet public and circulating libraries for the benefit of a large and increasing number of persons who read English.

In conformity with the increased scope and scale of its activities, the Ministry of Information branch in Moscow, which had hitherto been termed the Press Department of the British Embassy, was now elevated to the status of "Public Relations Bureau," which was officially rendered into Russian as "Department of Information and Cultural Ties."

The manifold and growing enterprises of the dynamic Mr. Smollet and his go-getters were matched by the almost total inactivity of the representatives of the United States—proverbial homeland of super-salesmanship and publicity. In January, 1943, U.S. Ambassador William H. Standley had publicly complained that the Russian people were not being given the facts about American aid to Russia by their own press. But the American Embassy made no efforts to set up channels of its own through which information about America might reach the Soviet public, even though at that time the *Britansky Soyuznik* had been a going concern for nearly half a year.

The *Soyuznik* was strictly and exclusively British. Even when it published a photograph of what to any practiced eye were obviously American Flying Fortresses, the caption read: "R.A.F. Bombers Enroute to German Targets." The sole American printed publicity matter that the Russians ever saw were the labels on cans and packages containing American food products—a powerful advertisement, admitted, but no substitute for special publications.

When Averell Harriman succeeded Admiral Standley as Ambassador to the Soviet Union in October, 1943, things took a slight turn for the better. Harriman was definitely publicity-minded and familiar with the work of the Office of War Information in London. He arrived in Moscow accompanied by Samuel Spevak, whose title in Washington was Chief of the proposed Moscow Office of the OWI. In Moscow, however, the OWI was simply the press section of the American Embassy, with no official identity of its own. To begin with, the only way of rendering "Office of War Information" into Russian was "Office of Military Information"—not a very auspicious title in a spy-conscious country.

Sam Spevak brought to Moscow a lot of rosy plans—some of which reflected his Hollywood background—for popularizing America among the Russians. These included the publication in Russian of slick-paper magazines whose technical layout alone would knock the Soviet reader for a loop.

After a few initial disappointments, Sam got discouraged—rather too easily we thought—and left Moscow not to return. But plans for the magazines, though they languished, did not fold up altogether. Today a Russian version of the OWI pocket-size magazine *USA* is being published in the United States for distribution in Russia. A Russian edition of the *Life*-like OWI picture magazine *Victory* is also in production. The Russian edition of the pocket-size magazine is entitled *America;* the picture magazine is called *America Illustrated.*

The plan is for them to appear on alternate months, other things being equal. The major difficulty is the distance between New York, where the magazines are being produced, and Moscow, where they are to be distributed. And because of censorship, all the copy must first make the round trip before it is printed; then the finished product must be shipped in bulk at the convenience of the U.S. Army Air Transport Command which operates no regular service into Moscow.

An added problem was to find in America translators capable of rendering the text into idiomatic and literary Russian. This was complicated by the fact that in the twenty-seven years since the Revolution the Russian language had undergone important changes; and though this applied less to straight literary material, it was a serious consideration when the subject matter involved colloquialisms or technical terms non-existent a quarter of a century ago.

A measure of the difficulties and delays is provided by the fact that the first issue of the pocket-size magazine was not ready for shipment to Moscow till the end of October, 1944, although it had been in preparation since early spring. It would be at least another month before it would be received in Moscow for distribution. Compare this with the *Britansky Soyuznik,* which got out a special Invasion Number on "D"-Day plus two!

The British are also far ahead of the United States in film distribution in Russia. When I first reached Moscow in December, 1943, the entire population was flocking to see a British effort called *George and the Dinky-Does,* so far as I could gather, a British imitation of a Hollywood musical show. During the winter, Noel Coward's *In Which We Serve,* with a poorly synchronized Russian sound track, had a big run. This was followed by Alexander Korda's *Thief of Baghdad* and another Korda fantasy in color film, which provided welcome distraction from the war. By contrast, the only two American pictures shown to the Russian public during the past year were Samuel Goldwyn's *North Star* and Frank Capra's *Battle for Russia,* both of which were well received, but neither of which told the Soviet movie-goer anything about America.

Practically all the latest American films eventually find their way to the American Embassy, where they are shown for the benefit of members of the foreign colony and sometimes to select audiences of Russians. A tremendous impression was made on such an audience by *Battle for New Guinea.* After the showing, one of the top-ranking Russian writers told me:

"I never imagined what your troops were up against in your war in the Pacific."

Yet my interlocutor was one of the best-informed persons in Moscow, one who had access to information sources inaccessible to the ordinary citizen.

Battle for New Guinea, though shown to a few more select audiences, including Red Army officers, was never released for public showing, any more than was *This Is the Army, Stage Door Canteen, The Human Comedy, Casablanca,* or any one of scores of pictures which the Russians would have enjoyed heartily.

The reason for this is simple. The Russian distributors are willing to show American pictures, but they want to do business on a reciprocity basis—one American film shown in Russia for one Soviet film shown in America. On the face of it this is a reasonable enough request. But the hitch is that whereas the Russian distributors are a state organization, in the United States film distributors are private concerns that operate not in terms of national policy but of profit. Their main objective is not the improvement of Soviet-American relations through mutual understanding, but a cash turnover. Some of the Soviet pictures they would have to take in exchange might be poor risk from the box-office standpoint.

Because of this deadlock, American films are kept from the Russian market, where they might contribute heavily to Russian knowledge about America, and thus bear indirectly on the whole central problem of world security. Obviously, it would be unthinkable for OWI to subsidize the film distributors' purchase of Soviet films. That would be aiding communist propaganda and inviting congressional investigation. Yet in Britain the Ministry of Information, confronted with the same situation, has solved it to everyone's satisfaction, distributing Soviet films and supplying the Russians with increasing quantities of British film and newsreels.

The conclusion to be drawn from the foregoing facts is self-evident. The fact that the war has brought the Western Powers and the Soviet Union closer together than ever before has opened up a golden opportunity for telling the Russians more about our countries. The British have taken full advantage of this opening and are effectively succeeding in spreading knowledge and sympathy for Britain among the Russian population. Up to the present, America has sadly missed out on this. A beginning has been made, but present plans are an insignificant drop in the bucket and are by no means keyed to the possibilities.

It is regrettable that the Office of War Information, which for the past two and a half years has expended gallons of ink and slick paper—not to mention greenbacks—on beautifully printed and illustrated pamphlets in most of the languages and dialects of the Middle East, where 90 per cent of the people are illiterate, has been so slow in reaching Russia where literacy runs above 90 per cent. Especially is it regrettable at the present juncture when it is far more important to inform the Russians about America than the Arab nomads of Kuweit.

So much depends on the future of Soviet-American relations. And the surest and best way to remove suspicion and misunderstanding, and thereby to cement friendship between the two countries and their peoples, is through the dissemination of accurate information. With the British example before our eyes to guide us, our neglect of this field has been nothing short of tragic.

RUSSIA AND AMERICA

☆ ☆ ☆ ☆ ☆ ☆ ☆ ☆ ☆ ☆ ☆ ☆ ☆

Taking the long or historic view, there is strong precedent for American-Russian friendship and co-operation.

Russia is the only major European power with whom the United States has never been at war. Never have Russian and American foreign policies conflicted; often they have coincided. It is as though these two great powers, stretching from ocean to ocean in opposite hemispheres, had been designed by Providence to be mutually complementary. One of the more enlightened Tsars, Alexander II, who by his liberation of the serfs in 1861 earned the designation of "Emancipator" two years before Lincoln, sensed that a strong United States was desirable from Russia's standpoint. On September 11, 1863, when long-threatened Anglo-French intervention on behalf of the South seemed about to materialize, the Tsar sent a naval squadron under Admiral Popov to San Francisco. Two weeks later another Russian squadron under Admiral Lessovsky put in to New York. The story at the time was that both these units had sealed orders to assist the Union if Britain and France aided the Confederacy. Although this was never verified, the Russian gesture proved enough to avert the threat. Though some die-hard Confederates may harbor a grudge against the Russians on this account, most Americans can thank Russia for the preservation of their country's unity and greatness in that most crucial hour. Pursuing the same policy of friendship, Alexander II in 1867 sold Alaska to the United States at a bargain price, and thereby removed the sole possible source of territorial conflict. Some thirty-eight years later the United States repaid these favors. At that time Russia was involved in a war with Japan that was going against the Russians. After steaming halfway around the world from its Baltic base at Kronstadt, the Russian Navy had been virtually wiped out in the Battle of

Tsusima Straits. The Russian Garrison at Port Arthur had surrendered. But the United States even at that time was not pleased with the prospect of too much Japanese expansion, and so, in the treaty of Portsmouth, that other President Roosevelt forced Japan to conclude a peace with Russia that prevented the Nipponese from reaping the full harvest of their victories and saved Russia's interests and face. Since then, we and the Russians have been allies in two world wars.

Russia's and America's foreign policies have never collided, but their internal political and economic structures have always differed as widely as their historical and cultural backgrounds. They have always strongly disapproved of each other's form of government and social philosophy.

Thus, when the Thirteen Colonies cast off their allegiance to the British Crown and set up a republic, to the Russians this was a denial of morality, righteousness, and law and order which in their eyes were founded on the sacred and inviolable principle of monarchy. And though England's loss of her colonies was decidedly not Russia's funeral, not yet the autocratic Tsarist Government could bring itself to recognize the upstart and dangerously revolutionary republic in the Western Hemisphere. The "American agent," Francis Dana, camped on the doorsteps of St. Petersburg, vainly seeking recognition from Empress Catherine the Great. Early in May, 1782, Count Osterman, the Russian foreign minister, instructed Prince Golitsin, Russian Minister to the Hague:

"With your dispatch came a portrait of Washington, to be delivered to one Dana, an American agent here. But as this man is not known to her Imperial Majesty or her Ministers, you are commanded by her Majesty to return it to the source from which it reached the courier. Her Majesty wishes Your Excellency, as well as Mr. Markov, in future not to receive for or from America any letter or anything else dispatched by the courier: for besides the reason given in my letter of the tenth of May it is not pleasant to deliver them to people with respect to whom Her Majesty's Ministers are ignorant who they are or why they are here." *

* Quoted in *Francis Dana* by W. P. Cresson Lincoln MacVeagh, the Dial Press, MCMXXX.

This cavalier treatment offers a close and striking parallel to the attitude of the United States Government some 140 years later, when the shoe was on the other foot and emissaries of the newly formed Soviet Government, beginning with Litvinov, were detained at Ellis Island. It took Tsarist Russia thirty-five years (from the Declaration of Independence) to recognize the United States. It took the latter fifteen years (from the October Revolution) to recognize Soviet Russia.

The long-standing mistrust has been based on lack of reciprocal knowledge and understanding. Though in the Far North Russia and the United States have long been neighbors, there have been few points of physical or intellectual contact between the two countries. In Tsarist times the educated and enlightened section of Russian society looked for cultural leadership to Western Europe, mainly to France. Seldom did their gaze or their travels take in America.

Likewise Russia was outside the ken of informed and well-traveled Americans. To the average U. S. citizen, Russia, if it existed at all, was a shadowy Asiatic "Land of the Hyperboreans," almost as remote and strange as it had been to the Italians of the time of Marco Polo, a disturbing *terra incognita,* inhabited by bearded semi-barbarians who spoke an impossible language with its own alphabet.

After the Revolutions of 1917 what tenuous contact had existed before was cut off altogether. Thereafter, for a decade and a half, Americans heard little about Russia save what they got from the anti-Soviet *émigrés* and the reams of propaganda dished out by others who hated and feared the new government and all it stood for. Nothing said against the Bolsheviks was too improbable to be discounted. And anyone who attacked the new regime in print or by word of mouth was sure of a ready and lucrative reception. This is almost as true now as it was then, even though Americans and Russians are bearing arms together against a common enemy.

But today the public has access to factual information on Russia. Besides that, the heroic record of the Russians on the battlefield speaks for itself more convincingly than volumes. And so, there is crystallizing in America a body of opinion which, without seeking to alter our form of government or our social system, is nevertheless willing to see good in someone else, and which, on the basis of the facts and the record, sincerely wants to be friends with Russia.

The cementing of friendly relations between the United States and the Soviet Union requires the removal of a tremendous amount of hostility, suspicion, and prejudice that has accumulated on both sides in the past quarter of a century. And the only way to do this is for Russians and Americans to get to know each other better. In his dealings with Chiefs of the other Allied powers, President Roosevelt has always staked much on personal contact. When he and Churchill and Stalin could get together and talk things over eye to eye, they were almost sure to reach an agreement. The same should apply to the peoples of various nations. It is of course impossible to bring the millions of Russians and Americans into the same room and seat them around a conference table. But it is possible to bring them into closer intellectual contact—to promote mutual understanding—and in the process much of the mistrust and misinformation will automatically melt away. Russians and Americans will then discover that they have much in common.

There is, to begin with, the vastness of their respective countries, the vistas uncircumscribed by hedgerows, the habit of thinking in bold sweeping terms, of planning and achieving on a huge scale. Both America and Russia are young nations with mixed populations yet to be assimilated. Both are accustomed to developing their own broad homelands and rich natural resources, rather than looking toward expansion beyond their borders or abroad. If in America the Frontier is still a vivid memory of the recent past, in Russia it is part of the living present. The pioneer spirit is molding the character of future Russia today as it molded that of America in the last century.

It may help Americans to revaluate their attitude toward Russia to hear what the average Russian thinks of America. Just as the average American for twenty years was fed anti-Soviet propaganda, so the common man in Russia was chiefly informed of the flaws in the American social order—the extreme contrasts of wealth and poverty, the want amid plenty, the distress of the depression years, the injustice to the Negroes. More modern American books were

translated for Russian readers than vice versa, but the most widely
circulated were Upton Sinclair's *The Brass Check,* Sinclair Lewis'
It Can't Happen Here, Theodore Dreiser's *An American Tragedy,*
and John Steinbeck's *The Grapes of Wrath.* No book dealing with
the favorable aspects of American life has been translated and
printed for mass distribution, and I have talked to more than one
Russian who regarded *The Grapes of Wrath* as a complete portrayal of typical American life.

These one-sided selections from American literature have been
supplemented by books and articles by Soviet authors who had
visited America. Thus the great modern Russian poet Vladimir
Mayakovsky, who toured the United States in the middle 1920's,
recorded his impressions in a collection of unforgettable prose
essays and poems. But his observations were inevitably circumscribed by his lack of knowledge of the English language and the
fact that he associated mostly with the Union Square communists.

In the middle 1930's the two noted Soviet humorists Ilya Ilf and
Evgeni Petrov toured America by automobile from coast to coast.
The product of this tour, a book entitled *One-Storied America*,* is
full of sparkle and humor. But as the title implies, in the selection
of subject matter it cleaves closely to the authors' preconceptions.
Like certain American visitors to Russia, they saw chiefly the things
they were looking for.

There has been a lack of balance in the picture. There are no
serious works or textbooks in the Russian language on American
history, government, or institutions; nor are these subjects included
in the Soviet curriculum save in the most cursory fashion and in
strictly Marxist interpretations.

In the early days of the New Regime an important crack in the
otherwise thick insulating wall that cut the Russians off from the
outside world was provided by American motion pictures. Soviet
audiences were as familiar with Douglas Fairbanks, Mary Pickford,
Jackie Coogan, William S. Hart, and Theda Bara as American
movie-goers.

But in latter years, as the Soviet Union developed a motion-
picture industry of its own, the importations from Hollywood

---

* Published in the United States under the title, *Little Golden America.*

gradually dwindled to a tiny trickle, and at present the only Hollywood star still well known in Russia is Charlie Chaplin. This restriction has been partly due to the necessity for saving precious foreign exchange for the purchase of machinery, but it also fits in with the Soviet policy of excluding "class-alien" influences.

Yet in the course of the past quarter-century the Soviet public has developed a fairly strong sales resistance to certain types of propaganda, and the average Russian's picture of America, though inaccurate and at times fantastic, is by no means all negative. No amount of adverse criticism of the American political and social order has been able to shake his admiration of what to him is the fabulous country of a push-button machine civilization.

To say that no other country in the world has fired the Russian imagination to the same extent as America would be an understatement. As a result of the isolation of the past twenty-odd years, America has retained for Russians the pristine glamor it once possessed for the middle and southern Europeans—in those halcyon days before immigration laws and reports of business recessions and unemployment, brought back by disillusioned uncles who had failed to find bonanza, rubbed some of the gold off the gold-paved streets of the steamship company advertisements. Because of this lack of contact between Russia and the U.S.A., in many Russian quarters the legend of America as the land of get-rich-quick survived the Revolution to plague the Marxian economists with their doctrine of the inevitable impoverishment of the workers and enrichment of the exploiters.

So strong was the hold of America on popular thought that Soviet propaganda made use of it. Premier Joseph Stalin sought to describe the scope of industrialization by coining the phrase "American efficiency plus Russian breadth." When in 1927 the first of the stupendous Five-Year Plans for the conversion of a backward agrarian country into a highly industrialized nation was launched, the main slogan was "Overtake and excel America."

This slogan appealed to the young people. For the better part of three Five-Year Plans, right up to the German attack, American achievement became the standard of excellence which every Soviet worker strove to emulate.

Soviet engineers and technicians showed a marked preference for American equipment and machinery, for American production and construction methods. American experts were hired for large valuta salaries, with expenses paid, to come to the Soviet Union and help in the building of everything conceivable—from the Dnieper Dam to the Moscow meatpacking plant that, in the best Chicago tradition, used every part of the animal but the squeal.

The new automobile plant at Gorki (Nizhni-Novgorod) was designed and staffed by Soviet engineers who had been schooled on the production line at River Rouge, and the plant was built and launched with American advice and assistance. It produced a slightly modified version of the Model-A Ford and later shifted to the 1933 model Ford, which continued in production until 1939 when the plant was converted to military purposes in anticipation of the German attack.

As the Russians grew more mechanically minded, any American manufactured article—from nail clippers to portable radios—would evoke ecstasies of admiration, cries of "What workmanship!" "How clever!" "How original!" and a wishful "When will we start making things like that?" And the ambition of every self-respecting young Russian was to acquire some American gadget—a fountain pen, a razor, an all-purpose penknife.

Even when, just before the war, Russian home industry began producing some very creditable copies, sometimes with improvements of its own, the Russian consumer would prefer the American product for the glamorous ingredient of the name.

Yet prior to the present war, Russian admiration for things American and instinctive liking for Americans as individuals could not bridge the gulf of political and social difference that divided Soviet Russia from the capitalist world, including America. The imponderable sense of hostility and distrust remained.

The common purpose of the wartime alliance has brought the two countries closer together than they have ever been before. Lend-Lease supplies reaching the Eastern front have become a powerful American propaganda weapon. Even before the Soviet Government began publishing complete data on Lend-Lease, Russia's fighting men were well aware of the extent of America's contribution to their victories.

Red Army officers acknowledged to me that it was American motor vehicles—mainly six-wheeled Studebaker heavy-duty trucks, of which the Russians received over 200,000, as well as jeeps—which kept the Red Army rolling through once impassable mud. It was this that enabled the Russians in the spring of 1943 to clear the Germans from the Ukraine in record time.

It will not surprise me if the rising generation of Russians includes a quota of little Studebaker Ivanoviches and Willys Ivanoviches (the Russians call the jeeps "Willys," after the firm making most of them) in token of appreciation.

Besides arms and vehicles, the Russians are deeply grateful for the food shipped from America. American canned goods, sugar, egg powder and other food products are to be found on the shelves of shops throughout the Soviet Union where the population buys its rations. The average Russian Army man is as familiar as his G.I. counterpart with Spam and other standard U.S. army rations. Only the emergency "K" ration caused some confusion in the beginning as the packers neglected to include any printed instructions in Russian, and so the Red Army men at the front had to learn what to do with the various items by trial and error. There were instances when they tried to make soup from the chewing gum and coffee from the cheese or dextrose tablets. Such minor misunderstandings were easily straightened out—a good augury for the future of American-Russian relations.

FRIENDSHIP—OR ELSE

☆ ☆ ☆ ☆ ☆ ☆ ☆ ☆ ☆ ☆ ☆ ☆ ☆

U NTOLD harm has been done to the cause of Soviet-American relations by some of the visiting firemen whose snap judgments reported back from a quick tour have contributed to the general misunderstandings. I have mentioned elsewhere Russian observers who came to America and saw just what fitted their preconceptions. But the most numerous offenders in this respect have been Americans.

When Eric Johnston made a trip to the Soviet Union in June, 1944, as the guest of Marshal Stalin, his party included one member who modestly described himself at the time as a hitch-hiker. He was William L. White, of the *Emporia* (Kansas) *Gazette* Whites, Roving Editor for the *Reader's Digest*. Restive under the regimentation of a continuous round of official tours and banquets, Bill White moved out of Spasso House and down to the Hotel Metropole, where for a few brave days he shared the rigors and discomforts of the regular Moscow correspondents. The reason for this slumming expedition was to gather first-hand information for his *Report on the Russians*.

It took Bill only one week, he says, to figure out why Moscow shops and buildings were so shabby. It was not because the Russians in their total mobilization had been forced to neglect everything not contributing to winning the war, but it was due to lack of private ownership and competition. To White it was as plain and simple as all that.

The fact that he had never seen either Moscow or the Soviet Union in peacetime, and therefore had no basis for comparison, troubles him not at all. Without one word of caution or qualification, he sounds off on all kinds of controversial issues, with splendid recklessness.

Thus, judging Soviet factories by appearances, he concludes that they, too, are inefficient and for the same reasons—because they are state-owned and -operated. Nor does White seek to square his cursory observations with the overall fact of Russia's showing in the war. That to him is apparently secondary and incidental. It was birds of passage like White who made work more difficult for serious correspondents.

Johnston himself wrote in *Life* magazine:

"One of the most impressive episodes in all my travels in the Soviet Union occurred at a dinner given for me by a Communist Party leader in Asiatic Russia. In offering a parting toast, he said:

"'It is always difficult to bid good-by to a guest. It leaves a vacancy in one's heart that cannot be filled until he returns. But there is one exception. That is when the guest accepts the hospitality of the host and, after departure, proves himself unworthy by making disparaging remarks.'"

Fortunately the spirit and content of Johnston's writings and public utterances since his return differ widely from those expressed by White, though the latter slily suggests that "Eric Johnston and I agreed in general on the significance of what we saw."

The hospitality lavished on Eric Johnston and his party was indicative of the new warmth and friendship for the United States. Never in the history of the Soviet Union had the red carpet and the banquets been spread the way they were for Johnston and his party. The head of a state could not have asked for or expected more. The abuse of Soviet hospitality is the shabbiest aspect of the White episode.

Both during and after his visit, Eric Johnston behaved with a dignity and courtesy in keeping with the consideration shown him.

The most important lesson Johnston learned on his tour of the Soviet Union was that the country is not returning to capitalism. All future political as well as economic relations with Russia must be grounded on acceptance of that fact.

The war has indeed speeded the return to Russian life of many old features previously discarded. The more liberal attitude toward religion, the revival of the old moral virtues, the rebirth of nationalism, the tightening of Army discipline, the restoration of old insignia of rank, the importance ascribed to money, the piece-rate system—one could go on almost indefinitely listing the developments which are often cited as evidence that Russia has forsaken the Revolution. The flaw in this marshaling of evidence is the inability to distinguish the essential from the incidental.

Actually, the fact that the Soviet leaders have, in the interests of war unity, restored so many of the older features of life, far from implying a weakening or repudiation of the Soviet economic and political system, is an indication of its stability. For the Soviet leaders could only afford this new tolerance and re-established continuity with the past because they were sure that the basic economic and political changes ushered in by the Revolution were now secure beyond challenge. In this all-important respect, the war, far from demonstrating the impracticability of the Soviet system, has had the opposite effect. Socialist industry and collective agriculture have come through the severest test history has ever imposed on the economy of any nation, stronger and more securely established than ever. Those who cite unequal wages, the piece rate, and the widespread use of money as signs of reversion to capitalism are simply demolishing their own straw man. At no time has the Soviet Government advocated complete equalitarianism. The slogan written into the Soviet Constitution is: "From each according to his ability, to each according to his work." Which is the piece rate, pure and simple.

Politically the power and prestige of the Communist Party is higher in Russia today than it has been in its whole history. Meanwhile, though the Comintern has been abolished officially, though religion has received some leeway and Soviet life seems likely to evolve toward ever more and more freedom, the official State philosophy is still Marxism-Leninism, not one of whose doctrines has ever been officially repudiated or revised. Of late, in particular, there has been a notable tendency to stress the importance of theory.

The war has failed to budge the Soviet leaders from the purpose of completing the program of industrialization launched back in 1927 with the First Five-Year Plan. In the decade following the war, Stalin intends to concentrate entirely on the reconstruction of heavy industry, on the building of machines to build machines, rather than on the production of consumers' goods. In other words, the damage to the industrial foundation must be repaired before any move is made seriously to increase the production of consumers' goods; and the Soviet population, after all the sufferings and privations of war, must and will take in their belts another notch if need be and build for the future.

In one respect the war has promoted Stalin's industrial program. By forcing the evacuation of basic industries eastward, together with a sizable proportion of the technicians and skilled workers, it has permanently shifted the country's center of gravity eastward into Asia.

Like the thirty thousand workers and engineers from the Kirov plant in Leningrad, thousands of others from Moscow and every city and industrial center in European Russia and the Ukraine were moved in 1941 beyond the Urals. Later they learned that they were to stay on permanently in their new location, together with the plants and factories that had been carted off piecemeal and reassembled.

Wrote *Pravda* last September:

"Enterprises with a considerable number of workers, engineers, and technicians, were evacuated to the Urals, Siberia, and Central Asia. These enterprises will remain in the East. People," continued *Pravda,* unconsciously paraphrasing Irving Berlin, "have gone there not for just a day, not for just a year. It is understandable that people from Moscow, Leningrad, Kiev or the Donbas love their native cities. But the interest of the Socialist State demands that evacuated enterprises remain in the East, since the process of parallel restoration of factories is going on in the liberated regions. This means that all conditions must be created for the evacuated workers and office employees to settle down in the new places—to settle down permanently and feel themselves satisfied."

It is hard in writing on Russia to avoid the charge of partisanship and yet convey some adequate picture of the Russian people's heroism and self-sacrifice, powered by an underlying faith in themselves and their country's future. It is this unwavering hope of a new and better world that has carried them through the ordeals of the recent past.

By her own effort and with Allied material aid, the Soviet Union has saved herself and in so doing has saved us as well. But no other nation in history has paid such a price in human lives and destruction and survived. In the absence of any census figures, the Ukrainian Soviet Government has recently estimated on the basis of ration cards, that the war and the invasion have reduced the Ukrainian civilian population by about 30 per cent. This would amount to around fourteen millions. Assuming that losses in the remaining occupied area—White Russia, the Baltic Republics, the Central, Northern, and Southern portions of the R.S.F.S.R.— Russia proper—the total civilian losses may well exceed twenty-five millions. This is exclusive of several million soldiers killed in battle, drawn from all areas of the country.

From the standpoint of vital statistics the extent of the damage is by no means fully expressed by mere numerical percentages of the whole. For it was the healthy, virile male population that sustained most of the loss. Consequently, until a new generation comes of age, the birth rate is likely to decline considerably, while the mortality rate, as an aftermath of the war, will continue above the average for several years. As a result, the natural increase may be wiped out altogether for some time. But even at the prewar average of an annual growth in population of about three million, it would take more than a decade to replace the war losses.

The extent of the damage to the country's economy may best be conveyed by pointing out that of the Soviet Union's five largest cities, only Moscow has survived virtually intact, despite the airraids of 1941. The second largest city, Leningrad, though never captured, was in the front lines for two and a half years, the constant target for German siege guns. The damage was especially heavy in the outskirts where most of the large factories were located. The next three largest cities—Kiev, Kharkov, and Odessa—were all under Nazi occupation for two or more years, and subject in varying degrees to the scorched-earth policy. The destruction of industry in the devastated regions, which included most of the industry in the

European part of the Soviet Union, added up to about 90 per cent of total plant equipment.

These human and material losses provide the most conclusive answer to the "Red Imperialism" talk. Regardless of all other considerations, Russia would be in no physical condition to launch a policy of aggression until her grievous wounds are healed, until her depleted population is restored, and until her ruined cities and industries are rebuilt. And this will take several decades at the very least.

Even people in America who are strongly opposed to the Soviet system, if not blinded by prejudice, must admit that in its preparation for the Nazi attack and in its conduct of the war, the Soviet Government has shown considerable foresight and a capacity for leadership. It is impossible, as some writers attempt, to distinguish in this respect between the Government and the people. Without this preparation and leadership, not all the heroism of the Russian people would have availed against the Nazis.

Under the circumstances, is it likely that Government heads who have shown such foresight in the past should harbor the insane desire to fight the other most powerful nation on earth? That would be a suicide gesture, appropriate to the Japanese, but not in the Soviet tradition.

It is an accepted truism that in this day of radio and aviation, not to mention buzz-bombs and robombs, this one world is constantly shrinking in size. It should therefore scarcely require demonstration that two great nations like the USA and the USSR must either cohabit this dwindling planet in friendship, or else inevitably end up by quarreling and fighting each other.

On the basis of the record, no sensible and patriotic American would deny that being friends with the Russians is far preferable to fighting them. Not that friendship will always be smooth and easy. Differences of background, custom, and outlook are bound to cause snags and irritation. We should build our policy on the things we have in common rather than on the points of disagreement. Anyone who deliberately sets out to pick a quarrel with Russia can always find a pretext. The same has applied and does apply to the British, even though we speak the same language more or less. For that matter, it applies to every individual citizen's dealings with his next-door neighbor or the members of his own family. In international as in personal relations there must always be a measure of give and take, a shock-absorber of tolerance, an allowance for the other fellow's (or nation's) peculiarities. It's either that—or good-by humanity.